Stress & Coping

The Eye of Mindfulness

Kendall Hunt
publishing company

Jonathan C. Smith
Roosevelt University

Cover image © Shutterstock.com

Kendall Hunt
publishing company

www.kendallhunt.com
Send all inquiries to:
4050 Westmark Drive
Dubuque, IA 52004-1840

ISBN 978-1-5249-3322-7

Published in the United States of America

DEDICATION

To the many courageous students taking courses in Coping with Stress.
Their adventures have paved the way.

ACKNOWLEDGMENTS

I wish to acknowledge the generous support and contribution of
Chicago's Roosevelt University, my home for decades.
Special note goes to the University
Research and Professional Improvement Leave Committee.

CONTENTS

LESSON 1

STRESS AND COPING

Chapter 1

The Key To This Book

© Circlephoto/Shutterstock.com

Chances are that you are already a stress expert. You've had your share of crises and know how it feels to be frustrated, overwhelmed, and in a word "stressed out." You may even have some insight that stress may not be good for your health, your job, sports performance, relationships, or your studies. Yes, these are topics we will explore throughout this book. But first things first. The first question you might ask when you open a book on stress is, What can I do? We begin our journey by outlining our coping options.

The Coping Equation

This is a book on coping. Let me start by giving away the ending. Our message is simple: First, we live in a stressful world of challenges and unsolved problems. We augment this stress through stressful negative thinking and worry and by creating and sustaining needless physical tension—that is, by tensing up our posture, muscles, and breathing when we don't need to. This can be summarized in a stress formula:

Stress =
Problems + Negative Thoughts + Tension

And there are three general types of stress management, three coping options: fixing problems, rethinking needless stressful thinking, and reducing needless tension by relaxing. All work best when done with undistracted sustained focus, that is, mindfully. This is our coping equation:

Coping =
Fix it + Re-think it + Relax
Mindfully

Let's elaborate. We cope when we fix external problems. This might involve something as simple as repairing a broken computer to something more complex like "fixing" ineffective study habits, a stressful work schedule, or even "broken" relationships.

We cope by re-thinking problems. We realize how our thinking and worry needlessly creates stress by over personalizing, catastrophizing, and blowing things unrealistically out of proportion. We reduce stress by seeing things realistically and in perspective.

But the core approach to stress management is the last part of our formula, relaxation and mindfulness. Superficially, this may be obvious. After our problems and worries are solved, we can relax and mindfully enjoy the present moment. A focused, restful break can prepare us to cope more effectively. And putting to rest needless mind wandering and tension can assist coping even more. But this is just the surface.

Mindfulness

Mindfulness is the organizing idea and practice for this book. To be mindful is to maintain focus on the present moment, without mind wandering and without needless strain. This is a very powerful skill we use every day of our lives. We gaze outside of the window and simply watch the world flow by. We take a deep breath and let go of our tensions and concerns. At the end of the day sink into a soothing bath. All of these reflect mindfulness.

We can be mindful at work, school, and sports. When we set out to write a report, and put aside other tasks, concerns, and worries, and simply tend to the job calmly and efficiently, we are being mindful. When we are absorbed in a game, giving it everything, focused, centered, and undistracted, we are actively mindful.

Put differently, mindfulness is the opposite of mind wandering, worry, needless strain, and rumination. To be mindful is to focus, not for a brief moment, and not with great effort, strain, or thought.

Although mindfulness has been around for thousands of years, we are witnessing an explosion of interest among health professionals today. Mindfulness is the most widely researched approach to relaxation. It is taught in most universities and major hospitals and clinics. It forms the foundation of the book you are reading. Indeed, there are hundreds of texts and stress manuals that deploy mindfulness. But this success has had an unfortunate consequence, the *great mindfulness confusion.*

The Great Mindfulness Confusion

Is mindfulness a religion? Is it a secular technique? This confusion has been around for decades. The fact is not all approaches to mindfulness are the same. Thousands of years ago, Buddhism incorporated mindfulness as part of a religious path to enlightenment. But Buddhism is not the only religion to use mindfulness. We see it in Christianity, Islam, Hinduism, Native American Religion, and even Pastafarianism. We see it in thousands of poems, parables, stories, chants, song lyrics, prayers, and literary wisdom passages outside the realm of religious thought.

In the 1970s, psychologists introduced core elements of Buddhist mindfulness into stress management, while omitting some (but not all) Buddhist features. The most famous is Jon Kabat-Zinn's Mindfulness-Based Stress Reduction (Kabat-Zinn, 1990). This was followed by other approaches, including Mindfulness-Based Cognitive Therapy, Acceptance and Commitment Therapy (ACT), and Dialectical Behavior Therapy (Brown, Creswell, & Ryan, 2015). Taken together, these represent *first-generation mindfulness training* (Shonin & Van Gordon, 2015). Collectively they incorporate partially secular versions that include key Buddhist meditative focusing and breathing exercises (supplemented by stretching), while omitting much (but not all) of Buddhist philosophy. More recently, mindfulness teachers and scholars have reintroduced key elements of Buddhism in *second-generation mindfulness training* (Shonin & Van Gordon, 2015).

First- and second-generation mindfulness are variations of Buddhism, more or less secularized. First-generation approaches might be described as "light Buddhism" and second-generation approaches as "medium Buddhism."

Third-Generation Mindfulness: The Eye of Mindfulness

This book is based on *third-generation mindfulness.* Our approach is:

1. Not Buddhist
2. Not wedded to any religion
3. Based on the brain-based skill of quiet, sustained simple focus. This core attentional act serves as a basic exercise and a template for understanding all levels of mindful practice, experience, and insight.
4. Informed by the universal natural language of relaxation and mindfulness, words used by actual everyday practitioners to describe their experiences. This is in contrast to the esoteric or scientific terminology used by experts.
5. Inclusive of a wide spectrum of techniques, strategies, and perspectives. Key to this inclusiveness is the recognition that all approaches to relaxation have elements of mindful focus and can serve as preparations or expressions of mind-

fulness. Indeed, many approaches to active stress management have elements of mindful focus.

6. Supportive of active, creative, and authentic engagement in a challenging world.

From this point forward, when we refer to "mindfulness," we are referring to the *third-generation type.* Our interest is in pure quiet, sustained simple focus, which we somewhat poetically describe as the Eye of Mindfulness. In sum, ours is an approach that is not only "secular," but non-Buddhist, religion-neutral, and truly inclusive.

Two Revolutions

Over the past decade we have witnessed two revolutions. Once relaxation and mindfulness were viewed as just techniques, tools in the toolbox of coping. Things have changed.

Revolution #1: Different approaches have different effects

The menu of relaxation approaches is vast—yoga, breathing exercises, massage, self-hypnosis, meditation, and so on. Once professionals considered these to be more or less equivalent, like generic aspirin tablets. It didn't matter what you used. Everything, from muscle relaxation to meditation and mindfulness, works the same. If you went to a stress clinic or stress counselor, typically you would get just one technique. Why? Again, because the general assumption was they all work the same. This was the official position taught by experts up until the end of the 20th century.

© Dmitry Lobanov/
Shutterstock.com

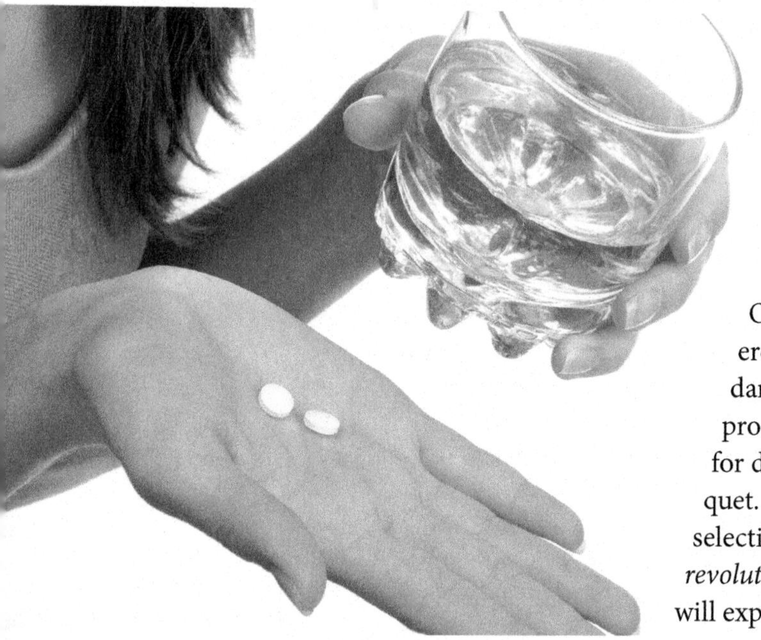

Relaxation is not like generic aspirin.

Over three decades of research, scholars have discovered something quite revolutionary—that is, the standard idea of relaxation is simply wrong. Different approaches to relaxation have different effects. They work for different people. Learning relaxation is more of a banquet. Practicing relaxation is like finding a balanced diet, selecting items from different food groups. This is the *first revolution of relaxation and mindfulness.* It is a revolution we will explore throughout this text.

Revolution #2: The Eye of Mindfulness

Mindfulness is a type of relaxation. However revolutionary new research shows that it is also a neurobiological skill, one of quiet sustained simple focus. This skill is associated with increased health, well-being, and productivity. And it is a brain-based skill, something like a "mental muscle" that actually grows through practice.

Relaxation is like a balanced diet.

© Monticello/Shutterstock.com

There's more. The brain-based skill of mindfulness is required in any type of relaxation, whether it be yoga, muscle relaxation, or self-hypnosis. There is a little bit of mindfulness in any relaxation technique. Indeed, any relaxation is a variation of mindfulness. Furthermore, all of stress management, even change-it and rethink-it approaches, can be viewed as active applications of mindfulness. To cope effectively is to cope mindfully, with full efficient focus, with minimum thought, worry, distraction, and mind wandering. In this text, we view the universe of stress and coping through the Eye of Mindfulness. The Eye of Mindfulness will be our guide.

The Book of Mindfulness

Good news! This book is actually two books. In our main text we consider stress and focus on active approaches to coping, including problem-solving and dealing with negative thinking. We also explore more complex topics that incorporate both, topics such as desensitization, relapse prevention, assertiveness, shyness, anger and aggression, job stress, and crises and catastrophes.

Our second book reviews relaxation and mindfulness. This is something of a book within a book, a handy guide we can return to again and again as we explore stress and coping. We'll call this our *Book of Mindfulness (Third-Generation Edition)*. It presents our suggested protocol as three groups of exercises: (1) the core Eye of Mindfulness, (2) basic relaxation exercises, and (3) mindfulness strengthening exercises. So you can clearly detect the unique effects of each strategy, we will prevent exercises in pure form, rather than as mixtures. Later on you can combine those exercises that work best.

The following graphic summarizes our *Book of Mindfulness*. We'll present it throughout so you can better understand the path we are travelling.

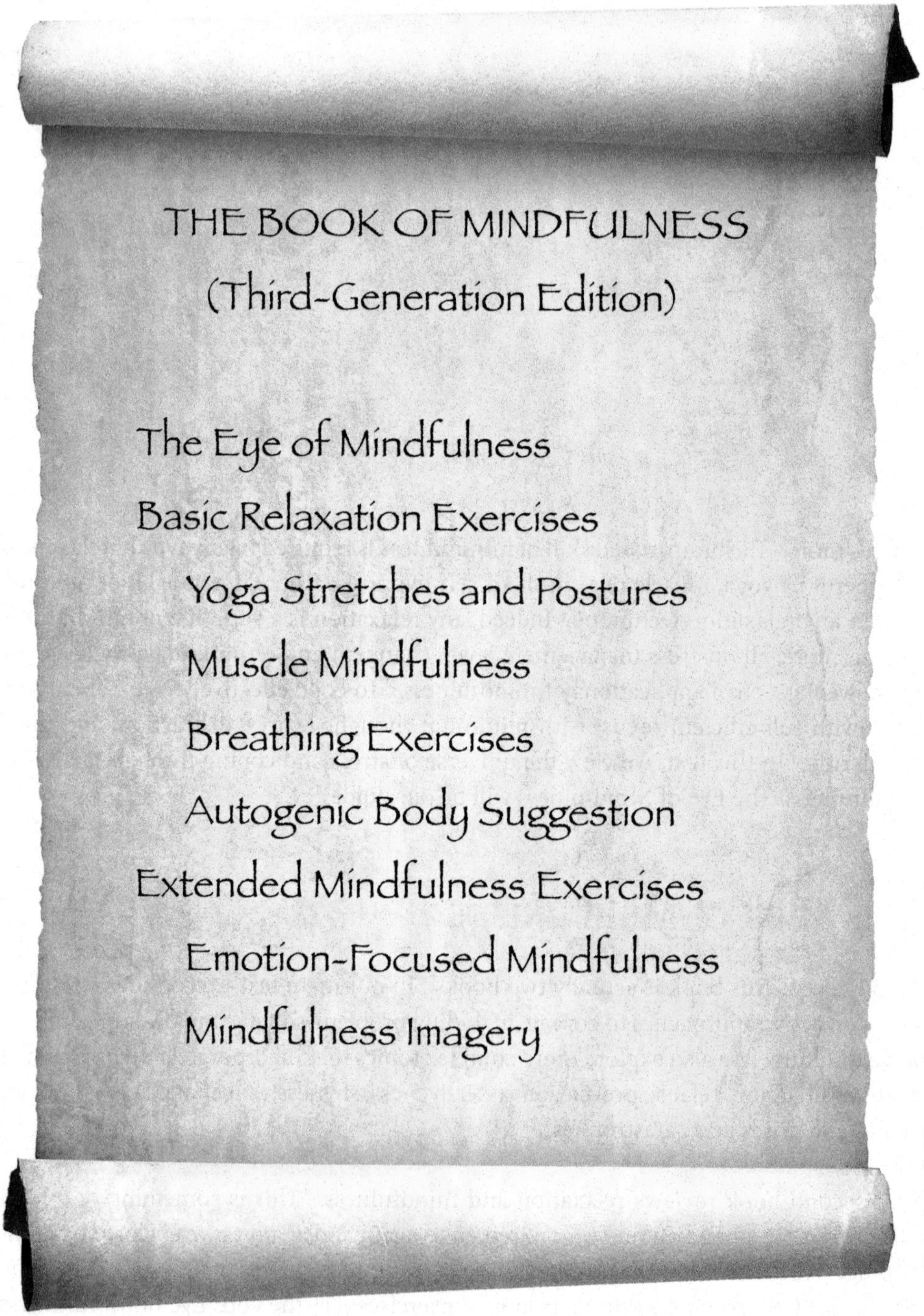

Relaxation and Mindfulness Breaks

You may wonder why exercises from our Book of Mindfulness are scattered throughout the book rather than put in one section. Actually, this is how most of us practice relaxation and mindfulness in actual life. First we engage in work. Then we take a break and relax. The *Book of Mindfulness* is a companion guide we will return to again and again as we progress through the challenges of stress and coping. And so it is with life.

Actually, there's a scientific reason for this. We do much better when we intersperse relaxation with work. It is best to relax every 90 minutes or so. Studies show that memory increases and sports performance improves. Indeed, studies have examined elite performers in music, athletics, acting, and chess, and found that the best performers typically work uninterrupted for no more than 90 minutes, and then take a renewal break (Schwartz, 2013; "*The Multitasking Paradox*," 2013). This pattern may be wired into our brains, and may be reflected in our 90-minute sleep cycles. On a larger scale, this is how most societies organize the work week. We devote five or six days to work, and take the seventh day, perhaps Saturday or Sunday, off for renewal. In the following section we get to work and consider the definition and sources of stress.

Targeted Exercises and Journaling

We learn best when we think about and apply what we're reading. This involves trying out exercises, practicing them enough to get an effect, sharing ideas with other students, and processing our own experiences in a longhand journal. To this end, most of our chapters end with specific exercises you can do, either by yourself or with other classmates. At the end of each set of exercises you will find an invitation to start or continue a *Stress & Coping: Eye of Mindfulness Journal.* I invite you to begin the regular practice of longhand (not on a "device") journaling. In this you write down your thoughts and experiences as they relate to what you have been reading. This includes stress and coping as well as relaxation and mindfulness exercises. What worked? What didn't work? How have you changed? What is new and different? Some students complete a journal every day, some every three days, some once a week. You may complete a journal page after every chapter, or every lesson, or even after a month of lessons.

Stress & Coping
Eye of Mindfulness Journal

Your experiences, insights, and discoveries. What worked? What didn't work? What's new? What changed? If you are practicing relaxation / mindfulness, what states of mind have you experienced? How do you interpret them?

Chapter 2

Stressor Warning Signs

Sometimes stress is good. If you are crossing a street and suddenly notice a truck barreling in your direction, a shot of stress helps you dash to safety. If you do poorly on an exam, perhaps a little worry is what you need to get you studying. If you are concerned about a persistent cough, perhaps your anxiety serves you well by prompting you to see a doctor. Indeed, a life without stress is hard to imagine. Doses of stress can even make us tougher and more resilient (Greenberg, 2017).

But too much stress is not good. It can subject the body to excessive wear and tear and upset the immune system's ability to deal with infection and illness. We are more likely to experience a legion of afflictions, ranging from the common cold and the flu to heart disease and cancer. Although stress may not cause many diseases, it can prolong their course and impair recovery. Wounds take longer to heal. Inflammations are exacerbated. That cough just won't go away.

And excessive stress can get in the way of living life. We aren't as happy. Performance at sports is impaired. Work productivity goes down. Grades suffer. As we shall see throughout this book, the costs of stress can be profound and extensive.

The Stressor–Distress Model

Is there a type of warning sign that can inform us of danger ahead on the road of life? Is there a way of telling good stress from bad? Early stress researchers thought of stress as something like physical wear and tear. Just as any household tool, gadget, or vehicle can wear out with prolonged and excessive use or "stress," so can people. With this notion, to determine how much stress a tool has received, one can look at how much it has been used, or put differently, how many changes it has had to endure. If we apply this to humans, a stressor is a change event, one that requires that we put to use our adaptive resources. *Distress* is the wear and tear we experience, including physical symptoms, illness, negative emotion, and impaired performance.

Put more formally, outside or external situations or events that require adaptation are *stressors*. Stressors eventually contribute to physical and psychological costs, or distress:

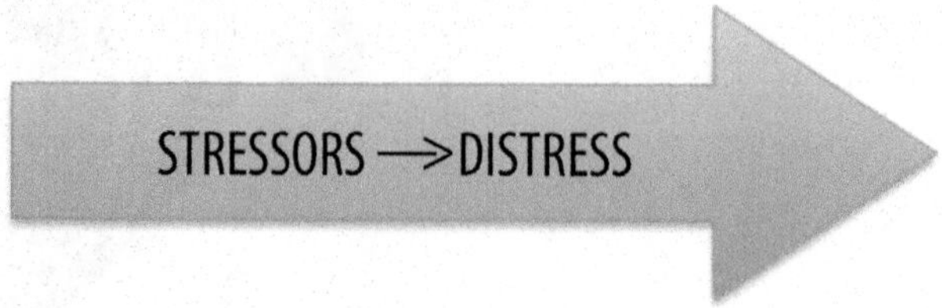

The Social Readjustment Rating Scale

This formula is similar to how psychologists first looked at stress. One might assess the level of change by simply adding up the stressors you have encountered. Perhaps the sheer number of stressors in your life is a good warning sign. A highly stressed bicycle may have been put through many rough rides—the snow, mud, rocky terrain, city traffic, speed racing, and so on. All this leads to wear and tear and potential breakdown. But how do we add up the changes humans accumulate?

Two physicians, Thomas Holmes and Richard Rahe (1967) were among the first to think of how stressors accumulate. They created one of the first stress tests ever, the Social Readjustment Rating Scale. They likened human stress to the notion of "stress" or wear and tear in physics. Their test consisted of 43 life events, ranked from those deemed most stressful to least stressful.

But psychologists eventually found problems with the Social Readjustment Rating Scale and using the sum or stressors as a warning sign. Is a change in financial status equally stressful for different people? Is marriage really all that stressful? The more you think about it, the more problems this approach seems to have. It is not surprising that psychologists quickly started looking for more precise stressor-based warning signs.

Four Stressor Warning Signs

Researchers have examined hundreds of stressors and compared their relative impact. Summarizing these studies, Segerstrom and Miller (2004) concluded that there are four general characteristics of stressors that can be truly destructive. We can view these as the scientifically validated warning signs of toxic stress.

Social Readjustment Rating Scale

Life event	Life change units
Death of a spouse	100
Divorce	73
Marital separation	65
Death of a close family member	63
Imprisonment	63
Personal injury or illness	53
Marriage	50
Dismissal from work	47
Marital reconciliation	45
Retirement	45
Change in health of family member	44 ✓
Pregnancy	40
Business readjustment	39
Gain a new family member	39
Sexual difficulties	39
Change in financial state	38
Death of a close friend	37
Change to different line of work	36
Change in frequency of arguments	35
Major mortgage	32
Foreclosure of mortgage or loan	30
Change in responsibilities at work	29
Child leaving home	29
Trouble with in-laws	29
Outstanding personal achievement	28
Beginning or end school	26 ✓
Spouse starts or stops work	26
Change in living conditions	25 ✓
Revision of personal habits	24
Trouble with boss	23
Change in residence	20
Change in schools	20
Change in working hours or conditions	20
Change in church activities	19
Change in recreation	19
Change in social activities	18 ✓
Minor mortgage or loan	17
Change in sleeping habits	16
Change in eating habits	15
Change in number of family reunions	15
Vacation	13
Major Holiday	12 ✓
Minor violation of law	11

INSTRUCTIONS: Add up the life change units for events experienced over the past year.

Score of 300+: At risk of illness.

Score of 150–299: Risk of illness is moderate (reduced by 30% from the above risk).

Score <150: Only have a slight risk of illness.

Bad news is an unwanted stressor.

1. Is your stressor unwanted?

Imagine your job requires that you move to a different part of the country. Obviously, the stressfulness of this change depends partly on whether or not you wanted to move. Undesired events are more serious stressors than neutral or desired events. What makes an event unwanted? Think about the one thing you don't want to happen in your life (other than your own serious illness or untimely demise). Most people would say that it is some type of loss, such as loss of a loved one. Loss is a part of life. People lose their parents and loved ones, their jobs, their homes, and so on. When considering whether a stressor is serious, ask yourself how much loss is involved.

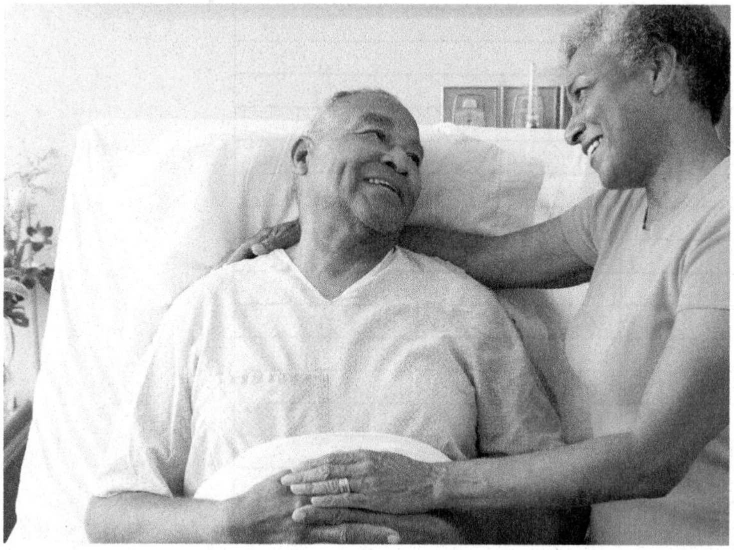

Illness can be a chronic stressor.

2. Is your stressor chronic?

A chronic stressor lasts (or has the potential of lasting) a long time. It is persistent, with few breaks or periods of relief. It can be part of a chain of stressors, part of a "domino effect" of interconnected problems. Serious examples include chronic illness (cancer, AIDS, heart disease), unemployment, living in a war zone, and so on. Although these are very serious examples, they point to an important warning sign question: How long lasting, or chronic, are the combined stressors in your life?

3. Is your stressor uncontrollable?

A stressor is worse if there is little or nothing you can do about it. Unemployment isn't so bad if you are going back to school to learn a new skill. AIDS is less stressful than it was in the 1980s because it can be effectively controlled with medications. Stressors that are realistically hopeless are most likely to be serious.

© AP17/Shutterstock.com

An earthquake is an uncontrollable stressor.

4. Does your stressor require major life change?

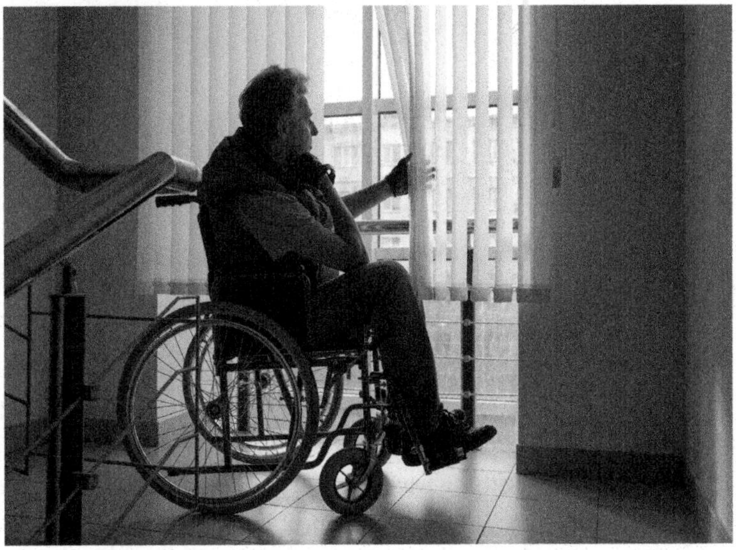

© SERGEI PRIMAKOV/Shutterstock.com

Permanent confinement to a wheelchair can lead to major life change.

The effect of a stressor is made worse when it requires that you make serious changes in your life, especially in your identity and social role. Living with and taking care of a parent may be a chronic and uncontrollable stressor. Your parent is aging, and will not get any younger. The stressor may involve serious loss. You can no longer do the things you used to do with your parent. However, stress is worsened if you have to change your life, for example, and quit your job for one that gives you more time to be with your parent. You may have to change your role, and perhaps see yourself as essentially a "live-in nurse" rather than a "work supervisor," "student," or even "independent."

The Stressor Meter

We can summarize these four warning signs with a tool you can use to evaluate the stress potential of any situation or event in your life. It's the Stressor Meter. Simply check how unwanted, chronic, and uncontrollable your stressor is. Indicate how much life change is involved Finally, estimate its overall stress level.

THE STRESSOR METER

	LO			HI
How Unwanted is it?	①	②	③	④
How Chronic is it?	①	②	③	④
How Uncontrollable is it?	①	②	③	④
How much Life Change is involved?	①	②	③	④
Average (Estimated)	①	②	③	④

Here's a simple stressor. On a recent boat trip, Chris was playing cards on an outdoor table. He put a $20 bill on the table and the bill blew away. Clearly Chris didn't want this to happen, but the loss wasn't serious. Was this a chronic, long-lasting stressor with lots of ramifications? Not really. It was more of an acute, time-limited event. Is his predicament uncontrollable? Just a little, but not much. Chris had several options: He could ask his friends for money, phone his wife, or walk. Things were relatively under control. Any life changes required? None. In sum, Chris had a mild stressor, as indicated here:

CHRIS LOSES $20

	LO			HI
How Unwanted is it?	●	②	③	④
How Chronic is it?	①	②	③	④
How Uncontrollable is it?	①	②	③	④
How much Life Change is involved?	①	②	③	④
Average (estimated)	●	②	③	④

Here's a more serious problem. Rose and Bill were planning to get married. Much preparation went into making this a big celebration. On the day of the marriage, everything was in order. All the guests were there with many gifts. The pastor was present. But there was a problem: Bill had not arrived. Rose tried phoning him at his apartment, but there was no answer. She eventually got through to his roommate, Josh. Unfortunately, Josh did not know where Bill was, except that two days ago he had packed all his belongings, taken them to an undisclosed place, and left a check for next month's rent. Bill also left Josh a note: "Sorry, something came up and I may not be coming back soon. Love, Josh." Rose now not only faces a wedding disaster, but all the negative ramifications. How will she pay for it? What happened to Bill? Will she have to resign to living the life of a single woman? Here's Rose's rating:

THE WEDDING?

	LO			HI
How Unwanted is it?	●	●	●	●
How Chronic is it?	●	●	●	④
How Uncontrollable is it?	●	●	③	④
How much Life Change is involved?	●	●	●	④
Average (estimated)	●	●	●	④

Rose is facing a serious stressor. It's unwanted. It's chronic because the negative effects and ramifications may well be long lasting. Although it seems uncontrollable, there are things Rose can and must do. The loss is large, especially if she must give up her marriage plans and she ends up living an unwanted single life. That consequence would also represent a significant life change. So, Rose estimated that her overall stressor score is high.

What would Rose's rating be if (a) her parents decide to pay for the wedding, (b) Bill sends Rose a letter saying that he's gay and has had a lover for five years, and (c) Rose decides to start over and move to Chicago and start school?

THE WEDDING (VERSION 2)

	LO			HI
How Unwanted is it?	①	②	③	④
How Chronic is it?	①	②	③	④
How Uncontrollable is it?	①	②	③	④
How much Life Change is involved?	①	②	③	④
Average (Estimated)	①	②	③	④

There's Hope!

If your Stressor Meter is high, that doesn't mean you're out of luck. It is a warning sign that you should do something effective about stress, and perhaps try the ideas in this book.

Most people can think of a friend or acquaintance who probably has a high Stressor Meter score, and isn't doing well. These are the unfortunate people who have more than their share of catastrophes, and are "taking it hard." Perhaps they look very unhappy. Perhaps their performance at work is suffering. Perhaps they are suddenly coming down with unexpected illnesses. I suspect these are individuals with poor stress management skills.

You may also know someone who has had a hefty dose of misfortune in life, has a high Stressor Meter score, and is doing just fine. They seem healthy, in relatively good spirits, and are surviving. I propose these individuals possess effective stress management skills.

Examples of High Level Stressors

Four common severe stressors are economic uncertainty, job loss and stress, discrimination, and stereotyping (including gender role and homophobia). Each can lead to high Stressor Meter scores in multiple ways. We can see this in poverty.

Ewart and Suchday (2002) studied urban stress on poverty in inner-city high school students. Looking at census data (income, education, unemployment, poverty) with violence and neighborhood disorder (drugs, shootings), they found that poverty and the violence and disorder associated with it contributes to stress. High school students had higher levels of anger, hostility, distrust, and irritability. Poverty imposes other chronic conditions: crowding, poor housing, financial problems.

Stressors, Mindfulness, and the Mindful Observer

It may surprise you that our Stressor Meter exercise introduces an idea central to this text—mindfulness. Later on we will learn more fully what mindfulness is all about. The Stressor Meter teaches us one mindful idea: to stand back from the storm of stressors and observe the situation realistically and objectively. When completing a Stressor Meter you are taking the role of a mindful observer, calmly considering what you have experienced. Later we will learn more about this special stance.

EXERCISES

2.1 The Social Readjustment Rating Scale

Stress experts frequently criticize the Social Readjustment Rating Scale. Do you think it accurately reflects the stress in your life? Why not? How would you improve it?

2.2 Stressor Meter Practice

Estimate a Stressor Meter score for each.

JOSE FAILS THE FIRST QUIZ

Jose is a nursing student at a local junior college in a large city. This is his first year and he is just learning the ropes of college life. His first course, Biology, is a bit tougher than he thought. College is not the same as high school. And living away from family for the first time in a big city offers many temptations and distractions. Jose has been attending all the classes, and doing the required homework. However, he is apparently doing something wrong. His first quiz grade was an F. How would you evaluate the degree of stress associated with this stressor? Of course, there are some facts you do not know, so you will have to guess. You will quickly discover that Jose's score will vary depending on the facts.

	LO			HI
How Unwanted is it?	①	②	③	④
How Chronic is it?	①	②	③	④
How Uncontrollable is it?	①	②	③	④
How much Life Change is involved?	①	②	③	④
Average (Estimated)	①	②	③	④

JILL GOES TO COLLEGE

Jill has lived with her family for 18 years and is moving across the country to start her undergraduate work at a strict church-run college in the middle of South Dakota. This is the first time she has spent time away from home and away from her high school friends. And there was Jon, her boyfriend-prospect who is going to a college far away from Jill. Jill will have to pay her way through college. She has no friends in her new town.

	LO			HI
How Unwanted is it?	①	②	③	④
How Chronic is it?	①	②	③	④
How Uncontrollable is it?	①	②	③	④
How much Life Change is involved?	①	②	③	④
Average (Estimated)	①	②	③	④

2.3 Your Stressors

In the following spaces, create your own stressor test. List all the potential stressors someone like you (your age, your job or level in school, marital status) might encounter. Then check the stressors you have actually experienced in the past six months. Give your guess as to whether you are experiencing a low, moderate, or high number of stressors.

- ☐ Change in school
- ☐ Change in job
- ☐ Change in health of family member
- ☐ Economic Uncertainty
- ☐ Change in social activities
- ☐ Difficult family dynamics
- ☐ Upcoming family reunions/get-togethers
- ☐ Change in friends' marital/parental status
- ☐ Work/School/Social Life balance
- ☐ Keeping up w/ health goals
- ☐ Drastic Change in Weather
- ☐ Change in finances

2.4 Your Stressor

Describe a typical stressor you are currently dealing with. Give it a Stressor Meter score.

The majority of my friends are having children & moving to the suburbs. As their families grow and then the physical distance of where we live from each other grows, I realize my social circle is shrinking drastically

	LO			HI
How Unwanted is it?	①	②	③	④
How Chronic is it?	①	②	③	④
How Uncontrollable is it?	①	②	③	④
How much Life Change is involved?	①	②	③	④
Average (Estimated)	①	②	③	④

2.5 Common Stressors

Your text mentioned four common severe stressors:

- Economic uncertainty
- Job loss and stress
- Discrimination
- Stereotyping, gender-role stereotyping, homophobia

Describe how each might be stressful. Then score it on your Stressor Meter.

Stress & Coping
Eye of Mindfulness Journal

Your experiences, insights, and discoveries. What worked? What didn't work? What's new? What changed? If you are practicing relaxation / mindfulness, what states of mind have you experienced? How do you interpret them?

Chapter 3

The Stress Engine

© Fabio Berti/Shutterstock.com

Bernie is a waiter at a small vegetarian restaurant. For the last few weeks, he has had problems at work:

> *"I'm making a lot more mistakes when waiting orders. I forget orders or get them mixed up. I seem to be wasting lots of time asking customers to repeat themselves, or serving tables in the wrong order. I think I'm under lots of stress, and it's beginning to show at work."*

Mouna is a busy accountant with a medical problem. She's seeing a specialist about a persistent abdominal pain. Here is her account:

> *"I get this stomachache and queasiness about midday, and it lasts until bedtime. Sometimes I feel so bad, I have to take a break and just rest. My specialist says I have acid stomach, aggravated by excessive stress. She wants me to take time off and deal with my stress."*

Sid is an art student specializing in computer graphics at the local college. He also works full time as a bartender. For the last year or so, he's had more than his share of colds. It seems that every three or four weeks be begins coughing and has to stay home. Sid started to worry about why he catches so many colds, and finally visited the school doctor. He now suspects where his problems are coming from.

> *"My doctor says its stress. Stress builds up in my body and eventually reduces my resistance, and I am more likely to catch a cold. Several colds a year."*

Each of these accounts has the same message: One of the first signs of stress is distress. And stress-related distress can appear as:

- Illness and physical symptoms
- Reduced effectiveness at work, school, sports, and home
- Negative emotions: frustration, anxiety, depression, and anger

In Chapter 2 we discussed stressors. We now consider an early perspective on how stressors create symptoms of distress. Understanding this remarkable process can give us powerful tools for detecting when we are under stress and what to do about it.

The Fight-or-Flight Response

Have you ever met a superman, or superwoman? This is a serious question because people sometimes do acquire near superhuman powers. We encounter them every day. Think about a recent football game. The game is near its end. Players are exhausted. If you were this exhausted, you would almost certainly plop yourself on a sofa and sleep. Amazingly football players find the energy to run to the goalpost.

Here's another example. A letter carrier fights off a barking dog. Suddenly she finds energy and endurance she didn't know she had. Or, a camper lifts a tree that has fallen on a tent, trapping the family puppy. Although not a weightlifter, he easily lifts 100 pounds. You may well have heard of similar accounts of apparently miraculous strength and endurance—and often they are accurate.

Each of us has an automatic ability that awakens and energizes us for emergency action. This is the body's stress engine, which when revved up can do remarkable things. Unfortunately, this same engine is often in "overdrive," running fast when we're doing nothing, and creating the symptoms of distress.

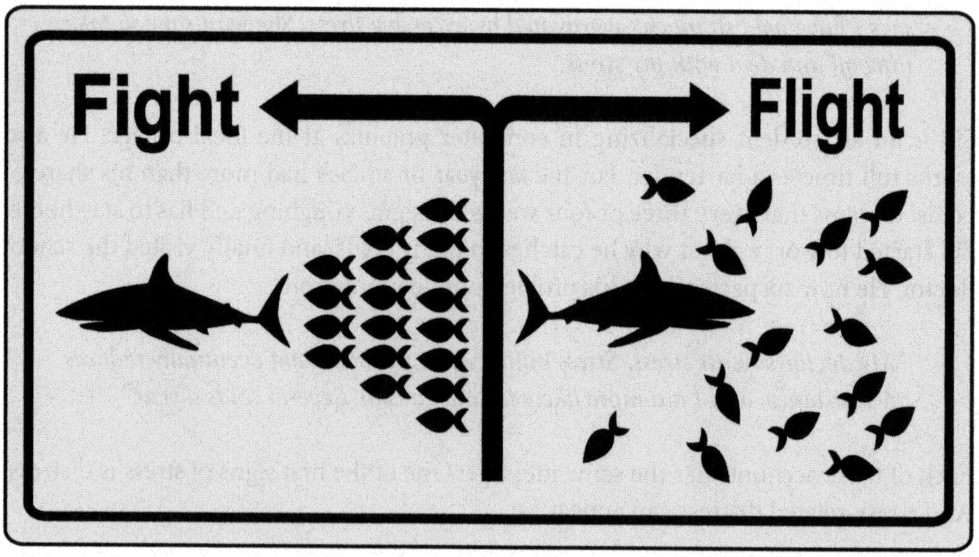

Physiologist Walter Cannon (1929) noted that our ancestors in the wild evolved an automatic lifesaving ability called stress arousal or, as he called it, the *fight-or-flight response*. Ancient humans hardly had time to figure out how to ready their bodies to fight off attacks from gorillas, bears, or hostile tribes. Other animals, even the dinosaurs, had this ability. One of the most successful products of evolution is the brain's stress engine and its ability to automatically, without thought or planning, bring about the fight-or-flight response.

THE SAM PATHWAY

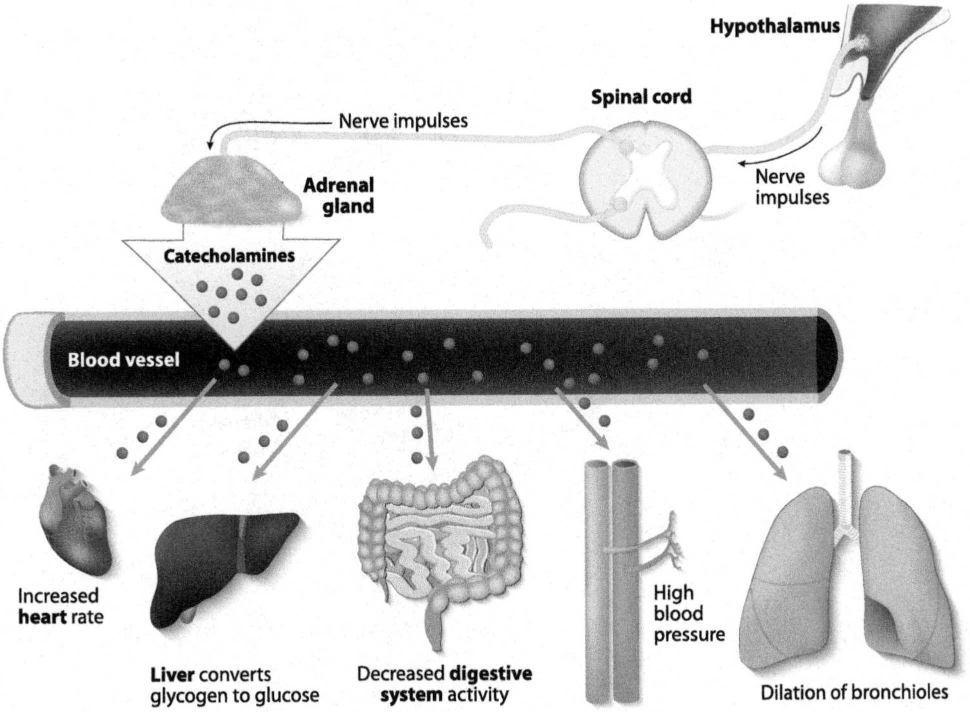

The SAM Pathway

Here's how the stress engine works. Deep within the brain is an almond-sized organ, the hypothalamus. This is the body's "stress trigger." When activated, the trigger begins an immediate response for acute stressors and a long-term and lingering stress response. The short-term response is sometimes called the sympathomedullary pathway in that signals are sent down the sympathetic nervous system in the spine to the central part of the adrenal gland, the adrenal medulla (SAM; S = Sympathetic nervous system, AM = adrenal medulla). Put simply, the SAM pathway can be summarized by key organs involved:

HYPOTHALAMUS -> ADRENAL MEDULLA -> STRESS HORMONES

Stress hormones called catecholamines, specifically adrenalin and noradrenaline, are released triggering an increase in heart rate. The liver releases fuels into the bloodstream by converting glycogen to glucose. Digestive activity decreases. Blood pressure increases. The lungs take in more air and oxygen by dilation of tiny lung passages called bronchioles. This response occurs within seconds to prepare for immediate stressors.

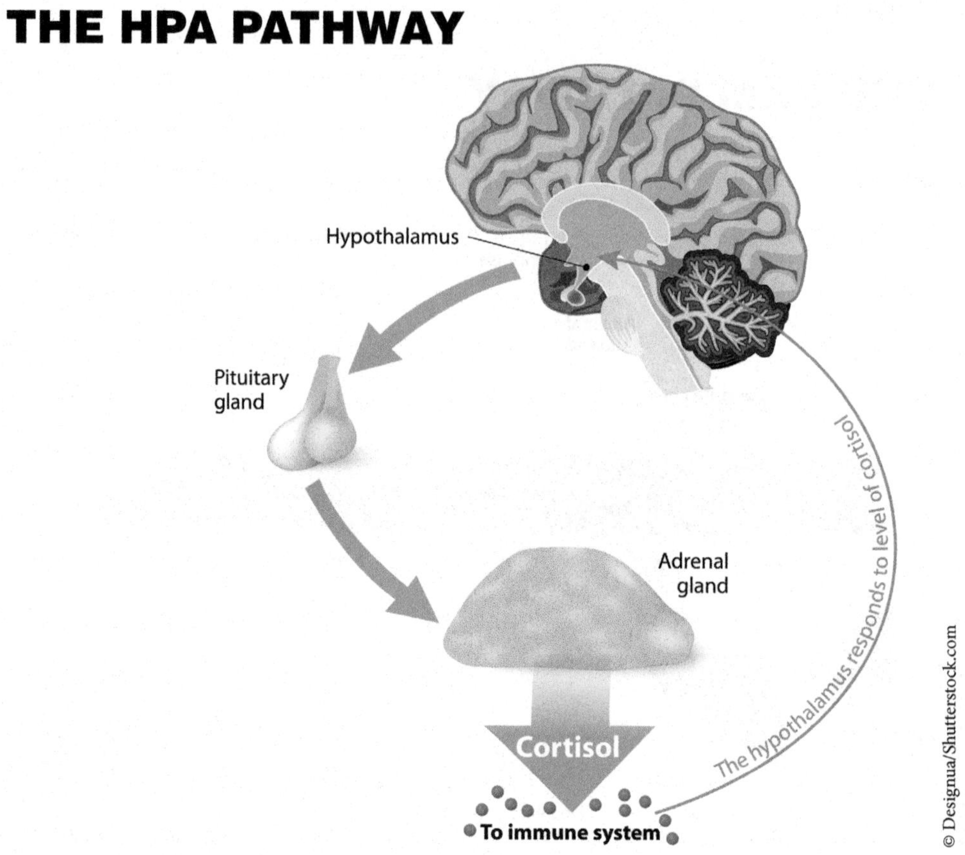

The HPA Pathway

The hypothalamus also triggers a longer-lasting version of this stress response, one that can last for days and weeks, prolonging the effects of stress even after a threat is long gone. The path of this response is a bit more complicated. Here the hypothalamus triggers a small nearby organ in the brain called the pituitary gland, which in turn sends signals to the adrenal glands (the outer portion or "cortex") which secrete an important set of stress hormones called corticoids, notably cortisol. This is sometimes called the HPA (H = hypothalamus, P = pituitary, A = adrenal cortex) pathway. This pathway can be summarized by key organs involved:

HYPOTHALAMUS -> PITUITARY GLAND –> ADRENAL GLANDS -> STRESS HORMONES

The HPA pathway supports many of the effects evoked by immediate stress, including increased blood pressure and release of sugars into the bloodstream. In time it also impairs the functioning of the immune system for fighting off and recovering from illness. One way to keep the fast-acting SAM and the slower lingering HPA systems distinguished is to remember that the SAM operates primarily through quick-acting nerve impulses, especially in the spine's sympathetic nervous system (the "S" in SAM). The HPA is slow lingering because it operates by chemicals secreted into the bloodstream, which in turn are somewhat more slowly distributed to relevant organs.

Summary of the Physiological Effects of Stress

These are the mechanics of the stress arousal engine, responsible for the fight-or-flight response. But just how do the combined effects of the SAM and HPA prepare us?

- Whether you are a football player, a boxer, or simply a child chasing a runaway cat, it takes energy to deal with an emergency. We get our stress energy from fuels in our body. The hypothalamus complies by triggering the liver to release sugars, fats, cholesterol (yes, cholesterol is also a body fuel), and proteins into the bloodstream.
- Whether fighting or fleeing, we need oxygen to "burn" fuel (including cholesterol) in a process called metabolism. To increase oxygen flow, the hypothalamus signals the lungs to breathe faster. And breathing passages in the lungs (bronchial tubes) expand to let in more air.
- Enriched with fuel and oxygen, blood must quickly and efficiently go to the muscles that will be doing the "fighting" or "fleeing." The heart beats more quickly, and as more blood is pumped with each beat, blood pressure increases.
- The muscles responsible for vigorous activity must take in increased blood supplied by the heart. Blood vessels to the heart and big muscles expand, providing more fuel to parts of the body that may be involved in emergency action. Tiny blood vessels to the skin, particularly the palms of the hands and the feet, constrict. Blood is not essential here for vigorous action. Hands feel cold and clammy.
- As we work hard to fight or flee, fuels are burned and body heat increases. Heat is carried away as we breathe more quickly and perspire.
- Functions not needed for emergency action are reduced: Stomach and intestinal activity are limited, and blood flow to the stomach, kidneys, and intestines decreases.

In addition, secondary changes occur that enhance our mobilization for emergency action:

- The body prepares itself for possible injury. Surface blood vessels constrict, reducing the possibility of serious blood loss. Clotting substances are dumped into the bloodstream, easing the formation of protective scar tissue.
- The immune system increases activity in anticipation of possible infection, or reduces activity to minimize the potentially damaging effects of infection and conserve resources for fighting and fleeing.

- Natural pain killers, endorphins, are released by the brain, to help us keep on going in the face of considerable discomfort.
- Finally, the body readies itself for active involvement with the outside world. Pupils of the eye enlarge to let in more light and enhance vision, palms and feet become moist to increase grip and traction when running, and brain activity increases.

Three things about autonomic stress arousal are important to recognize.

1. It is adaptive, supplying quick energy for fighting off or fleeing attack, quickly responding to unexpected physical assault, and so on.
2. It can have a delayed and prolonged effect, important for maintaining stress-fighting resources at a high level over the weeks.
3. The response is automatically integrated. All relevant body systems are energized together—heart, lungs, circulatory system, and so on. One does not have to plan for increased stress arousal, as one might deliberately prepare the proper stance for striking a golf ball or running a race. In times of severe crisis, our ancestors in the jungle needed complete automatic, quick energy.

We now have a better understanding of our stressor–distress formula. Physiological arousal is a key component of distress. Our formula can be refined:

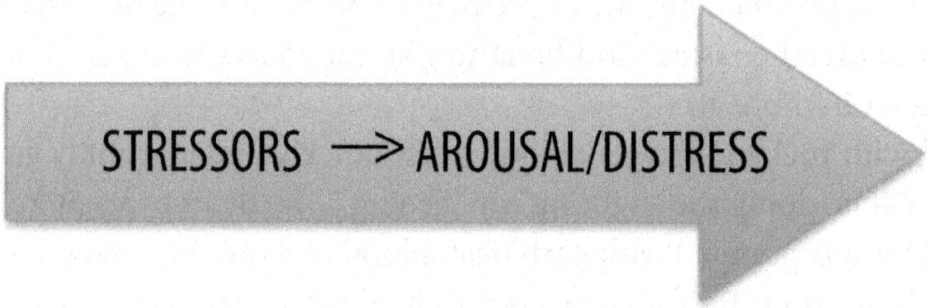

The Costs of Fight or Flight

People may think of stress as always negative. However, the fight-or-flight response can be very useful, even life saving. It provides quick energy for the football player catching a pass, the secretary who must prepare for an immediate emergency, and the jogger running from a dog in the park.

The General Adaptation Syndrome

At this point we take a slight historical detour. Hans Selye, an endocrinologist from Canada, is sometimes seen as a founding father of current work on stress. Seyle extended Cannon's idea of the fight-or-flight response. He found that if you subject laboratory animals to sustained environmental stressors, such as freezing, constant light, noise, or constant swimming, the demands eventually become too great and the animals die.

Furthermore, it appeared that all test animals displayed a general *nonspecific response to demand.* Seyle developed a model for this breakdown, calling it the *General Adaptation Syndrome*, or GAS. It has three stages: alarm, resistance, and exhaustion.

1. The alarm, or fight-or-flight response, is the initial emergency reaction to a stressor. It's as if a fire triggers the fire department to send all its fire engines to the emergency.
2. Eventually, in the resistance stage, the body devotes only the resources needed. Most of the fire engines are sent home. However, if the stressor is prolonged, the resources devoted to resist wear down (especially "weak links"), and more resources are again allocated to dealing with the stressor.
3. When these are worn out, the organism experiences the third phase, exhaustion, and often dies. (Incidentally, these three stages of stress might technically be seen as three stages of strain, if we were to use words correctly.) We will reconsider Selye's GAS near the end of the book when we discuss environmental stress. Here his ideas have some relevance.

Selye thought his GAS was indeed general and applied to just about any lab animal subjected to an extreme and prolonged environmental stressor. However, today experts have concluded this model is too simple, extreme, and misleading to apply to most human stress. Rarely do humans reach exhaustion. Furthermore, when stress is positive (which Seyle called *eustress*) rather than negative (*distress*), the costs are minimal. Finally, when stress energy is focused on the task of dealing with a challenge, it is put to productive use, minimizing potential harm. Furthermore, the idea that everyone displays the same global nonspecific response is a myth that appears again and again in the field of stress, as we will discover in this text.

What is important to know is that the fight-or-flight response can be triggered by nonemergencies like alarm clocks, worries, negative emotions, interpersonal conflict, and excessive work. These do not have to be at such catastrophic levels described in Seyle's research. Even for stressors not leading to Seyle's exhaustion stage, stress energy increases and is not discharged through vigorous emergency action. Over days and weeks, stress arousal continues to rise, eventually contributing to distress on body organs and illness. In sum, short-term stress isn't particularly bad for you; however, chronic and uncontrollable stress clearly impacts health and well-being (Segerstrom & Miller, 2004)

It would take many books to describe how stress arousal, or excessive running of the stress engine, can contribute to distress, to symptoms, illness, and ineffectiveness at work, school, sports, and home. If you are interested in the details, check out Table 3.1.

TABLE 3.1 The Costs of Chronic Fight-or-Flight Arousal

Physical Symptoms and Illness

High blood pressure. The stress engine pumps up blood pressure so that more blood gets to muscles for emergency action. If this goes on nonstop, blood pressure remains continuously high, a serious medical condition.

Coronary disease. In coronary disease, cholesterol and fats clog the arteries; occasionally a blood clot may break away and create a blockage in the heart (causing a heart attack) or the brain (causing a stroke). The stress engine dumps more cholesterol and fat into the blood as "fuel," as well as blood clotting substances to reduce excessive bleeding in case of injury. However, when prolonged these very same beneficial effects become problems.

Cancer. The relationship between stress and cancer is still in question. People with suppressed immune systems seem are vulnerable to some, but not all forms of cancer. However, stress can probably impair the body's ability to fight off some of the negative side effects of cancer and cancer treatment.

The common cold and influenza. The immune system helps us fight off and recover from a wide range of respiratory diseases. If suppressed by stress (see "Cancer" above), we are more likely to catch a cold or the flu, and our illness is more likely to be prolonged.

Other disorders related to stressful wear and tear and immune system disruption. Just about every illness patients report to physicians can be influenced by stress-related immune impairment: AIDS, angina, asthma, back pain, bradycardia, cancer, cardiac arrhythmia, chemotherapy side effects, colitis, common cold, coronary heart disease, diabetes, gastrointestinal disorders, hypertension, hyperventilation, inflammation and infection, influenza, injury/healing, insomnia, irritable bowel syndrome, migraine headaches, multiple sclerosis, muscle cramps, myocardial infarction, nausea, peptic ulcer, psoriasis, Raynaud syndrome, spasmodic dysmenorrhea, tachycardia, and tinnitus.

Negative Emotions

Negative stress emotions include fear, anxiety, depression, feeling blue, anger, and irritation. All of these are exaggerated by worry. Although negative emotions are not a direct result of stress arousal, they are connected.

The Yerkes-Dodson Law

Some arousal can be good. Too little or too much can get in the way. Psychologists Robert M. Yerkes and John Dodson (1908) noted that increased arousal improves performance, but only up to a point. Then arousal interferes. Yerkes and Dodson found this was true for rats learning to complete a maze. A little electrical shock motivated rats to learn a maze more quickly, but too much shock caused the rats to run around trying to escape, never learning the maze.

A pessimist might say that life is something like living in a maze. More seriously, the relationship between arousal and performance is complex. Why is it that football players try to stir themselves up to high levels of arousal before a game, whereas you might relax by taking a few deep breaths before completing an exam? Relaxing before football, or screaming and jumping before an exam, would not work.

Different types of tasks call for different levels of ideal arousal. Too much, or too little, gets in the way. Very simple tasks that are mostly physical can tolerate higher levels of arousal. Indeed, you may even perform better. However, complex and mental tests, like completing a college exam, reading a textbook, or doing homework, require some but not high levels of arousal.

Is Your Stress Engine in Overdrive?

You can be unaware of stress arousal through a process called *habituation*. The brain can tune out constant, unchanging stimuli, whether it be the background drone of air conditioners, traffic noise, or stress. The signs of stress arousal can also habituate so that we become "numb" to or unaware of them. One step of stress management is to be mindful of your distress/arousal symptoms. Generally, they fall into three categories:

- Worry, feeling distressed, anxious, fearful, irritated, angry, depressed, blue
- Fight-or-flight physical symptoms
- Attention deficits (trouble concentrating, forgetfulness, being easily distracted, feeling confused)

Over the years I have developed a simple stress test that can help you determine if you have excessive stress arousal. Researchers around the world have used this test on thousands of individuals. When asking if you are experiencing high levels of stress arousal, our test can be a useful starting point. However, keep in mind that a high score can mean many things, including an underlying medical condition (so you might consider seeing a physician if your scores are high). It is more likely that a high score is stress related if you have a lot of stressors in your life.

The probability is even greater if any of the additional stress-enhancing behaviors described in the next chapter are a factor (e.g., engaging in needless negative thinking, stirring up exaggerated feelings of arousal and upset, or doing the wrong thing in an attempt to make stress better). More on that later. First, let's address your stress arousal/distress level.

SMITH STRESS TEST

Your Level of Arousal/Distress

To what extent do the following statements generally or typically fit you?

Please rate each item using the following key.

① DOESN'T FIT ME
② FITS A LITTLE
③ FITS MODERATELY
④ FITS VERY WELL

PART 1: WORRY

①❷③④ I worry too much about things that do not really matter.
①❷③④ I have difficulty controlling negative thoughts.
①❷③④ I feel distressed (discouraged or sad).
①❷③④ I am depressed.
①❷③④ I am anxious.
❶②③④ I have difficulty keeping troublesome thoughts out of mind.
①❷③④ I am afraid.
①❷③④ I find myself thinking unimportant, bothersome thoughts.
①②❸④ I feel irritated or angry.

WHAT IS THE SUM OF YOUR RATINGS? 18
DIVIDE IT BY 9.
THIS IS YOUR NEGATIVE EMOTION / WORRY SCORE. = 2

PART 2: FIGHT OR FLIGHT

①❷③④ I have a nervous stomach.
❶②③④ I lose sleep.
❶②③④ My breathing is hurried, shallow, or uneven.
❶②③④ My heart beats fast, hard, or irregularly.
❶②③④ I lose my appetite.
❶②③④ My mouth feels dry.
①❷③④ I perspire or feel too warm.
❶②③④ I feel the need to go to the restroom unnecessarily.

●②③④ I feel fatigued.
①●③④ My shoulders, neck, or back are tense.
①②●④ My muscles feel tight, tense, or clenched up (furrowed brow, tightened fist, clenched jaws).
●②③④ I have backaches.
●②③④ I have headaches.

WHAT IS THE SUM OF YOUR RATINGS? __18__
DIVIDE IT BY 13.
THIS IS YOUR PHYSICAL SYMPTOMS SCORE. 1.38

PART 3: ATTENTION DEFICITS

①●③④ I become easily distracted.
①●③④ I lose my memory and forget things.
●②③④ I feel confused.
●②③④ I lose my concentration.
①●③④ I feel disorganized.
①●③④ I feel restless and fidgety.

WHAT IS THE SUM OF YOUR RATINGS? __10__
DIVIDE IT BY 6.
THIS IS YOUR ATTENTION DEFICITS SCORE. 1.67

SCORING KEY

Generally, our research shows that an average score from 0–2 is rather low. A score from 2–3 is average. Anything above 3 is a little high.

Stress & Coping
Eye of Mindfulness Journal

Chapter 4

Stress Booster Buttons

© Tashatuvango/Shutterstock.com

It is easy to think of stress in simple cause-effect terms. Any stressor causes us to feel upset and distressed. We might blame our noisy child for our headaches, our insensitive coworkers for our work frustration, or our crazy schedules for our fatigue. Here stress is something like an arrow:

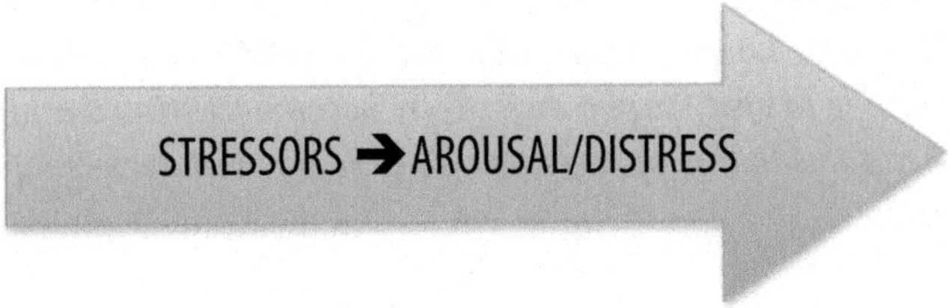

But if you think about it, there is something wrong with the cause-effect arrow. If things were that simple, our problems, although painful, would quickly pass. You might stub your toe on the steps (stressor) and feel stirred up and in pain (arousal/distress), and get over it. In reality, the world is much more complicated. Your boss may unfairly deny you a raise (stressor) and you get angry with an upset stomach (arousal/distress). But the story, of course, doesn't end here. You may worry. Work may suffer. You may start drinking, etc.

There is a very important missing part to our stress arrow. Stress is not automatic. We can make stress worse through our choices. Three booster buttons can crank up the severity and duration of both stressor and arousal/distress:

① We can make **coping mistakes.**
② We can **distort** through needless negative thinking.
③ We can create and sustain arousal through **physical self-stressing**.

Here's our improved stress arrow, complete with three new booster buttons. Let me describe how it works.

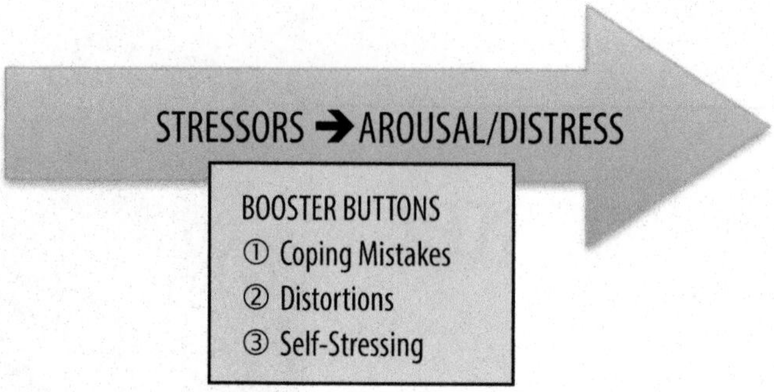

First, note the placement of the booster buttons. Distortions, coping mistakes, and self-stressing can impact any part of our stress equation. Indeed, any booster button can have an effect on any other booster button. Your distortions can interfere with your coping.

In the following example Tony is facing a modest stressor and is experiencing some arousal/distress. However, he is boosting his problems in three ways:

> *Tony is a beginning college student who has moved away from his mother to live in a college house. One weekend his mother called and announced that she was going to visit for two days. Tony became frustrated and upset because had other plans and wanted to be alone. So far we have a simple cause-effect stress arrow.*
>
> *MOTHER ANNOUNCES HER VISIT -> TONY GETS UPSET.*
>
> *However, there's more to the story. Immediately after the call, Tony started thinking, "She's checking up on me. Mother doesn't trust me. She always treats me like a child." Actually, this was a bit of an exaggeration, a distortion. In addition, Tony started thinking about how awful it is when his mother visits. He clenched his fists and held his breath. Tony was stirring himself up through self-stressing. And not wanting to be bothered, he yelled at his roommate not to bother him, probably a coping mistake in this situation.*

In sum, Tony aggravated and probably prolonged his stress through coping badly, engaging in distorted thinking, and making himself unnecessarily tense. We now consider each stress booster in detail.

© Gearstd/Shutterstock.com

STRESS BOOSTER ① Coping Mistakes

There is no end to the specific mistakes people can make when attempting to cope with the problems of living. However, it is useful to view stressors as problems waiting to be solved. In this context, one can make several general types of mistakes:

- Denying and avoiding the situation

  John has graduated from college and moved to a new city. He is living with friends and looking for a job as a cashier in a restaurant. Having little luck, he thinks, "I'll just hang around. Something will turn up. Things have a way of working out." Unfortunately, this line of thinking leads John to avoid looking for a job, thus increasing his stress.

- Not looking at the real problem

  Maria has made an agreement with her husband Jose. They are to take turns cleaning house every other week. Two weeks have gone by, dirt is piling up, and Jose hasn't touched the broom. Maria decides that if she doesn't clean on her week, Jose will think she doesn't love him. So she figures out how to spend an extra afternoon cleaning house. Clearly, the problem is not how to keep Jose's love, or even how to schedule extra cleaning time. Maria probably wants Jose to keep his side of the agreement and needs to deal with this.

- Getting stuck on one possible solution and not generating others

  Roberta is trying to figure out the best way to meet guys. After school, she sits in her room with a pad of paper and decides to make a list. The first thing that comes to mind is, "Call my friend Amy. She'll help me out. She always does!" Roberta runs to the phone and makes her call.

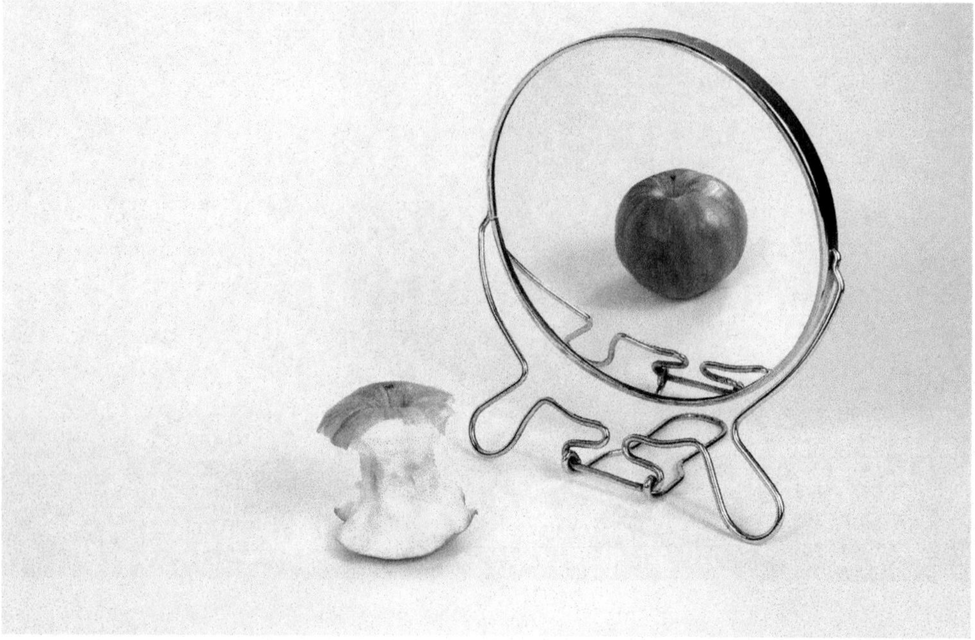

© Des Green/Shutterstock.com

STRESS BOOSTER ② Distorting Stress

Here are two items from the famous stressor test, the Social Readjustment Rating Scale invented by Holmes and Rahe:

Going to Jail
Divorce

How we think about stressors influences their impact. When we distort our stressors, we often make them worse. Consider these two unfortunate people who had to spend a night in jail (because of too many parking tickets):

Inmate 1: "I can't stand jail. This seems like forever."

Inmate 2: "It's only one night. I can take it. I'll get my life in order starting tomorrow."

Or consider these two divorcees:

Divorcee 1: "Divorce is a personal failure. I simply do not have what it takes to get along with others. No one will ever want to date me again."

Divorcee 2: "This divorce is unfortunate, but a challenge. I will have to learn from my mistakes. People who have been married once are more mature, and better candidates for good marriage."

It should be clear that Inmate 1 and Divorcee 1 are distorting their predicaments by needlessly catastrophizing, personalizing, and assuming things will always be bad. Inmate 2 and Divorcee 2, on the other hand, are treating their situations as challenging problems, not catastrophes, and are generally cool headed, realistic, and practical about their situations.

STRESS BOOSTER ③ SELF-STRESSING

Let us return to the stress engine, fight or flight. Picture an unlucky distant ancestor, whom we shall name Tena. Tena encounters an angry bear in the forest. In response to this perceived threat, she experiences a quick rush of energy. As we have seen, her hypothalamus initiates a series of body changes that provide blood and oxygen to organs for vigorous action.

Usually this process is more or less automatic. However, Tena boosts her stress whenever she makes a coping mistake or thinks in a stressful way. In addition, she intensifies and prolongs the fight-or-flight response through physical self-stressing. Specifically she leaps into action and tenses up. If this were a video, we could slow down the action and notice that she is engaging in three types of physical self-stressing:

1. **Stressed posture.** Tena assumes a physical posture of readiness for fight or flight. She crouches in a defensive position and holds her arms still so not to upset the bear. This posture keeps her tense and maintains stress arousal.

Self-Stressing

2. **Stressed muscles.** She tightens her muscles and gets ready to run or flee at a moment's notice. Tension continues and increases.
3. **Stressed breathing.** She holds her breath tightly, breathes in through her expanded chest, and takes an occasional deep sigh. This makes her even more tense.

Through self-stressing we intensify and prolong the fight-or-flight response. Although stress arousal is often automatic, self-stressing is a way we can choose to augment it.

Self-stressing has its place. Sometimes we encounter emergencies that require high levels of stress arousal. In such situations we learn to put up with associated distress. Such extreme situations may include engaging in vigorous sports, escaping an attacking animal, dealing with a prolonged highway emergency, and so on. In addition, we can experience self-stressing in less extreme situations, as illustrated in these examples:

> *Yoshi is a junior in college and is having trouble getting into the college routine. She enjoyed her summer vacation and is reluctant to get back to work. Unfortunately, Yoshi failed her English midterm. This really shook her up. The night after the midterm, she goes to the library, finds a good firm chair, and sits alert and upright* ***(stressful posture)****. With pencil clenched in hand, brow furrowed, and jaws clenched, she opens her book* ***(stressed muscles)****. She realizes that she has more chapters to read than she expected, and holds her breath* ***(stressed breathing)****.*

Here is another example:

> *Hector is a young legal assistant in a large law firm. Recently coworker Joe has been publicly putting him down. Hector is a bit shy, but feels upset and intimidated every time Joe jokes about his hair, clothing choice, and preference for hats. One evening, Hector finds himself thinking about Joe's most recent insult and decides to have a heart-to-heart talk. Because he sometimes has difficulty confronting others, Hector decides to practice what he is going to say. Alone at home, he stands, looks straight ahead, and folds his arms* ***(stressful posture)****. He carefully furrows his brow, lowers his voice, and lifts his hands for emphasis* ***(stressed muscles)****. He takes a deep breath, holds it a little, and then breathes in a very careful, controlled way* ***(stressed breathing)****.*

What was your fight-or-flight score on the Smith Stress Test in Chapter 3? Can you identify ways you self-stress? Identify two or three serious stress situations. Imagine you are in them. What are you doing and thinking? What happened? What went wrong. Now, how did your posture reflect stress and tension? Were you tightening up any muscles? Was your breathing shallow, uneven, or rushed?

Stress & Coping
Eye of Mindfulness Journal

Chapter 5

The Coping Toolbox

© Ilin Sergey/Shutterstock.com

The stress management toolbox is overflowing. If you search the Internet for stress management tools you will quickly uncover a never-ending list, with "hits" ranging from acupuncture to Zen. Where does one begin? Actually, if you have read the first part of this book, or even the preceding page of text, you already know the answer.

We have seen that there are three things we do to boost and prolong stress:

1. Do the wrong thing through maladaptive coping.
2. Distort stress through unrealistic thinking.
3. Stir up tension and feelings through self-stressing.

These point to three general categories of stress management:

1. Cope effectively (fix it).
2. Think realistically (re-think it).
3. Learn to relax.

Do all of this mindfully.

This is our coping formula:

Fix it + Re-think it + Relax
Mindfully

© valdis torms/Shutterstock.com

1. Fix It: Effective Problem-Solving

There are many ways of doing nothing. One might pretend ("The problem will just go away on its own"), put things off ("I'll do it tomorrow, or the day after"), or even feign helplessness ("This is just too big for me. I'll just give up").

Problem-solving involves taking a realistic piece of a problem, identifying what one really wants, brainstorming options, and taking action. For example:

> *Kathy has just moved to a new town and is staying with a friend. She finally found a job and feels she must leave. But living with her friend is so easy. And because Kathy has never lived alone before, finding a place seems overwhelming. So one day she decides to get down to business and move. That evening, she goes to a local coffee house and lists what seems like realistic steps. How much rent can she afford? What neighborhoods does she like? How will she get to them? And most important, where can she call for help? She then proceeds with each question.*

The key to problem-solving is to accept that all parts of a problem can't be solved at once, and there may be many courses of action one could take. One then targets what can be solved.

2. Re-think It: Realistic Thinking

Needless distorted thinking makes stress worse. Realistic thinking involves catching ourselves in the act of thinking negatively, identifying and challenging our unrealistic thoughts, and figuring out what is more realistic. We see this illustrated:

> *Sergio promised to take his friend Peter out to dinner on his birthday. Sergio forgot and felt terrible. At first, he started putting himself down: "I'm a worthless friend. No one can trust me." Then he realized what he was saying to himself. "Gosh, I'm really doing a number on myself. Worthless? Untrustworthy? These are extreme words!" He took a deep breath, and re-thought the situation. "Well, I shouldn't call myself worthless and untrustworthy. I was just very careless and perhaps sloppy for not putting Peter's birthday in my calendar." And he figured out a more realistic way of thinking. "I care for Peter and will take him out when he wants, maybe even twice. He's worth something to me, and I know him well enough that he thinks I'm worth something."*

Such rethinking is easier said than done, and in following chapters we will look at a variety of powerful strategies for breaking bad negative thinking habits and approaching problems more effectively.

© gornostay/Shutterstock.com

3. Relax: Relaxation and Mindfulness

When we self-stress we create arousal and distress. Relaxation involves just the opposite, reducing arousal and distress. We will learn in our chapters on relaxation that each form of self-stressing has a corresponding relaxation family.

Mindfulness is a special type of relaxation that is more. It is also a way of quietly sustaining simple focus. As such, we will explore how all approaches to relaxation, as well as coping with stress, can be viewed through the lens of mindfulness as *mindful relaxation* and *mindful coping.*

We are now just about ready to immerse ourselves into the many worlds of stress and coping and explore *The Book of Mindfulness.* But first we take an important diversion. There are times when all of our efforts at fixing things, re-thinking things, and relaxing (or being mindful) aren't enough. An important part of successful coping is learning when to rely on others and our deeper beliefs. We consider these important facts of life in our next chapter.

Stress & Coping
Eye of Mindfulness Journal

Chapter 6

Social Support and Meaning

© Lightspring/Shutterstock.com

Social support and supporting beliefs are important parts of stress and coping (Wills, 1985). These are the resources we can tap when our efforts at coping aren't enough. They are also resources that can grow when we apply the tools and strategies of this book.

© Lorelyn Medina/Shutterstock.com

Tangible Social Support

© Robert Kneschke/Shutterstock.com

Informational Social Support

© Lorelyn Medina/Shutterstock.com

Emotional Social Support

Social Support

Experts identify three types of social support: *tangible*, *emotional*, and *informational* (House & Kahn, 1985). People who offer tangible support provide physical help, such as help in getting groceries, going to the hospital, paying bills, and so on. Other examples include:

- Sharing work to complete a job
- Giving money when needed
- Allowing use of a car or cell phone
- Offering a place to stay
- Providing food
- Babysitting
- Lending a pencil during an exam

Emotional support involves showing care and acceptance as well as providing a listening ear to others. One does so without judgment or ulterior motives. When someone offers you emotional social support, you are more likely to think:

> *"This person accepts me for who I am, regardless of what I've done or what I feel."*
> *"I can really open up to this person and share my feelings."*
> *"I don't have to worry about making a good impression or being judged or evaluated."*
> *"My friend takes time to listen, and doesn't preach or lecture me."*
> *"This person seems to know what I'm feeling and knows what it's like to be in my shoes."*

Informational support involves useful instruction, facts, advice, and feedback, for example:

- Giving directions
- Explaining where to get help
- Showing how to do something
- Practicing ahead of time ways to deal with potentially stressful situations, such as giving a speech
- Interviewing for a job
- Asking someone out for a first date
- Giving feedback as to one's appearance, behavior, etc.

Social support can serve as a stress *buffer* by "providing psychological and material resources needed to cope with stress" (Cohen, 2004, p. 677). Social support can have a beneficial *main effect* regardless of whether or not one is under stress. Being with people and having healthy relationships in itself is conducive to good health, which in turn can enhance coping. That is, one's social network may promote behaviors that reduce vulnerability to stress (exercise, meditation, relaxation, diet, not smoking, abstaining from dangerous drugs) and increase sense of responsibility to take care of oneself and others (Cohen, 2004). In general, people with healthy social ties are healthier and live longer than those without these ties, regardless of socioeconomic status, race, gender, or general health (Cohen, 2004; Karren, Hafen, Smith, & Frandsen, 2001).

The Meaning of It All

Both personal spirituality and commitment to organized religion can provide sources of hope, strength, and comfort beyond social support. Spirituality and religion sometimes involve, and at times not involve, the idea of a personal God. In fact there are people who find deep meaning in life who do not believe in a personal God, and there are those who do believe in such a God who live stressful lives with little meaning. Let's begin by focusing on a tangible concern: meaning.

What is more important than your personal concerns, pleasures, and frustrations? What tells you to "keep on going" even when you are about to give up? Why take the time and effort to keep healthy, go to school, and learn stress management skills? These are the "deep meaning questions" of life. Sometimes, our first answers to such questions are somewhat restricted, for example:

I want to perfect my coping skills in order to be healthier.

Limited answers are important, but partial. Why do you want to be healthier? Eventually, if you keep asking "Why do this?" you encounter a deep meaning question, a justification for your choices and actions that is larger and more important than yourself. This is a meaning resource. Your meaning resource answers questions like:

- What in life is larger and more important than yourself?
- What bigger direction or purpose justifies doing things you might find temporarily frustrating or uncomfortable?
- Why bother resisting the immediate gratification of short-term pleasure (including addiction and compulsion), procrastination, and inaction?

Of course, there is no one answer that is right for everyone. Here are a few answers students have shared:

- God wants me to be happy and productive.
- I am here to make the world a better and more loving place.
- Right now, I need to grow.

© Robert Kneschke/Shutterstock.com

EXERCISES

6.1 Social Support in Your Life

What are the sources of tangible support in your life? What types of tangible support might you expect?

What are your sources of emotional and social support?

6.2 Social Support Banquet Table (Adapted from Blonna, 2005)

Imagine a large banquet hall with a single table. Now imagine you are inviting your social support people to a banquet. You need chairs for everyone. Your chair is in the center. In this exercise indicate where you would seat each source of social support. Put each chair close or far away from your seat depending on how much support you get. If you are not completely sure of what kind of support they can give, put a question mark by their chair.

Indicate on each chair whether the person provides tangible, emotional, or informational support (label the chairs "T," "E," "I," or any combination).

ONCE AGAIN, A PERSON IS A VERY IMPORTANT SOURCE OF SOCIAL SUPPORT. PLACE THIS PERSON'S CHAIR VERY CLOSE TO YOUR CHAIR. IF ANOTHER'S SUPPORT ISN'T AS IMPORTANT, OR IS UNCERTAIN, PLACE THE CHAIR FARTHER AWAY.

YOUR SOCIAL SUPPORT BANQUET TABLE

Social Support Table

© TheBlackRhino / Shutterstock.com

6.3 You as a Support-Giver

In this exercise, return to your social support banquet table. Include all of the people you introduced in the room on the previous pages. This time indicate to what extent you have offered tangible, informational, or emotional social support to each person. Draw arrows from you pointing to each person to whom you have offered support in past. Label each arrow "T," "I," and/or "E" to indicate the type of support you have given.

YOU AS A SUPPORT GIVER TABLE

6.4 Your Meaning Candle

Now, imagine everyone has left your banquet. Your table is once again empty, with one chair, you. In this exercise, answer the question, "What is the greatest source of meaning in my life?" Place this source of meaning as a candle on your banquet table. Beside the candle, give it a brief name. Place the candle close to you if it gives you much meaning and you have actively incorporated it in your life. A close candle represents a source of meaning is something that gives you daily strength, meaning, and direction. If your source of meaning is something you don't think about very much, but it's there in case you might need it in the future, put it farther away from your chair on the table. It might even be a potential source of meaning you consider relying on in the future. In this case, put your candle on the floor, away from the table.

YOUR MEANING TABLE

Stress & Coping
Eye of Mindfulness Journal

LESSON 2

THE BOOK OF MINDFULNESS

Chapter 7

The Relaxation Response and Its Benefits

© Lidiya Oleandra/Shutterstock.com

In this section we begin our journey into the worlds of relaxation and mindfulness. We explore the *Book of Mindfulness*, our book within a book. First we consider basic science and theory, and end with our definition of mindfulness. Then we return to our main text on stress and coping. However, we will return again and again, introducing a new exercise at the end of each lesson. In the final chapters you have an opportunity to develop your own relaxation and mindfulness program.

Return to the Fight-or-Flight Response

The first defense against excessive stress is relaxation and, more generally, mindfulness. How they work is a story worth telling, one that can help you understand the whys and hows of relaxation and mindfulness practice. It begins with the stress engine, the brain and body processes that contribute to increased stress arousal/ distress.

When confronted with a threat, a tiny stress trigger in the brain, the hypothalamus, initiates hundreds of body changes that automatically awaken and energize the body for emergency action. Blood pressure and breathing increase, fuels are released into the blood, blood vessels expand, energizing hormones are released into the bloodstream, and so on. This is the body's fight-or-flight stress response, the engine of arousal/distress, as discussed in Chapter 3.

This amazing process can be seen with sensitive stress laboratory equipment similar to the well-known lie detector polygraph. If you were hooked up to such a machine, sensitive detectors, about the size of small coins, would be stuck on your arms, chest, and forehead. These sensors work something like thermometers except that in addition to measuring body temperature, they measure other aspects of arousal including blood pressure, how

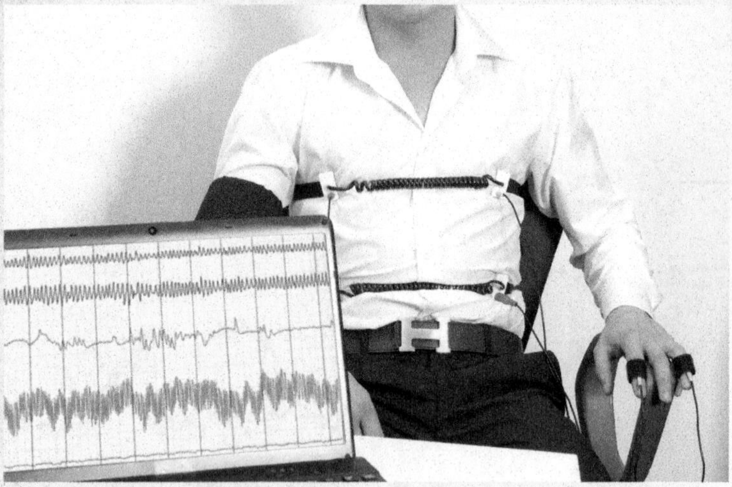

quickly and deeply you breathe, how tense your muscles are, and so on. These sensors are then attached to a computer that processes signal input.

Imagine after you have been hooked up, someone drops a large book on the floor with a loud bang. You feel startled and a bit nervous, in other words, a bit of arousal and distress. A series of squiggles on our computer monitor shows that the fight-or-flight response has been triggered. If you were asked to think about a bad day at work, we would see another jump in arousal. Thinking about a variety of stressors will cause the computer to register stress arousal. Indeed, many of the assaults of everyday living trigger bits of stress arousal so that over time we experience chronically high levels of the fight-or-flight response. This causes strain and distress. Health suffers. Resistance declines. Ability to attend productively at work, school, sports, and home is harmed.

The Relaxation Response

Psychologists and physicians have known about the fight-or-flight response since the start of the 20th century. However, in the early 1970s scientists made an interesting discovery. They selected individuals who learned relaxation or meditation and hooked them up to the same type of polygraph machinery we just described. Only this time, instead of inducing stress, participants were asked to practice whatever relaxation or meditation technique they had mastered.

What the researchers found revolutionized our understanding of stress. Almost immediately after they started relaxing, a constellation of changes automatically appeared, including reductions in blood pressure, breathing rate, muscle tension, levels of stress hormone, and body temperature.

What the researchers had discovered was the mirror opposite of the fight-or-flight arousal/distress response, what physician Herbert Benson (1975) called the **relaxation response**.

Just as the brain has an innate capacity to automatically trigger emergency stress arousal/distress, it has a parallel innate capacity to trigger an opposing, recuperative, and healing relaxation response. Furthermore, the relaxation response proved to be rapid and deep, more than one could achieve through just listening to music, sleep, or even hypnosis. The relaxation response is truly an important human capacity, a basic life-giving skill one acquires through a relaxation, meditation, or mindfulness technique.

How to Evoke the Relaxation Response

The relaxation response is one of the most powerful ways of cooling off the stress engine and reducing the arousal/distress part of our formula. However, doing this is no simple task. Watching television isn't enough. One must learn and master a special set of exercises. To understand the tools available, we need to review how we can augment and maintain our levels of stress. First, let's review the three types of self-stressing:

Stressed posture. You take on and maintain a stressful posture or body position, like crouching, bending over a computer terminal, straining your neck to read a book, holding your arms partially upright to grasp a car's steering wheel, and so on. Physically your joints become stiff. In addition, blood begins to stagnate, carrying less energy to your body and mind and carrying away less fatiguing waste.

Stressed muscles. You tighten your grip on a steering wheel, hold your hands over a computer keyboard, lift heavy objects, strain at attention during a lecture. Muscle tension increases.

Stressed breathing. You hold your breath in anticipation, deliberately subdue your breathing so as not to disturb a sleeping child (or people in a library), breathe rapidly while running away from an attacking dog. Stressed breathing is rapid, shallow, and uneven; it also involves breathing through the chest.

These three types of self-stressing point to basic family groups of relaxation exercises. To elaborate, there are hundreds of relaxation techniques. However, nearly all can be organized into family groups. Each has as an initial effect reducing a different type of self-stressing. Once this happens, techniques can have deeper effects.

Yoga stretches and postures. You correct stressed postures and positions. You undo joint stiffness and increase energizing and cleansing blood flow.

Progressive muscle relaxation (or "Muscle Mindfulness"). You learn to detect when your muscles are tense, and release or let go of muscle tension.

Breathing exercises. You learn to breathe in a way that is slow, usually deep, and even. Relaxed breathing involves breathing in and out through your abdomen, a skill called *diaphragmatic breathing.*

Yoga, progressive muscle relaxation, and breathing exercises are physical. It is possible to mentally create the relaxation response mentally?

First, one can use targeted self-suggestion. To explain, with *autogenic body suggestion,* we focus on suggestions or images targeted to relaxing self-stressed body organs or processes. In our minds we might say the words, "Hands and arms warm, heavy, and relaxed," or "Heart is beating calmly," or "Muscles feel heavy and relaxed."

Second, most, if not all mindfulness exercises have the potential for evoking the relaxation response. But mindfulness appears to go further, a topic we begin to explore in the following chapters.

Chapter 8

What Is Mindfulness?

© Dirk Ercken/Shutterstock.com

There is more to relaxation than the relaxation response. All of relaxation, indeed all of effective stress management, involves a bit of mindfulness. We can use the idea of mindfulness as a central organizing idea for this entire book.

In spite of its popularity, there is a confusing array of definitions of mindfulness (Brown, Creswell, & Ryan, 2015). There is general consensus that it is a type of awareness. But what type of awareness? Here, each expert has his or her definition, using such terms as "present-focused," "nonjudgmental," "nonelaborative," "open," "receptive," "curious," "equanimous," and so on. Furthermore, is yoga a type of mindfulness? Prayer? What about meditation?

First, part of the confusion arises from the fact that sometimes mindfulness is used as an umbrella term that applies to many techniques. More often it is a restricted term that applies to one type of approach. To make things more confusing, the term *meditation* is also used in the same general and specific way.

Here is my beginner's definition, one I use in orientation lectures:

Mindfulness is quiet sustained simple focus.

This definition can be expanded to a full definition:

Mindfulness is sustained simple focus with minimal judgment and effort.

In a very general sense, any exercise that requires such quiet sustained simple focus is an exercise done "mindfully." Some might even term such exercises types of mindfulness. However, pure mindfulness, as a specific exercise, involves quiet sustained focus and nothing else. We will consider this definition more fully later on, but first we need to consider the opposite of mindfulness, mind wandering.

© alphaspirit/Shutterstock.com

Mind Wandering

How do you spend most of your time? What do you do each minute of the day? Obviously, this is an unusual thing to ask, but imagine you had a special smartphone, one that called you randomly throughout the day and asked you what you were doing or thinking about. What would you say?

Believe it or not, scientists are actually doing this. Two Harvard researchers, Killingsworth and Gilbert (2010), used an iPhone app to contact 2,250 people from 83 different countries with ages ranging from 18 to 88. Phoners called randomly throughout the day and asked participants how they felt and what they were doing or thinking.

After studying a quarter of a million responses the researchers were surprised to find that their participants' minds were wandering about 47 percent of the time. (What percentage of your time is devoted to mind wandering?) In addition, people were more likely to be unhappy when their minds were wandering, and mind wandering seemed to contribute to future unhappiness. The researchers concluded: ". . . a human mind is a wandering mind, and a wandering mind is an unhappy mind. The ability to think about what is not happening is a cognitive achievement that comes at an emotional cost" (Killingsworth & Gilbert, 2010).

Checking your Smartphone

Often mind wandering has an ego-centric, self-centered quality. *"I need something." "I'm in trouble." "I don't want this." "I must have this." "It's all about me."* The most important actor in such dramas is "me." Formally, this is **self-referential thinking**, an important concept we will encounter again and again throughout this text.

It may surprise you to discover that **mind wandering** is actually a technical term (sometimes referred to in terms of the "default network" or "task negative network"), and has received serious scientific attention. When we are not mind wandering, we are focusing on and engaging with the world. We are attentive (using what some term the brain's "task positive network"). We do things consciously and deliberately chosen, and can generally describe our choices to others. When our minds wander, this stops. We are inattentive.

Mind wandering is sometimes *automatic*. Sometimes it seems as if our thoughts have been hijacked by some internal worry, desire, memory, or fantasy. We find ourselves unexpectedly and automatically choosing to pursue random and pointless rumination. "Is my hair too long?" "Why did John not pay for dinner?" "Will it be cold next week?" "Will I have a stomachache tonight?" Or our attention may have been commandeered by some external distraction, a stimulus evoking longing and desire, a threat, a reminder of unfinished business. The list goes on.

In contrast, attentive and engaged focus less likely to be automatic. Say you are reading this book. If asked what you are doing, you might say, "I have consciously and deliberately chosen to read this book." Obviously this choice is explicit in that you can explain it to your inquirer. Your mind was not wandering.

In sum, we begin our journey with mind wandering. Mindfulness is the opposite of mind wandering. It is the opposite of self-referential thinking.

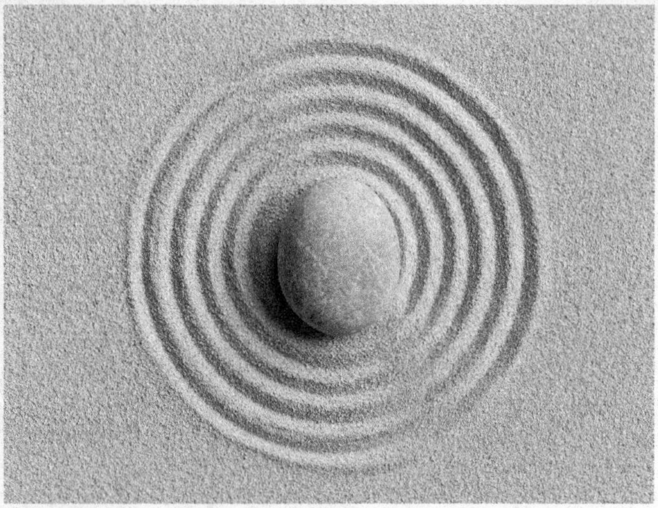
© Tischenko Irina/Shutterstock.com

Our Definition of Mindfulness

We can now return to our definition:

Mindfulness is sustained simple focus with minimal judgment and effort.

This needs unpacking. Mindfulness is *sustained* in that you deliberately chose to attend for more than a brief moment. Mindfulness is *focused* in that you direct your attention. You may restrict your focus to one stimulus, like your breath, a mentally repeated word or mantra, or more broadly the coming and going of the present moment. Your focus may be broad or narrow, like a wide-angle or telephoto camera lens.

Mindfulness is *simple*. You are engaged in just one task, attending. You focus on just one stimulus. Even if you are open to the flow of all stimuli that come and go, your openness is simple.

Mindfulness involves *minimal judgment* in that you do not appraise anything as incomplete, insufficient, needing attention, to be analyzed, rejected, or to be possessed. You do not judge as good or bad. You display an attitude of acceptance, one that says "leave it be" or "it is what it is."

Finally, mindfulness involves *minimal effort*. The task of doing all of this is perhaps something of a paradox. How does one try and not try? First, mindfulness involves minimal effort in that you cease your busy everyday activity. At the very least, you may begin by practicing a preparatory relaxation tension-release exercise. When practicing mindfulness you do not strive and strain at being mindful. And every distraction and instance of mind wandering provides an opportunity to again and again let go. But mindfulness does involve a type of effort, the choice to be mindful and awake. It is not dozing or taking a nap. It is the choice to sustain simple focus with minimal judgment and effort.

Minimal effort can have many layers of meaning. You remain receptive and open. You cease all trying. You surrender. Letting go can range from the simple act of releasing a tightly held breath, to quietly putting aside an instance of mind wandering, to being humble, to opening up in awe, wonder, and reverence. If we consider one's "self" as essentially a "doer," an "effort-entity" defined by a sense of agency ("I do this, I do that"), then a profound experience of selflessness also reflects minimal effort of the deepest sort.

We can view our definition in terms of mind wandering. All types of judgment, effort, and diversion from your target focal task represent mind wandering. To let go of these efforts is central to the task of mindfulness.

Concrete Examples

Enough abstract definition. Imagine you are spending an evening at a campsite. You might be experiencing this:

> *You are resting on the grass, simply watching the stars. All of the thoughts, plans, cares, and concerns of the day seem very distant. Your mind is at peace, as you easily gaze above. In this moment you are simply an observer, doing nothing to interfere. You notice a breeze. It caresses your skin and settles into silence. You put aside any thoughts about the breeze and quietly gaze overhead. In the distance a bird sings its song and becomes still. You note it and let go. Your mind is quiet, without thought, like a pond without ripples. You see a silver cloud, shining with the moon floating overhead. It quietly evaporates into complete silence. You simply attend. You are nothing more than a silent observer, doing nothing to interfere.*

Or you might be sitting by a slowly moving stream watching what floats by:

> *It is a peaceful, lazy day. You are comfortably sitting on a rock with your feet dangling in the stream. You gaze easily at the coming and going of the river. A green leaf floats into sight. You note it, and it floats away. Then you notice a shiny single bubble as it floats into sight. Very gently it pops and disappears into silence. You sit silently and attend to the flow of the river. Deep in the waters you see a goldfish and it swims away. Again, complete silence.*

Mindfulness is quiet sustained simple focus. You are simply the observer, doing nothing to interfere.

Stress & Coping
Eye of Mindfulness Journal

Chapter 9

The Mindfulness Response

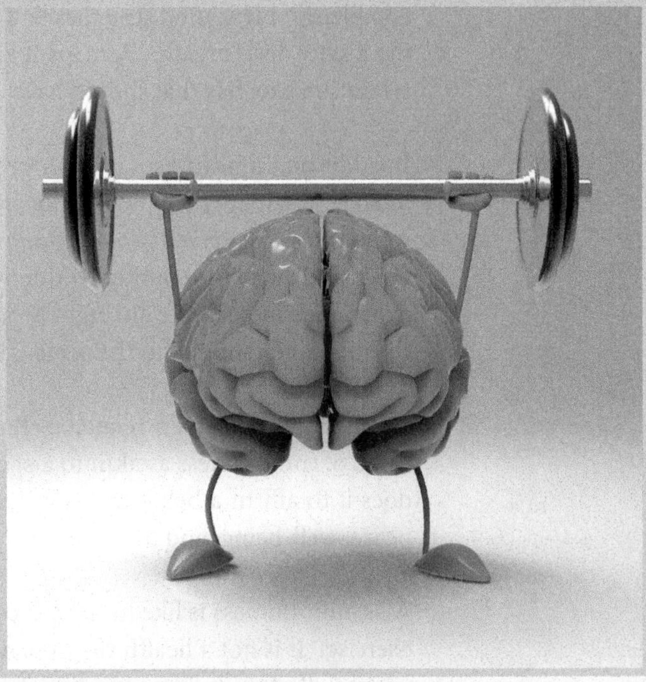

© Julien Tromeur/Shutterstock.com

We have seen that relaxation exercises work by evoking a generalized anti-stress relaxation response. Mindfulness exercises evoke a parallel body/brain *mindfulness response.* Much of the current explosion of interest in mindfulness was triggered and continues to be fueled by revolutionary research on this response.

Mindfulness training is like lifting weights. The results are not immediate. Muscles take time to grow. It might surprise you that one curious phrase is appearing with increased frequency in the mindfulness literature: mindfulness muscle. And mindfulness training is increasingly being compared to physical fitness training. Mindfulness training is a type of "cognitive fitness" training. For beginners, this is a useful place to start.

Every time you direct your attention to the present, without needless thought, and focus on the coming and going of the sensory world, you commit an act of mindfulness. Each time you do this something important begins to happen. You begin to develop mindfulness muscle. This involves many parts and processes We sample four commonly mentioned in research: the left prefrontal cortex, the anterior cingulate cortex, the posterior cingulate cortex, and the amygdala.

Barriers to Mindfulness

Before proceeding into the brain, it is useful to consider difficulties many have with mindfulness. Perhaps the first barrier to mastering mindfulness is the myth that it is quick and easy. It is perfectly understandable why people think this. Mindfulness is often presented side by side with yoga stretching and breathing, exercises that can have immediate effects. If you've been sitting at your desk for hours, simply standing and completing a few good stretches will instantly evoke relaxation and energy. So will taking a slow deep breath. Perhaps it is reasonable to expect that mindfulness is another relaxation exercise that should have quick results.

In addition, mindfulness is often presented along with various health tips, advice in a Sunday newspaper supplement or health web page. For example, *"List your priorities when you wake up, and do one thing at a time"* might immediately prompt you to slow down and avoid the counterproductive strategy of doing everything at once. You might experience increased calm right away. Perhaps the advice to "be mindful" and "live in the moment" should do the same. Read about it, "get it," and be mindful.

Given that mindfulness related techniques are often taught in a religious context, many think of mindfulness as akin to a spiritual ritual, something like prayer or chant. One does it to affirm a belief or commitment. After such ritual one may well feel a sense peace, well-being, and belonging.

Alas, mindfulness is like none of these. At the deepest level, it is not another relaxation exercise. It is not a health tip. It is not quite a religious ritual. Mindfulness is a *brain-based skill.* Mindfulness training is like lifting weights. The results are not immediate. Muscles take time to grow. Yes, mindfulness training is a type of "cognitive fitness" training.

How long does it take? No one has formally researched this question. We have practitioners reporting over 40,000 hours of lifetime practice. Perhaps the majority of famous instructors have about 10,000 hours. I hypothesize that about a month of daily practice, a half hour a day, should begin to yield measurable enduring brain changes. It took me about two months of daily practice (40 minutes a session) before I noticed measurable changes. A single session will trigger temporary changes, just as a single session of lifting weights will result in warming and blood engorged biceps.

Neuroplasticity

Years ago, conventional neurophysiological wisdom was that after a certain age, the brain was set and little new growth occurred. Then, in the 1980s a new set of remarkable studies showed the capacity of the brain for physical change, for what is termed *neuroplasticity.* Recent studies dramatically show that learning a skill, like learning the skill of lifting weights, results in tangible and measurable growth. This is true even for driving a cab.

London Cab

What does it take to be a cab driver? What are the required skills? Obviously you have to know how to drive, speak politely to riders, and make change. But one of the most important skills is to know how to navigate the streets of the city.

This is particularly true in London, a city blessed with 25,000 streets and thousands of tourist attractions. Furthermore, the streets are not arranged in an easy to remember grid, but often more resemble a chaotic batch of spilled spaghetti.

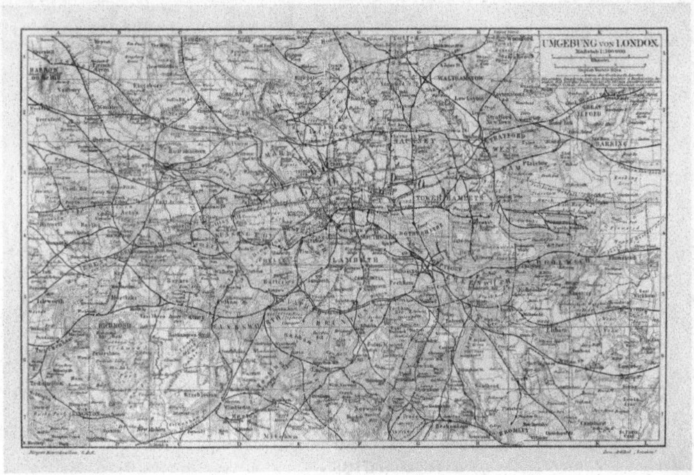

Streets of London

To become a London cab driver, you need extensive training involving learning thousands of miles of streets. Then you take a series of difficult exams (only 50 percent pass). Something interesting happens to the brains of London cab drivers in training. A part of the brain associated with spatial memory, the hippocampus, actually grows and becomes more dense (Maguire et al., 2000). The effect is as measurable and real as the biceps that grow on a determined weight lifter.

You may wonder how scientists made this discovery about London cab drivers. The invention of a remarkable device, the magnetic resonance imaging (MRI) scan, enables scientists to actually look inside the brain and examine distinct areas and how they work. Scientists can actually see what parts of the brain light up when one completes math problems, engages in visual imagery, thinks about playing tennis, and even has a sexual fantasy. MRI scans have been applied not only to cab drivers, but meditators, revealing a revolutionary portrait of the mindfulness response. Meditators are placed inside an MRI scanner, asked to meditate, and the scanner images what parts of the brain are active.

Magnetic Resonance Imaging

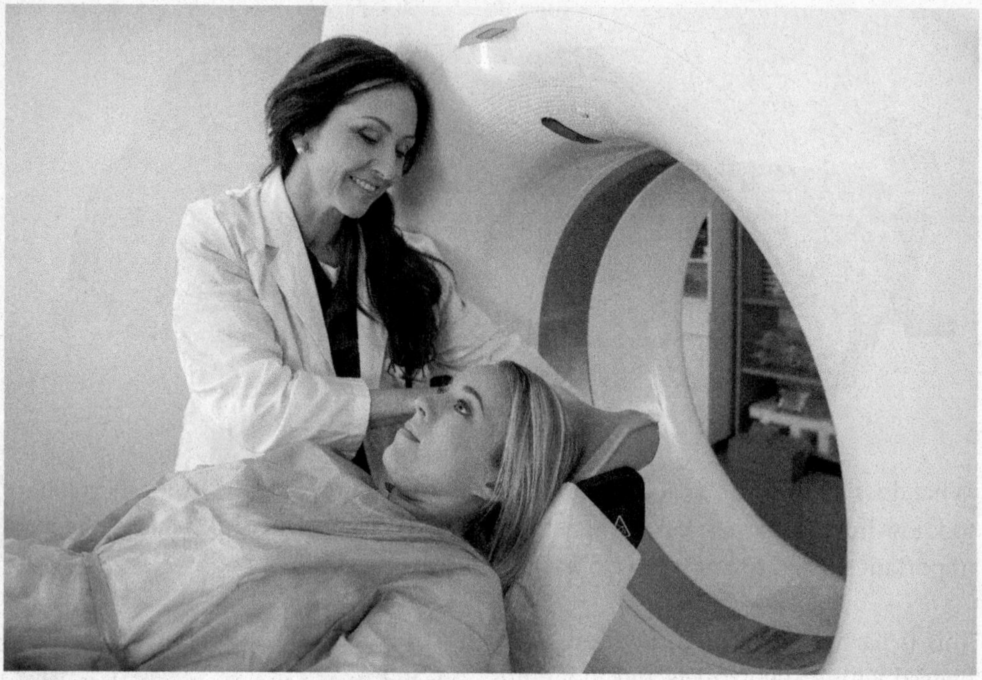

© Tyler Olson/Shutterstock.com

The Mindfulness Response: Brain Structures, Networks, and Brain Waves

When one practices mindfulness, important changes occur within the brain. These are far too numerous to be described in this text. We will focus on a sample four brain structures, and one general brain process. Together they constitute something of a *mindfulness response*, a set of body/brain changes associated with the practice with mindfulness.

Left Prefrontal Cortex

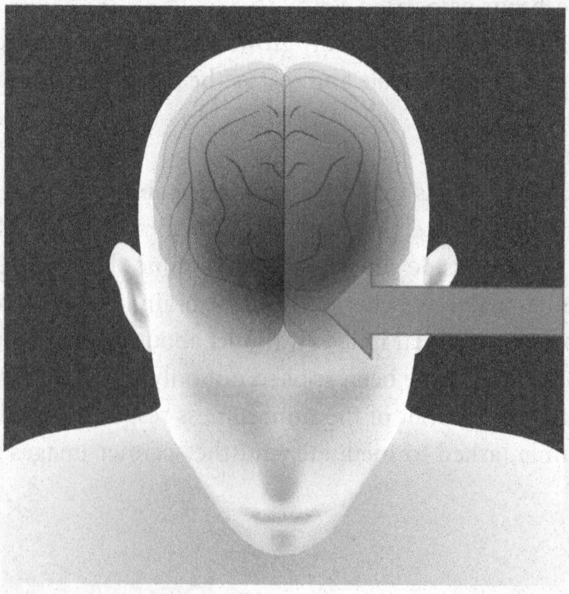

© Shutterstock.com

Brain Structures Associated with Mindfulness

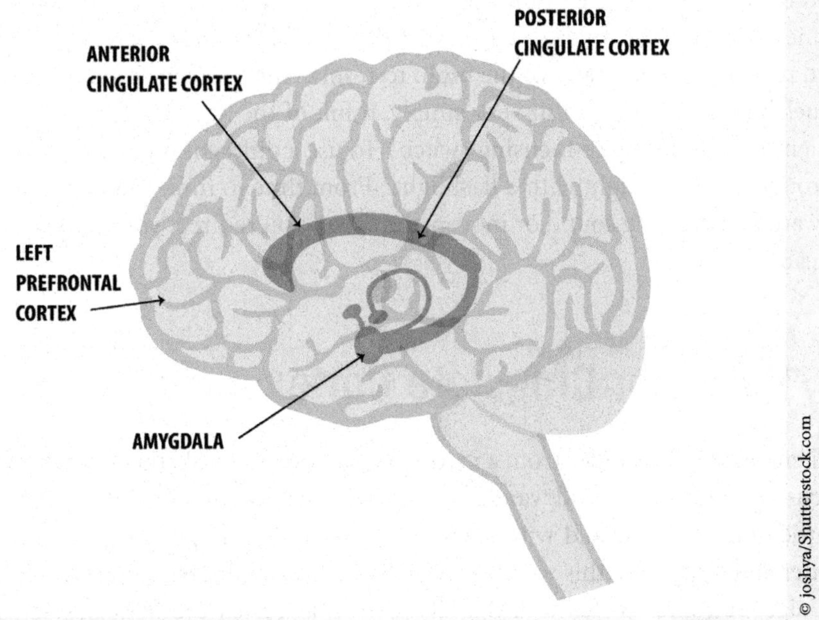

1. The Left Prefrontal Cortex

What "muscle" do we "grow" when we regularly practice mindfulness? We cultivate our brain's capacity to focus. Specifically, mindfulness involves directing attention to the coming and going of stimuli. This attentional act is often associated with an area at the front and left of the brain, just above the left eye, the prefrontal cortex.

The prefrontal cortex is part of the brain that is responsible for many of our most advanced human brain capacities—attention-direction, decision-making, working memory (task-specific short-term memory), and regulation of thoughts. Interestingly, the *left prefrontal cortex* is also associated with optimism and positive mood (the right prefrontal cortex is associated with more negative emotions).

The most frequent noted physical change associated with mindfulness is growth in the prefrontal cortex. As practice continues, this part of the brain becomes more active and remarkably grows in density and size.

2. Anterior Cingulate Cortex

Mindful attention isn't just attending. It is also pulling away from mind wandering and distraction. To the brain this is a conflict between focusing on one thing versus something else. The *anterior cingulate cortex* mediates such conflicts by spotting them and recruiting other parts of the brain to resolve the problem by amplifying focus and squelching distraction. Put very simply, think of the anterior cingulate as something of a mind wandering or focusing switch. To use a different metaphor, think of walking through a park at night with a flashlight. From time to time you direct your flashlight toward a distracting sound or movement. Then you redirect your flashlight to the path ahead.

3. Posterior Cingulate Cortex

When our minds wander from a meditative task, or any task, the brain switches from its focusing mode to its mind wandering mode. The *posterior cingulate cortex* in the center of the brain is associated with such mind wandering. Experienced meditators appear better at deactivating this worry-center during mindfulness. Connections between the medial prefrontal cortex and the left prefrontal cortex are better established (which actually shows up in brain imaging), implying a greater ability to disengage from mind wandering. Good connections make it easier to sustain simple focus.

4. The Amygdala

We complete our brief overview of mindfulness and the brain by noting the amygdala. The amygdala is an almond-shaped structure deep in the brain that plays an important role in emotion, particularly fear and stress. Indeed, the amygdala actually grows for those under stress. For seasoned practitioners of mindfulness, the amygdala shrinks and loses density. Our brain's focusing organ, the left prefrontal cortex, can contribute to such changes by how it focuses in stress and in mindfulness. In a way one learns to direct the spotlight of attention (left prefrontal cortex) away from the amygdala. By focusing in unproductive ways on life's challenges and worries, stress increases, and the amygdala becomes more active and grows. Mindfulness has the opposite effect.

If you are a bit overwhelmed by this brain physiology, there is a simpler way of summarizing what we have described. A brain *network* can be seen as a "collection of interconnected brain areas that interact to perform circumscribed functions" (Bresslor and Menon, 2010). If the brain can be seen as a huge forest, a large-scale network is a well-worn path to various places, say to the lodge, dining hall, or wilderness garden. Mindfulness researchers write of three popular networks. The *central-executive network* (CEN) is responsible for overall focusing of attention as well as high-level "executive" activity. It includes the left prefrontal cortex. The *default mode network* (DMN) is associated with mind wandering and includes the posterior cingulate and to some extent the amygdala. Finally, the *salience network* (SN) is the brain's mental switch that, like a 911 telephone operator, switches from less relevant or "salient" tasks to those that are most important. Put differently, the salience network helps us detect that current (salient) task we have chosen to do, perhaps meditate, and pull away from whatever distraction we have wandered onto.

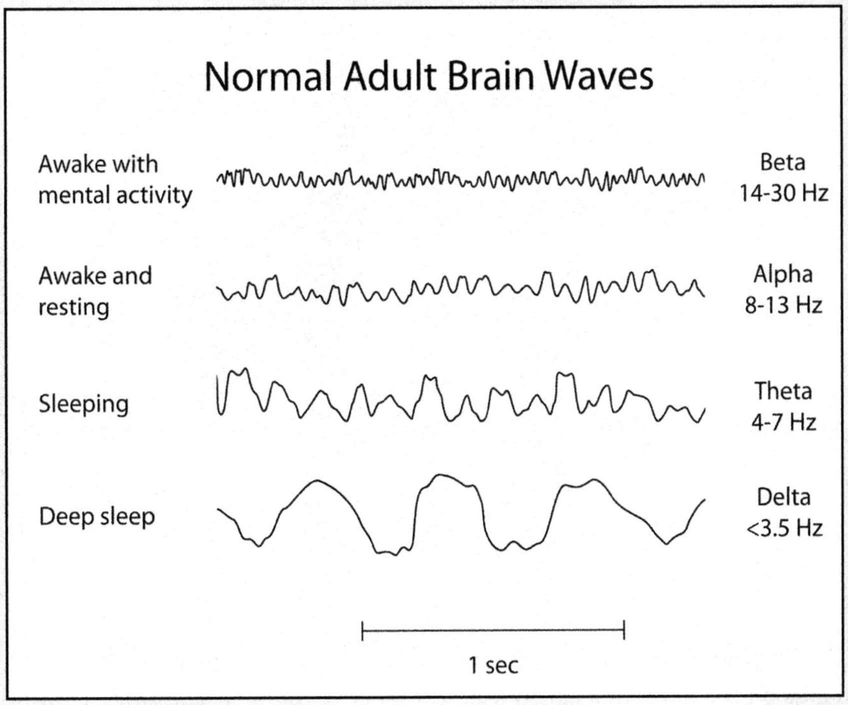

© Alila Medical Media/Shutterstock.com

5. Brain Waves

Another important change is less associated with a specific organ than with overall brain activity. The brain consists of billions of neurons. Their many interconnections generate electrical activity, detected by electroencephalographic (EEG) equipment and sensitive electrodes placed harmlessly on the surface of the skull.

EEG Electrodes Placed on Surface of Skull

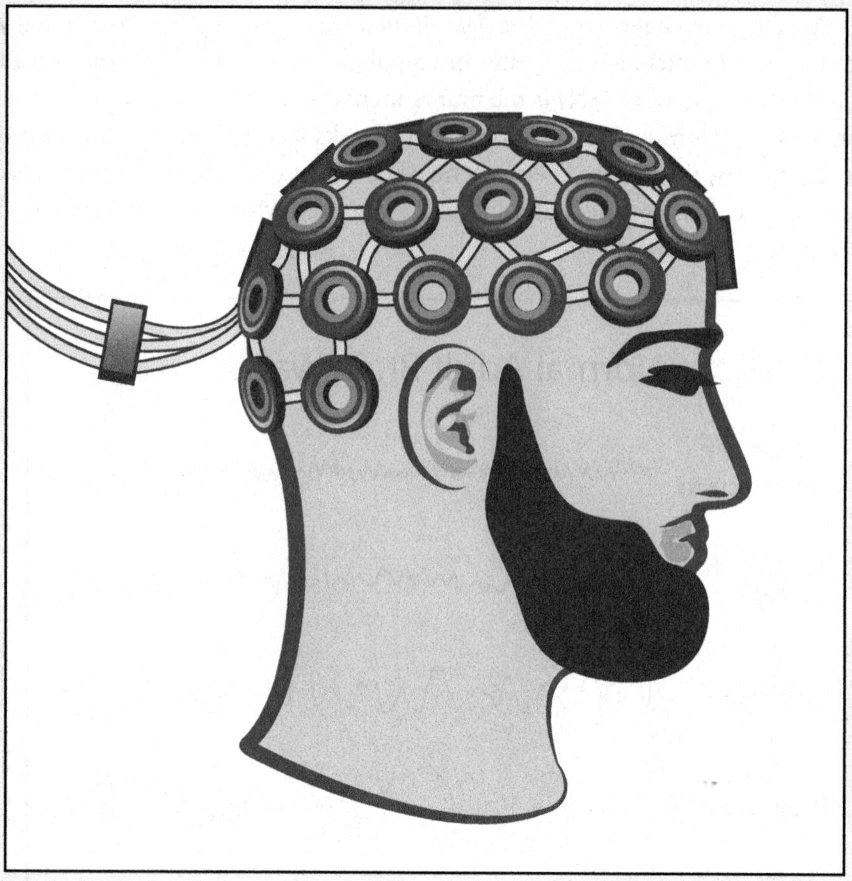

© VECTORWORKS_ENTERPRISE/Shutterstock.com

The EEG does not detect specific thoughts, but overall activity, much as if you placed your hands on the hood of a car to feel how fast the engine is running. However, this brain activity shows a wavelike pattern, and the speed of waves can say something about what the brain is doing. When the waves throb at 13 to 60 pulses per cycle, one is typically conscious, alert, and perhaps agitated. This is called beta brain wave activity. Alpha waves pulse at 7 to 13 cycles per second (cps) and are associated with physical and mental relaxation and awareness. Theta waves (4–7 cps) are associated with somnolence and reduced consciousness. Delta waves (0.1–4 cps) are associated with unconsciousness, deep sleep, and catalepsy.

Brain Wave Synchronization

In the 1960s and 1970s, researchers noted that meditators appeared to generate alpha brain waves (Kasamatsu & Hirai, 1966). A small industry emerged of techniques and devices to help people develop alpha waves. Quickly research focus shifted from the frequency of brain wave activity to the synchronization of brain waves—that is, waves oscillating in harmony (Cahn & Polich, 2006). Imagine the brain is an orchestra with many players. When all members are playing to the same beat, they are in synchrony. When each person is playing to a different rhythm, there is chaos, or lack of synchrony.

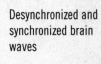

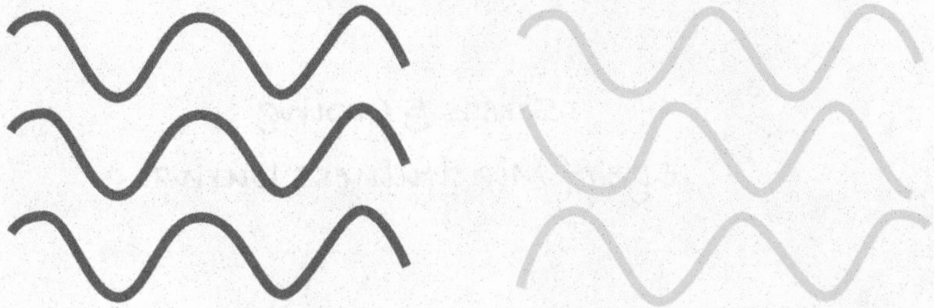

Desynchronized and synchronized brain waves

Researchers of transcendental meditation focus less on localized activity than activity in the brain as a whole. Alpha and theta activity increase, showing increased synchronization. This is speculated to be associated with restful alertness and a lessening of sense of self and division. In terms of the brain components we have discussed, one might speculate there is enhanced synchrony throughout the brain, perhaps associated with sustained focus and less mind wandering.

Alpha Filtering

Some brain waves are centered around specific areas of the brain. Imagine again an automobile. The muffler is not working and is rattling vigorously. You might feel this rattle if you placed your hand over the back bumper. You would not feel it by touching the front hood. The rattle is localized.

Localized alpha waves are associated with certain brain parts. This is important to know if you are feeling a distracting pain or discomfort. During a practice session, a small blanket of alpha waves actually settles over that small part of the brain associated with the pain or discomfort. If your foot hurts from too much exercise, the part of the brain where the foot is represented (technically the "primary motor cortex") gets an alpha blanket. As a result, the pain or discomfort is tuned or filtered out. This appears to happen automatically, just by engaging in quiet, sustained simple focus. It may be one reason why many people find mindfulness-related exercises useful for managing pain, discomfort, and even depression (Gaspar & McDonald, 2014; Kerr et al., 2013).

Stress & Coping
Eye of Mindfulness Journal

© iunewind / Shutterstock.com

Chapter 10

The Claimed Benefits of Mindfulness

© Nadly Aizat/Shutterstock.com

We have seen that relaxation evokes a general anti-stress relaxation response. Mindfulness is also associated with this as well as with a mindfulness response. We have also reviewed the benefits of tuning down stress arousal and protecting against and recovering from distress. One topic remains, what are the benefits of mindfulness?

Some would say I am a notorious skeptic when it comes to the claimed benefits of mindfulness related exercises. My very first research (Smith, 1975, 1976) concluded that the psychotherapeutic effects of meditation have yet to be determined. I even invented one of the most elaborate placebos ever used in mindfulness research. This research got me my current job as a university professor. Forty years later I still publish widely used textbooks on skepticism (Smith, 2010, 2018). What do I now think of the promise of mindfulness?

A few years ago, the most widely read journal in psychology, the *Monitor on Psychology*, published a review of the benefits of mindfulness, written by two very prominent mindfulness researchers (Davis & Hayes, 2012). Most psychologists subscribe to this journal. Indeed, you get it if you become a member of the American Psychological Association. The review in question is now offered for Continuing Education (CE) credits for psychologists desiring to renew their licenses. Although in my opinion the review has serious problems, it is the closest thing to an "official" professional endorsement of what mindfulness does. With an open mind, and skeptical eye, here are the claims.

Focusing on Your Laptop

© Jacob Lund/Shutterstock.com

Focusing Ability

One develops an increased ability to focus on a wide range of tasks, both within the practice session and in work and daily life. This includes an increased ability to suppress distracting information. One can monitor stimuli more accurately and show less interference from invalid cues. Translated, whether it be watching a movie, doing homework, listening to a lecture, or paying attention to a supervisor's advice, you should be better able to attend more accurately with less distraction and mind wandering.

© Boris Ryaposov/Shutterstock.com

Reduced Rumination and Self-Referential Thinking

Rumination is worrisome mind wandering. It is very characteristic of anxiety as well as depression. Most rumination is **self-referential** ("What is wrong with me? What will people think of me?") and future or past centered ("I feel bad about all that I have done wrong." "I am concerned about all that might go wrong."). Mindfulness is associated with reduced rumination, and thus reduced anxiety and depression. It is associated with reduced self-referential thinking.

© Nadya_Art/Shutterstock.com

Stress Reduction

Of course, rumination and negative mind wandering is part of stress. Such thinking contributes to triggering and maintaining the stress arousal response. Reducing such rumination should reduce stress. Increasing the ability of the left prefrontal cortex to redirect the attentional spotlight away from negative emotion, such as might be associated with the amygdala, may reduce neural reactivity. The mindful person confronting a stressful situation should be better able to view it neutrally, as a simple distraction, and not get caught up.

Boosts in Working Memory

Working memory is defined in terms of information you keep in mind when doing something, like studying or performing a job. If you are writing a term paper, your working memory is the mental bookshelf in front of you with all the information you need at your fingertips. When going grocery shopping, it is the shopping list you keep in mind. Working memory consists of all the facts you have readily available, easily accessible for immediate use.

© Mopic/Shutterstock.com

Working memory is like your personal library.

When taking a test on this chapter you want to have ready access to all the points made. Hopefully these points are in your working memory. Mindfulness training appears to reduce distracting thoughts and increase working memory.

Increased Metacognitive and Introspective Ability: The Observer

Metacognition is thinking about thinking. For example, if you are taking a multiple choice test, you presumably think about each question. This is direct thinking. But let's say you complete a question and then start thinking about the answers you are giving, or your test taking strategy. Maybe your concern is that you've been answering too carelessly. Maybe you realize you haven't been taking into account lecture material, and have focused too much on the textbook. Maybe you should be focusing on the easy questions first, and put the difficult ones off until later. In these instances you are "thinking about thinking," thinking about your answering questions. This is metacognition, standing back and objectively reviewing yourself.

Introspection is a bit similar. You stand back and observe yourself. You may take a stance of observing body sensations or emotion. For example, if I asked you to close your eyes and report how you are feeling now, and you said, "I'm feeling nothing," it is quite likely you are not introspecting. When you can report what's going on inside, your body sensations and emotions, you are introspecting. Mindfulness appears to increase both metacognitive and introspective ability.

Metacognition

© Syda Productions/Shutterstock.com

With both metacognition and introspection one assumes an **observer stance** toward oneself and the world. You stand back and with neutrality and objectivity simply observe what is happening, both inside of you and in the outside world. You do nothing to interfere.

Less Emotional Reactivity and Dereification

The previous claimed benefits imply that mindfulness should help people disengage from upsetting emotion. Indeed, research appears to show that one can more readily detach oneself from an emotionally distracting image and focus on a given task. One takes perspective, assumes the role of a neutral observer, and simply sees things as they are.

Much of the claimed reductions in emotional reactivity might be associated with a process called **dereification.** Let me explain this somewhat convoluted idea. Mind wandering perseveres because we reify, "fuse," and, literalize thoughts. We lose realistic objective perspective (Hayes, Strosahl, & Wilson, 2003). We take a simple distracting thought, urge, or feeling and treat it as if it were literally true, as if it were a real object. Thoughts becomes fused with facts. They become "fact-like, " the way things "really are," or "have to be." They acquire the same final qualities as such hard realities as rocks and trees – not products of our thinking. A rock is a rock, and that is that. Peas are intrinsically disgusting.

Extreme examples are easy to identify. Prejudiced persons may have distorted thoughts about what a gay person, African-American, or Catholic is like. And when they meet a gay, black, or Catholic, they see the person as "obsessed with marriage and fidelity,"

"needing racial profiling," or "dogmatic." In their eyes, that is the way such individuals really are. To take another example, your child may have picked up the idea that peas are "disgusting." Perhaps she heard these words on a cartoon show. Fusing the words with the fact of a plate of peas, she refuses to eat the "disgusting" vegetables.

We can reify thoughts about ourselves. At some time someone may have told you that you are "creative," "demanding," or "a bit selfish." Perhaps you took these words in, and began to see yourself in these terms. These are no longer just words. They are personal facts.

Our world of reified concepts helps define our perspective of just about everything. Because these concepts reflect how we think things really are, including ourselves, these thoughts are central to our reality. They define the dramas and soap operas of our universe. For example, a teen lover has lost his boyfriend. All day he is distracted by such wandering thoughts as:

> *"My interpersonal world is destroyed."*
> *"My boyfriend and I were a perfect couple."*
> *"There are other guys. But I will never find another man."*
> *"My life is over. I will always be depressed."*

Notice mix of facts and thoughts. "I live in an interpersonal world." This is most certainly a fact. He likely does know people. To this he adds, or fuses, an evaluative thought, "destroyed" -- he sees himself living in a "destroyed interpersonal world." To continue, it may well be an objective fact that our teen and his friend were lovers. To this he fuses the evaluation, the thought "perfect." And of course there are in fact "other guys." But our teen sees fuses the thought "never find another man." Finally, the simple and honest feeling of depression is reified to a hard, urgent, final rock-like fact, "I will always be depressed."

In summary, for our teen some thoughts have the quality of a drama or soap opera. These become attached to the facts of his life. The world is destroyed, as if the bombs have fallen. He has lost objective perspective. It is not surprising thoughts about his world persist, fueling more and more negative mind wandering. In six months, our friend most likely comes to his senses, or in mindful terms, he has dereified, "defused," "deliteralized," and "gained objective perspective." He may laugh at how he took so seriously the mental grade-B movie which so defined his earlier life.

More Cognitive Flexibility

You have your heart set on going to your favorite restaurant with a friend. Your friend announces she doesn't like their food and suggest another. You let go of your preference, and go with her suggestion. Here you have displayed **cognitive flexibility.** If you've spent an hour on math homework, and need to start reading a novel for English,

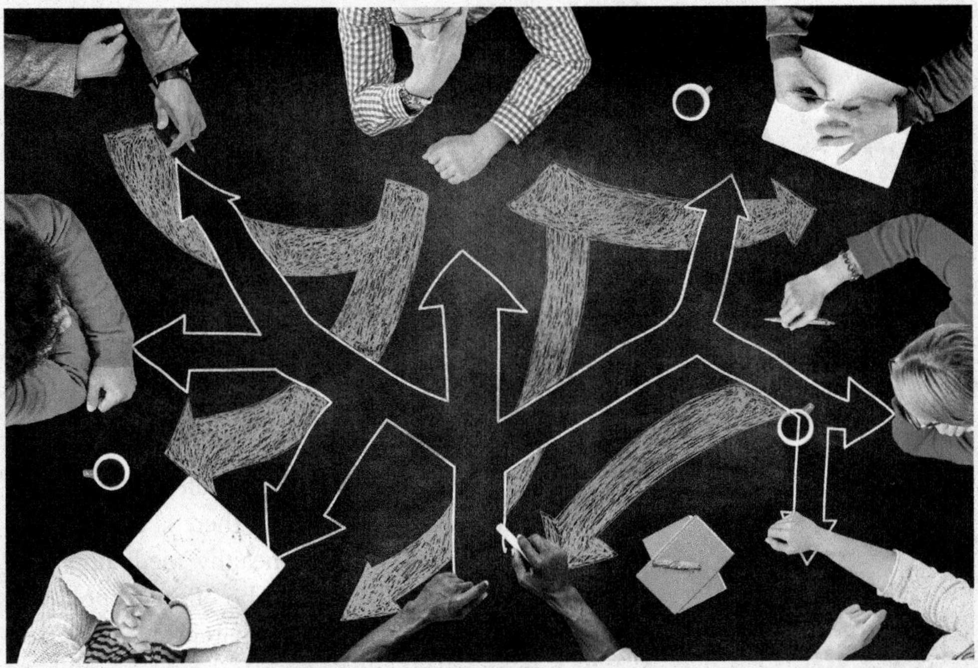

© Rawpixel.com/Shutterstock.com

the ability to switch gears is also cognitive flexibility. Such flexibility is a complex skill, one involving such mindful skills as focusing, noting mind wandering, letting go of mind wandering instead of getting caught up, and returning focus.

Relationship Satisfaction

A satisfying relationship involves many things, including what we have just discussed: an ability to focus (empathically on others), reduced rumination and self-referential thinking, stress reduction, working memory, metacognition, introspection, reduced emotional reactivity and reification, and cognitive flexibility. Can you identify the unmindful features of the following description of a troubled relationship:

© Akhenation Images/Shutterstock.com

> *Sue and Bart are having difficulties. When Sue describes a problem or concern, Bart is easily distracted and doesn't seem to pay attention. He seem self-involved, and finds it difficult to see things from Sue's perspective. He seems to spend much of his time thinking about his own concerns. Bart overreacts to even the slightest criticism from Sue. When they discuss their problems, Bart seems clueless and simply can't seem to recall specific incidents (not showing*

© ESB Professional/Shutterstock.com

up for a date, insulting Sue publically, promising to spend more time together, and the like). Rarely does Bart take time to look at himself and examine the part he plays in his relationship. Furthermore, he feels there are no problems and feels fine with Sue.

Health Benefits

A huge body of research has examined claimed health benefits of mindfulness and related disciplines. Most of this research suffers from serious methodological problems. There is the selection problem (perhaps only healthy meditators sign up for research); the placebo effect (expectation of relief can contribute to apparent gain); or extraneous variables that are not a part of mindfulness (finding companionship in a mindfulness group). This said, the most frequent health benefit claims appear to include:

- Pain reduction
- Depression reduction
- Anxiety reduction
- Increased immune functioning
- Addiction control
- Aggression management
- Insomnia reduction
- Hypertension control

If you search the web for the benefits of mindfulness, you will discover that this list is much longer. Indeed, every month seems to produce yet another scientific discovery of what mindfulness can do. To the extent mindfulness evokes the relaxation response, it could well contribute to prevention, treatment, management, or recovery of all the disorders and conditions listed in Table 3.1.

Finally, our APA article suggests benefits of mindfulness for therapists, counselors, and their trainees. These include increased:

- Self-reported empathy
- Compassion, especially not judging or reacting to clients as well as taking on others' perspectives
- Awareness of the therapy process and greater comfort with silence in therapy

Stress & Coping
Eye of Mindfulness Journal

Chapter 11

The Five Levels of Relaxation and Mindfulness

© Iva Vagnerova/Shutterstock.com

What is your experience with relaxation and mindfulness? How are your experiences similar to or different from the experiences of others? Sometimes do you feel you are growing? Maybe at times you feel stuck. Answering these questions requires that you know the language of relaxation and mindfulness. After all, a student chef who is learning various culinary traditions could not discuss her creations without a shared vocabulary of taste, for example, what constitutes "hot," "sweet," "savory," "spoiled," "burnt," "undercooked," and the like. If different schools of music students want to discuss their mastery, they need to understand the language of music, say "noise," "rhythm," "harmony," and "jazzy." And when travelling, the soothing wise voice from your smartphone GPS guides you on your way. If you were not conversant with the language of travel ("detour," "warning: speed camera ahead," "road closed," "intersection," "traffic jam"), you would indeed be lost.

Languages help us to communicate with each other. They sensitize us to experiences that may be hidden. They direct a flashlight on paths we might be on, pointing out when we are moving and when we are stuck. Is there a universal language of relaxation and mindfulness?

We could turn directly to the religious and spiritual texts. But here we find esoteric and technical terms limited to histories and traditions, and used by elites to communicate with each other. We might encounter such esoteric phrases as "astral body," "higher Self," or "detachment." These terms might be meaningful to one tradition, say Christian or Buddhist, and not to others. Similarly, secular scientists have their own technical language which might include such words as "dereification," "metacognition," or "sensory focus." Alas, this is hardly a natural language of actual practitioners. The question remains: *What is the universal natural language of relaxation and mindfulness?* What words are meaningful to practitioners across traditions at various levels of expertise?

Quest for the Natural Language of Relaxation and Mindfulness

Since 1999 I have embarked on a quest for the universal natural language of relaxation and mindfulness. My goal has been to create a master user lexicon, a dictionary of words and phrases. This would be a special dictionary not wedded to any particular religion, philosophy, or psychology, but based on the words practitioners actually use to describe their experiences.

I began by studying the basic instructional texts of yoga, progressive muscle relaxation, breathing, prayer, meditation, mindfulness, tai chi, imagery, self-hypnosis, and autogenic training. This search included ancient approaches as well as those that are new, approaches from the East and West, and approaches from spiritual and secular traditions. What words do teachers use when talking to their students? In all I came up with an initial dictionary of over 200 relaxation and mindfulness words.

Which are actually used by practitioners? In 1996 a talented Spanish scholar of mindfulness, Alberto Amutio, came to America to help me with this question. We gave my list to hundreds of practitioners. Our results triggered over two decades of similar studies involving over 6,000 participants and over 40 types of relaxation and mindfulness (Borgogna & Smith, 2016, 2016a; Smith, 1985, 1986, 1988, 1999, 2001, 2005, 2007, 2012, 2015; Smith, Amutio et al., 1996).

In addition to conducting this research, I have been teaching relaxation and mindfulness. Over the past 33 years I have taught over 150 classes including nearly 4,000 students a menu of exercises, including yoga, breathing exercises, muscle relaxation, autogenic self-suggestion, imagery, mantra meditation, and mindfulness. In my classes, every student is taught the full array. Students take shortened versions of my relaxation and mindfulness list to track progress and make technique comparisons.

Over time I used research and teaching findings to shorten my list to 25 relaxation and mindfulness states. I call this my Relaxation/Mindfulness (R/M) Lexicon. It is my best attempt at identifying a universal dictionary of relaxation and mindfulness based on the natural language of practitioners from diverse traditions.

Today when I teach, I use the Lexicon as a training questionnaire, the Relaxation/Mindfulness (R/M) Tracker. Students track their progress and growth, articulate experiences that may be subtle and hard to put into words, compare and contrast exercises, and identify what works best. Here is my latest R/M Lexicon:

The R/M Lexicon Used in the R/M Tracker

Basic Relaxation

1. FAR AWAY
2. PHYSICALLY RELAXED
3. AT EASE, AT PEACE
4. REFRESHED
5. PLEASANT MIND WANDERING
6. FANTASY, DAYDREAMING

Basic Mindfulness

7. FOCUSED, ABSORBED
8. CENTERED, GROUNDED
9. QUIET
10. UNBOTHERED
11. EASY, EFFORTLESS

Mindful Awakening

12. OBSERVER
13. CLEAR, AWAKE, AWARE
14. INTERESTED, CURIOUS, FASCINATED
15. BEAUTIFUL

Mindful Deepening

16. GOING DEEPER
17. SPACIOUSNESS, EXPANSIVENESS
18. SENSE OF SOMETHING GREATER
19. MEANING, PURPOSE, DIRECTION

Mindful Transcendence

20. REVERENT, PRAYERFUL
21 AWE/ WONDER, DEEP MYSTERY
22. SPIRITUAL MYSTICAL

Mindful Positive Emotion

23. HAPPY, OPTIMISTIC, TRUSTING
24. LOVING, CARING
25. THANKFUL

The Five Levels of Mindfulness

The R/M Tracker presents five levels of R/M States, all potentially supported by a set of states we call mindful emotions. Our five levels differ along four dimensions:

1. Lower-level states are associated with beginning practice. Higher-level states are often, but not always, associated *longer periods of practice.*
2. Higher-level states display less egocentric or self-centered "self-referential" judgmental mind wandering (Chapter 9, the brain's default network; Chapter 10, self-referential thinking). They are more likely to be "*other-referential,*" directed away from oneself and toward something else.
3. Higher-level states are more likely to be "*dynamic,*" and open to the potential for change and evolution.
4. Higher-level states are more *open and encompassing.* Their range of application is greater. They are larger tents that cover larger territories. Furthermore, higher level states imply that there is more to be experienced, something larger or greater than oneself. They are highly other-referential.

To summarize, the R/M Lexicon suggests something of a universal map of what can happen when one masters and explores the promise of quiet, sustained simple focus. Our map is religion-neutral, not wedded to, but compatible with the full rainbow of religions and philosophical perspectives. As such, the R/M Lexicon and Tracker are defining features of *The Book of Mindfulness* and Third-Generation Mindfulness (Chapter 1).

Here is a summary:

Five Levels of Relaxation/Mindfulness

Level 1: Basic Relaxation
Level 2: Basic Mindfulness
Level 3: Mindful Awakening
Level 4: Mindful Deepening
Level 5: Mindful Transcendence

All supported by mindful emotions:
Happiness, Optimistic, Trusting
Loving Caring
Thankful, Grateful

But it is important not to view this map as a simple grocery list of potential benefits. Let me explain.

The Dynamic Other-Referential Orientation: What Can Mindfulness Teach Us?

We have emphasized that the opposite of mindfulness is self-referential or ego-centric thinking (Chapter 8). There is an implied and profound twist in this observation. The opposite of a self-referential orientation is a **dynamic other-referential orientation.**

To elaborate, there is a risk in getting stuck on Chapters 7-10. There is a risk in viewing mindfulness only as a static health chore, something to "do" or a way to "get" certain desired payoffs. The Five Levels of Mindfulness suggest something of a growing, expanding, and moving path with potential for discovery. It has a potential meaning, direction, and unexpected insight.

A self-referential focus places primary emphasis or locus of control on oneself. (*"I do this."*). An other-referential focus places primary emphasis or locus on something else. (*"Something else is doing this."*) This "something else" could be "Love," a cause, a philosophy, a God or Gods (or the lack thereof), higher consciousness, or the powers that be. In terms of this book, the emphasis or locus is simple. *"What does mindfulness have to teach us?"* Not *"What can I get or make happen?"* Of course, if you believe in God or Gods, that could be how your mindfulness locus works. If you are an atheist, it may be some basic cosmic order. Or your own "creative unconscious." Or even "the flow of the way things are." It is not my goal to muddy the waters with feeble attempts at philosophy. Let's keep things simple. *What can mindfulness show us? Where can it lead us?* Such questions reflect a dynamic, other-referential orientation.

We now consider the five levels of relaxation/mindfulness.

Level 1: Basic Relaxation

Basic Relaxation consists of simple relaxation states most people experience when practicing relaxation and mindfulness techniques. We have found that relaxation is far more rich and differentiated than most experts recognize.

R/M State 1: FAR AWAY (Disengagement). One of the first achievements of training in relaxation, meditation, and mindfulness is simply getting away (or "letting go") from the day's stressors. When we experience R/M State Disengagement we feel distant and far away, indifferent to our cares and concerns, and nicely detached from the surrounding world. We may even lose awareness of our relaxation trainer, or of parts of our body. All these words clump together as a unified "factor" group, defined by the words "far away."

R/M State 2: PHYSICALLY RELAXED. As you disengage, you may feel R/M State Physical Relaxation. You let go of unnecessary muscle tension and your breathing becomes relaxed. This can be experienced in various ways. Often when our muscles are relaxed they feel nicely warm and heavy. This is a normal sign of muscle relaxation. You may feel tingling or heaviness. Your breathing may feel more even and effortless. There are many words we can use to describe when the body is relaxing, all of which form a unified "factor" group.

R/M State 3: AT EASE, AT PEACE. Distress comes in many forms, including frustration, pain, worry, fear, concern, or conflict. When distress is eliminated, we feel mental relaxation, that is, R/M State At Ease, At Peace.

Mental relaxation is associated with how we cope with problems. Imagine something is creating fear for you. Perhaps your child has gone out for the evening and is late. You feel fear. You call, and discover she is one block down the street coming home with her friends. Suddenly your mind is relieved—mentally relaxed. Imagine you are driving home and haven't eaten for hours. There is no place to eat in sight. Suddenly a favorite restaurant appears, and you quickly go for a delicious meal. Your hunger turns to contented satisfaction—again you are mentally relaxed. Maybe you are having an argument with your boss over her unfair demands. She realizes she has been pushing too hard, and agrees with your request for an easier schedule. The conflict is resolved, and you are mentally relaxed. Or you have burned your foot and are in pain. You apply a soothing lotion, and you feel soothing relief, mentally relaxed.

The dictionary reveals that all of these experiences have one thing in common, the relief of psychological tension, whether it be fear, craving, conflict, pain, and so on. Interestingly, such worlds clump into a "factor group," R/M State best described by the words *At Ease / At Peace*, or mental relaxation.

The absence of mental relaxation can be a barrier to growth in relaxation and mindfulness. It can suggest unfinished business requiring attention. If you are filled with fear that needs to be resolved, deal with it. Get out of the thunderstorm before meditating. If you are hungry, eat a banana. If you are in conflict, confront it. In pain, try to relieve it, and so on. If actions to relieve psychological distress fail, then relaxation and mindfulness may be your last, best solution. Or try active coping supplemented by relaxation and mindfulness.

R/M State 4: REFRESHED. One type of mental relaxation is the simple feeling of being refreshed and energized, R/M State Refreshed.

R/M State 5: PLEASANT MIND WANDERING. My students have taught me one type of basic relaxation rarely noted by experts. Sometimes when people relax, they simply let go of deliberately planning and doing things, and enjoy the pleasures of undirected fantasy and random mind wandering. This is both relaxing and possibly an easy type of mindfulness as long as one does not get caught up in planning, analyzing, or reacting to one's fantasy. I have found that R/M State Pleasant Mind Wandering is experienced by most practitioners of relaxation and mindfulness. Indeed, some practitioners identify it as a sign that their practice is working. Researches need to identify the role this R/M State plays in mindfulness.

R/M State 6: FANTASY, DAYDREAMING. Sometimes mind wandering becomes more directed, perhaps with a plot or story. Here it becomes a pleasant fantasy or daydream. Unlike pleasant mind wandering, fantasy and daydreaming are somewhat more coherent and directed and less random. Most of my trainees find R/M State Fantasy, Daydreaming to be a distraction to mindfulness. It is less likely to be reported by advanced practitioners. However, the role of this R/M State in mindfulness training is an interesting empirical question.

Note on Basic Relaxation: I suspect that Basic Relaxation is a rudimentary type of mindfulness, reflecting reductions in effort and judgment, and a degree of sustained focus. However, the focal task or stimulus may not be particularly simple. A practitioner of yoga may focus on a sequence of 15 stretches. A relaxing daydream may involve a complex setting of a peaceful church. However, even when complex, the focal task or stimulus serves to assist other components of mindfulness. Yoga, spiritual fantasy, breathing exercises, and the like may mindfully serve to reduce unnecessary judgment, effort, and perhaps stimulus complexity. We can term simple relaxation exercises activities done in the spirit of mindfulness as *mindfulness preparations or assists.*

Level 2: Basic Mindfulness

© Olga Lyubkin/Shutterstock.com

In addition to Basic Relaxation, most practitioners of relaxation and relaxation/mindfulness experience a degree of Basic Mindfulness. Our guiding definition of mindfulness expresses this formally: Mindfulness is *sustained simple focus, with minimal judgment and effort.* Research and student experiences suggest a natural language of terms students can relate to.

R/M State 7: FOCUS, ABSORPTION. Attention is directed to a target stimulus or task. One can sustain such focus for a period of time. When this attention is completely engaged to the exclusion of competing stimuli, one is absorbed.

R/M State 8: CENTERED, GROUNDED. Here sustained focus and absorption is comfortably stable like a rock or tree firmly planted in the ground.

R/M State 9: QUIET. Imagine you are on vacation and are sitting alone by a lake. Evening is approaching. The hustle and bustle of the day has settled down. At this moment you may feel a state our research has identified as mindful R/State Quiet. Specifically, you feel an inner silence and calm. Thought and emotional activity has settled and there is little mind wandering. Your mind is quiet and still. Even feelings of peace and serenity are absent. However, you are not "numb," "zoned out," or "in a trance." The R/M State Quiet reflects primarily an absence of judgment and effort, in the context of a single focus.

R/M State 10: UNBOTHERED. One is accepting. Negative thoughts or feelings might emerge, however one is not "caught up" in them. They may be seen as simple thoughts rather than final realities. Formally this is "dereification," or in terms of our guiding definition, reduced judgment.

R/M State 11: EASY, EFFORTLESS. It is easy to let go of mind wandering and distraction, return to task, and sustain focus. It is easy to let things be, accept what is, and go on. The task at hand, whether it be relaxation, mindfulness, or even work or recreation feels effortless.

Level 3: Mindful Awakening

Once one has acquired the brain-based skill of quiet sustained simple focus, new experiences may emerge. These generally reflect an increased awareness of oneself and the world. This reflects the beginning of a *dynamic, other-directed orientation.*

© Olga Lyubkin/Shutterstock.com

R/M State 12: OBSERVER. Here one simply stands aside and watches things come and go, as a neutral and objective witness. You don't get caught up in what's happening.

Imagine you are sitting at the edge of a pond watching two fish scramble for the same worm. It is a bit interesting, a curious incident unfolding in the world of the pond. Now imagine you are sitting at the edge of a playfield and your two young nephews are fighting for the same toy. You get upset and start shouting for them to "play nice." You get personally involved as they yell at you to leave them alone. In both examples you are an observer. In the playfield incident you lost your neutrality and got caught up in the moment. However, when sitting by the pond you were neutral and objective and simply watched the event unfold. This is the stance of the mindful observer, R/State Observer.

R/M State 13: CLEAR, AWAKE, AWARE. As an observer one may have a sense of experiencing things as they really are. Things may seem "vivid" or particularly "real." One's mantra may cease to be a mechanical chant, but a sound with a life and direction of its own. A prayer may become more than a mechanical chant, but words from god. The flow of the present moment may be seen clearly, as for the first time, perhaps as seen by a child.

R/M State 14:INTERESTED, CURIOUS, FASCINATED. When one is interested, curious, or fascinated in a task, whether it be mindfulness, yoga, relaxation, or even work or recreation, one is displaying a type of focus, a type of mindfulness. Perhaps this is a step beyond simple awareness as an objective observer. It is more than viewing a stimulus vividly as "really real." An important new dimension is added: There is more than first appeared. The deeper reality of breath is more than the inflow and outflow of air. The deeper reality of the mantra is not just a repeated sound or syllable. The reality of the present moment is more than a series of events. What is this more? We experience R/M State Interest, Curiosity, and Fascination.

At a deeper level, mindfulness begins to prompt us to ask such questions as, Why be mindful? Why let go of judgment and effort? Why become relaxed? Why become focused? At the very least, we can say "because the world is beautiful." This leads to our next R/M State.

R/M State 15: BEAUTIFUL. Things seem beautiful, harmonious.

Level 4: Mindful Deepening

I hypothesize that when mindfulness develops, R/M States emerge that reflect a slightly different facet of mindfulness. In Mindful Deepening, one sustains simple focus with minimal judgment and effort. In Level 3 we discover a new feature of such quiet focus and openness to the potential of something more. In Level 4 another feature emerges: Our focal target is no longer a static state but one that changes and evolves.

R/M State 16: GOING DEEPER: Things are unexpected, new, interesting. Things are changing, opening up, being revealed. It may feel like you are in a different place or space.

© Olga Lyubkin/Shutterstock.com

R/M State 17: SPACIOUSNESS, EXPANSIVENESS. One has a sense of spaciousness and expansiveness.

R/M State 18: SENSE OF SOMETHING GREATER: You may feel the sense of something greater than yourself (God, a higher power, spirit, energy, love, or consciousness). If religiously inclined, you may feel that God is with you.

R/M State 19: MEANING, PURPOSE, DIRECTION.

Level 5: Mindful Transcendence

© Olga Lyubkin/Shutterstock.com

In rare and special moments of mindfulness one comes in touch with the deeper side of life. Transcendent states reflect awareness of a world larger or greater than oneself. They represent something of a living "relationship" to the world outside of self-referential concern. This last point can be difficult and calls for a bit of discussion.

Think of a relationship in your life, perhaps a friend. You do not treat your friend as a tool or object. You respect your friend. He or she has an autonomous identity (not a puppet of your desires). He or she can change and evolve independently. You recognize back-and-forth interactions are equally real. You may say or do things for your friend that are important, and he/she may say or do things that are important for you.

In a way we can have a relationship with our perceived transcendent world, a universe larger or greater than ourselves. We can respect this world as having an autonomous identity, one that changes and evolves on its own. We can recognize that this world affects us. And we can recognize that our thoughts and actions affect this world. But it is very important to note that R/M States require no supernatural beliefs. Meditating atheists as well as believers can experience and find meaning in them. To put this simply, *respect your mindfulness.* Here are the transcendent R/M States.

R/M State 20: REVERENT, PRAYERFUL. Feelings of reverence and prayerfulness reflect an emotional response to something larger or greater than oneself. These are expressive states, coming from oneself. One "reveres," one "prays."

R/M State 21: AWE/WONDER, DEEP MYSTERY. R/M State Awe and Wonder reflects a nonanalytic and goal-less awareness of a larger and greater reality that is new, awesome, beyond ordinary familiar comprehension and expectations. We don't have words for "it."

We may experience a release from adult, verbal, analytic thinking; one might feel like a small child facing a wonderful, larger world. The Grand Canyon can leave one "struck with awe." Here the intensity and immensity of an external stimulus leave one temporarily "shocked" or "blinded."

Our language provides many phrases that convey this notion: "shock of the new," "blinding truth," "dumbstruck," "speechless," "far out," "mindblowing," "knocks one's socks off," or simply "Wow!" or "Amazing!" However expressed, one's adult, verbal, analytic thinking cap has been knocked askew; one is temporarily freed or released from these constraints and sees things anew.

R/M State Deep Mystery is somewhat familiar to most people. We all have discovered things we do not understand, and sometimes we encounter profound questions and mysteries that seem to transcend any possibility of understanding.

There is a subtle difference between Awe/Wonder and Deep Mystery. R/M State Awe/Wonder suggests we simply do not have the words to describe what we experience. Deep Mystery implies we do not understand it. You may not have words to describe the Grand Canyon, a magnificent temple, or the night sky, but understand the geology of how the Canyon developed or how the temple was built. In contrast, you may well have words to describe the sky you see, for example, the differences between planets, stars, and galaxies. However, the fact that the universe is infinite, or is expanding faster than the speed of light, may be a mystery, something beyond your comprehension.

R/M State 22: SPIRITUAL, MYSTICAL: This constellation of R/M states reflect a profound and personal meaningful experience—a sudden awakening or insight.

- This might include feelings of an underlying hidden truth. One might feel as if one has special and important insightful and intuitive knowledge. There is a sense of certainty of encounter with ultimate reality, a sense of seeing or knowing what is "really real," ultimate reality.
- One might have feelings of being "at one" with the universe or others, a sense of selflessness.
- One common feature of transcendent experiences is that they are difficult to describe or communicate to others. One feels unable to justify the experience by simply putting it into words. This goes beyond the R/M State of awe and wonder, which reflects more an emotional experience that is ineffable.

Mindful Emotions

Many strong positive emotions can emerge in relaxation and mindfulness. Such emotions can help one sustain simple focus, reduce needless effort and judgment, and let go of self-referential thinking and mind wandering.

R/M State 23: HAPPY, OPTIMISTIC, TRUSTING. A wide range of joyful feelings can spontaneously bubble up when one practices any form of relaxation and mindfulness. They can be released when one withdraws from stress, releases tension, relaxes one's mind, and becomes more aware and accepting. Happiness, optimism, and trust can be mindful when attention is not self-referential. One might feel like saying "I am happy for your health," "I am optimistic things will turn out OK; I have done all I can and can leave things be, " "I trust the powers that be will guide us."

R/M State 24: LOVING, CARING. Occasionally practitioners of relaxation and mindfulness report that strong and unexpected feelings of love, kindness, compassion, and caring emerge during their practice. It is not surprising that many traditions use love and compassion as a meditation focus. A natural consequence of all R/M States is a reduced self-referential thinking and increased awareness of others. This is the heart of love and compassion. One may feel more giving and generous, wanting others to be safe and happy and experience R/M States. In everyday life it is important to remember the value of acts of thankfulness, love, compassion and forgiveness. Not only do they help us let go of pressures that may not matter, but they nurture the practice of relaxation and mindfulness.

R/M State 25: THANKFUL: One experiences thankfulness towards the source of a gift. One is grateful for the gift itself. ("I am grateful for this; thank you for sharing it with me.") To be thankful is to be mindful. You are fully aware of a gift, and fully aware that you did not create or give the gift to yourself. Self-referential mind wandering is minimized. You are fully and clearly aware of the gift in and of itself. Acknowledgement and cultivation of gratitude may be another way of cultivation mindfulness.

Summary of the Five Levels of Mindfulness

Level 1: Basic Relaxation
I relax and put distracting tensions, judgment, and effort aside; I focus on and enjoy the pleasures of relief and relaxation.

Level 2: Basic Mindfulness
I sustain quiet simple focus with minimal judgment and effort, minimal self-referential thought.

Level 3: Mindful Awakening
I am mindful of a real world outside of my self-referential focus. There is more than me.

Level 4: Mindful Deepening
I am mindful that the world outside of self-referential focus changes and evolves. It may have direction, meaning, and purpose.

Level 5: Mindful Transcendence
I am mindful that the world outside of self-referential focus is not only real, changing, and evolving, but is much larger and greater than myself. It is a world that commands reverence, awe, and wonder. It is a world beyond words. It deserves my respect.

Mindful Emotions
I feel happiness, optimism, and trust.
I feel love and care.
I feel thankful.

The R/M Tracker

The R/M Tracker measures R/M States. With it you can measure your progress and compare and contrast the effects of various exercises. See the Appendix.

THE R/M TRACKER

DID YOU FEEL OR EXPERIENCE DURING **THE EYE OF MINDFULNESS EXERCISE?**

CLICK BOXES USING THIS KEY

(SKIP ITEMS YOU DON'T UNDERSTAND OR DIDN'T FEEL OR EXPERIENCE)

☒❑❑❑	☒☒❑❑	☒☒☒❑	☒☒☒☒
Felt this SLIGHTLY	Felt this MODERATELY	Felt this VERY MUCH	Felt this EXTREMELY (the most ever)

*1. **FAR AWAY** and distant from the troubles around me.*	❑❑❑❑
*2. **PHYSICALLY RELAXED**. Muscles relaxed, loose, limp, warm and heavy. Breathing slow, even, and easy.*	❑❑❑❑
*3 **AT EASE, AT PEACE**.*	❑❑❑❑
*4. **REFRESHED**.*	❑❑❑❑
*5. **PLEASANT MIND WANDERING**. Undirected, random positive thoughts.*	❑❑❑❑
*6. Lost in **FANTASY** and **DAYDREAMING.***	❑❑❑❑
*7. Periods of sustained, continuous **FOCUS. ABSORPTION.***	❑❑❑❑
*8. **CENTERED, GROUNDED.***	❑❑❑❑
*9. **QUIET.** Still, few thoughts. Little mind wandering.*	❑❑❑❑
*10. **UNBOTHERED.** Accepting. When I had a negative thought or feeling, I didn't get caught up in it. No judging, clinging, pushing away, figuring things out.*	❑❑❑❑
*11. **EASY, EFFORTLESS.** Effortless to let go, put thoughts aside, sustain focus.*	❑❑❑❑
*12. I felt like an **OBSERVER** standing aside and watching what happens.*	❑❑❑❑
*13. **CLEAR, AWAKE, AWARE.** I saw things as they really are.*	❑❑❑❑
*14. **INTERESTED, CURIOUS, FASCINATED**.*	❑❑❑❑
*15. Things seemed **BEAUTIFUL.***	❑❑❑❑
*16. **GOING DEEPER**. Things seemed unexpected, new, changing, opening up,being revealed. Felt like I was in a different place or space.*	❑❑❑❑
*17. Sense of **SPACIOUSNESS, EXPANSIVENESS**.*	❑❑❑❑
*18. I felt the **SENSE OF SOMETHING GREATER** than myself (God, a higher power, spirit, energy, love, or consciousness.); God is with me.*	❑❑❑❑
*19. A sense of **MEANING, PURPOSE, DIRECTION.***	❑❑❑❑
*20. I felt **REVERENT, PRAYERFUL**.*	❑❑❑❑
*21. **AWE / WONDER, DEEP MYSTERY** of things beyond my understanding.*	❑❑❑❑
*22. I felt a profound personal meaningful "**SPIRITUAL**" or "**MYSTICAL**" experience -- sudden awakening or insight.* • *Felt an underlying hidden **TRUTH.*** • *Feeling **AT ONE.*** • *Feelings so profound they **COULD NOT BE PUT INTO WORDS.***	❑❑❑❑
*23. **HAPPY, OPTIMISTIC, TRUSTING.***	❑❑❑❑
*24. **LOVING, CARING.***	❑❑❑❑
*25. **THANKFUL.** Grateful.*	❑❑❑❑

Stress & Coping
Eye of Mindfulness Journal

Chapter 12

The Eye of Mindfulness and the Mindfulness Protocol

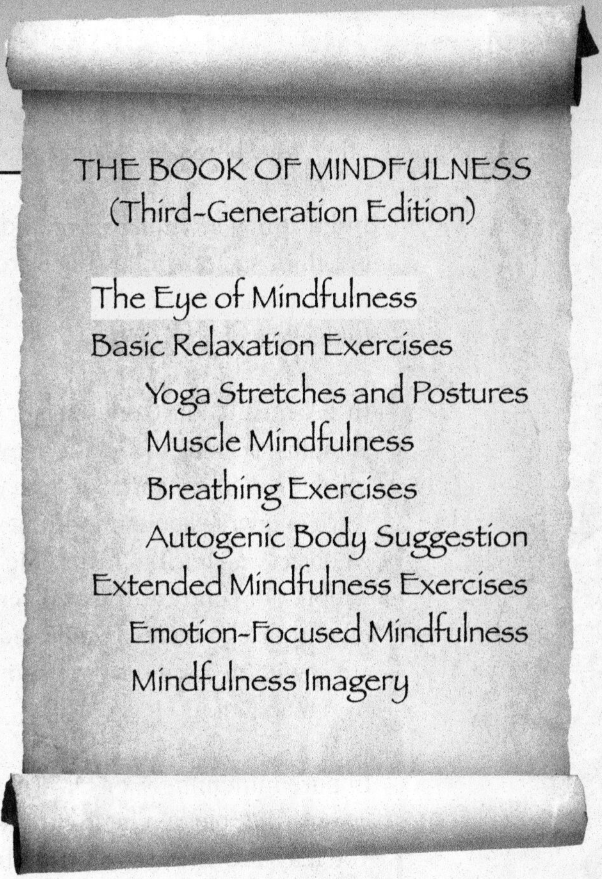

There are thousands of instructions for mindfulness. Most involve developing the "muscle" of *sustained simple focus with minimal judgment and effort.* I have organized the key universal elements into a system I call *The Eye of Mindfulness.* Basically, the Eye of Mindfulness system incorporates four types of exercises:

1. Body scanning
2. Breathing scanning
3. FA Meditation (focused attention meditation)
4. OM Mindfulness (open monitoring / open awareness meditation)

All four are forms of mindfulness in that they instruct you to sustain simple focus with minimal judgment and effort. You direct your attention to a very simple stimulus or task, and gently return every time you detect mind wandering or distraction. Put simply, in each exercise you assume the role of a calm observer, doing nothing but attending. You remain neutral in face of all mind wandering and distraction, letting thoughts come and go on their own.

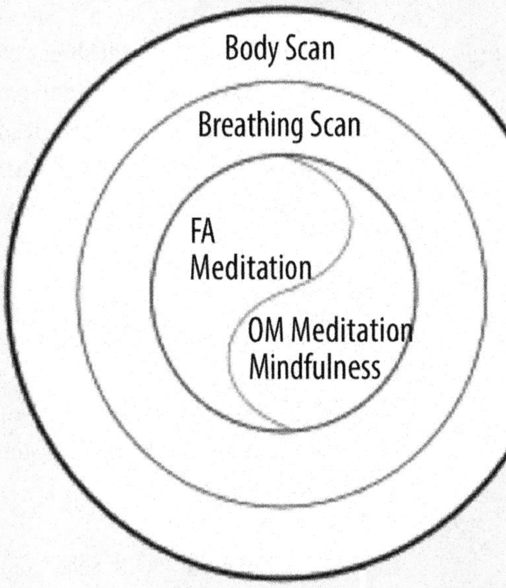

The Four Elements of the Eye of Mindfulness

In body scanning meditation, or the "body scan," you attend to one body part after another, note how it feels, and simply let go of any tension you may feel.

In breathing scanning meditation, or the "breathing scan," you attend to the flow of breath in and out, following it from the nose, throat, chest, and abdomen. You do not force yourself to breathe. You simply assume the role of a neutral observer, attending to the flow of breathing.

In FA meditation (sometimes called "concentrative meditation") you select a target stimulus, such as the gentle movement of rocking back and forth, a neutral word or syllable called a mantra, or a very simple mental image like a spot of light. Those who teach and write about mindfulness typically pick a simple breath-related or body-related object on which to focus. Here FA meditation might be called FAs (somatic) meditation. In contrast, transcendental meditation, Christian/Jewish/Islamic meditation often utilizes a mentally repeated mantra, or possibly an image. These mental objects are cognitions, and the corresponding type of meditation might be called FAc (cognitive) meditation.

In pure mindfulness, or OM (or open monitoring / open awareness) meditation, you assume the role of a neutral observer, and attend to the sounds as they come and go. You may also attend to all stimuli as they come and go, observing sights, sounds, body sensations, and even fragrances. You are simply the observer, not getting caught up in any stimulus, not getting involved in thought.

In all forms of mindfulness, you will experience mind wandering. This, as we have seen, is perfectly normal. Gently return your focus to your task after every mind wandering incident and distraction. It's like taking a puppy for a walk on a forest path. The puppy will of course run off again and again and again. This is normal, nothing to get all fussed about. You simply and gently return the puppy to the path again and again and again.

The Core Mindfulness Cycle

We have defined the act of mindfulness as quiet sustained simple focus. Experts (Lutz et al., 2008, 2015) have noted that this is actually a complex act. Here is my summary and elaboration:

1. **ORIENT**. One selects some "thing" or "task" on which to mindfully focus. To do this one must identify and put aside either involvement in default mind wandering or discursive purposeful activity. In a more general sense, one makes a sincere choice to practice.

2. **RELAX**: As preparation, one disengages from the busy world, from stimuli that evoke mind wandering. In addition one calms the body and mind, reduces distraction, and lets go of cognitive or bodily arousal.
3. **FOCUS.** One directs attention to a simple stimulus or task ("target," "object," or "focus") with minimal effort;
4. **DETECT.** One maintains a stance of monitoring, an unconscious vigilance to potential distraction and mind wandering. In terms of our definition, one is prepared to detect needless judgment, effort, stimulus or tasking complexity, or deviation from one's chosen stimulus. One is primed to expect interruptions to focusing. By monitoring one does not become frozen in rapt attention waiting for the next distraction. Monitoring is not like playing a high-stakes video game in which one anxiously waits for the next alien attack. Instead, perhaps through practice, one is easily ready for distraction. One has already accepted that mind wandering is of no importance, nothing to get upset about. One is a quiet observer. Each instance of mind wandering might be interesting and evoke curiosity. But one detects each distraction, each instance of mind wandering as neutrally as possible, with minimal disruption.
5. **LET GO.** One lets go or releases involvement with a distraction or mind wandering after detection, doing so with a minimum of additional default thinking. This may be accompanied by a brief instance of supportive letting go and relaxation. In terms of our definition, one lets go of needless judgment, effort, or distracting stimuli. One might find oneself reaffirming orienting instructions or practicing a brief segment of a basic relaxation exercise (like shifting or stretching, letting go of muscle tension, taking a deep breath).
6. **REFOCUS.** One promptly redirects attention to one's chosen focus, again with a minimum of default thinking or effort. I differentiate initial focusing from refocusing. Refocusing incorporates recognition that one has been distracted, one's mind has wandered, or default activity has occurred. However, this recognition is minimally disruptive.

This sequences is the **core mindfulness cycle:**

ORIENT – RELAX - FOCUS - DETECT - LET GO - REFOCUS

This cycle reminds us that mindfulness isn't just focusing. When you are struggling whether it is worthwhile to devote a portion of each day to simply being quiet, you are doing something mindful (ORIENT). When you stop your day's hectic routine and related mind wandering, and spend some time in deep relaxation, you are also doing something mindful (RELAX). When you detect a distraction early on (rather than halfway through a practice session), when you can let go of a pressing or tempting diverting thought, and when you can easily get back to the task of mindfulness, you are being mindful (DETECT, LET GO, REFOCUS).

Our Mindfulness Protocol: Four Training Tasks

The key to making mindfulness work is to pick the right exercise, practice regularly, and supplement and extend your practice with additional strengthening exercises. Let's consider each of these basic tasks:

TASK 1, SELECT: Select your Home Exercise (from the Eye of Mindfulness Introductory Exercise)

We begin with the Eye of Mindfulness Introductory Exercise at the end of this chapter. It introduces body scanning, breath scanning, FA meditation, and OM meditation. Have someone read the exercise script to you as you practice. If you are in a self-study group, assign this task to a group member with a soothing voice. Or record the script yourself. Practice the Introductory Exercise 3-5 times. Eventually you will pick FA meditation, OM meditation, body scanning, or breath scanning (or some combination) as your preferred core technique. This will be your "home" exercise.

TASK 2, CHALLENGE: Increase the Length of your Home Exercise through Exercise Duration Challenges

Throughout this program you need to practice your home exercise every day. Without regular practice your mindfulness muscle won't grow. (Be patient, it may take up to a month.) Most students start with short sessions. This is good for a start, but not enough for serious growth. I have found it useful to encourage "exercise duration challenges." Here's how it works.

Once you have selected your home exercise, you have a new task, increase the session length you can tolerate. I have my students start with five minute sessions. At their own pace they continuously challenge themselves with slightly longer sessions: 5 – 10 – 15 – 20 – 30 minutes. When I began mindfulness, my sessions were 10 minutes long. Now my daily sessions last at least an hour.

TASK 3, STRENGTHEN: Strengthen Practice with Relaxation and Extended Mindfulness Exercises

Throughout this program I invite you to strengthen your practice with basic relaxation and extended mindfulness exercises. These can serve as powerful preparation "warmups" for your home exercise, and tools for exploring and expressing mindfulness beyond the practice session.

We will systematically explore a variety of supplementary exercises throughout this text. I recommend that for any strengthening exercise, you give it at least three tries. In the first session you become familiar with the instructions. In the second session you increase your familiarity with the instructions, and begin to enjoy the effects of the exercise. By your third session, you should get a good taste of what the exercise does. In other words, never judge an exercise by practicing it just once.

Finally, you will always be returning to and practicing your home mindfulness exercise, regularly challenging the session length you can tolerate.

TASK 4, TRACK: Describe your experiences on an R/M Tracker

After practicing and exercise, fill out an R/M Tracker to describe your experiences. If you practiced an exercise several times, fill out a Tracker for your best session. In this program, we present a fresh Tracker whenever a new exercise is presented. Of course, you will continue to practice your home mindfulness exercise. For your home mindfulness exercise, copy a tracker from the Appendix. (Copy as many as you want.) Keep all of your trackers so at the end of the program you can look at your progress, compare approaches, and identify what R/M States changed most.

We are now ready to begin with the Eye of Mindfulness. Simply practice the following exercise. Then fill out the concluding R/M Tracker mindfulness questionnaire to describe your experiences.

EYE OF MINDFULNESS

INTRODUCTORY EXERCISE SCRIPT

MAKING YOUR OWN RECORDING: Read very slowly and calmly. Your voice should be deliberate, focused, and clear. Be generous with pauses. Speak quietly with little inflection. Imagine you are meditating while making your recording.

ORIENTATION (The Orientation can be skipped after the first week of practice.)

To understand mindfulness we need to start with its opposite—idle worry, getting stressed out, simple mind wandering. Mindfulness is the opposite of this. It is a powerful brain-based skill developed through practice, just as muscle develops through exercise.

Mindfulness is quiet, sustained simple focus. It's easy. Attend to something very simple. Whenever you get caught up in a distraction, note the distraction, and gently return attending to your mindfulness focus. Whenever you get caught up in mind wandering, just note what has happened, and gently and effortlessly return to attending to your mindfulness focus. You are nothing more than a quiet observer.

Our mindfulness exercise is called the Eye of Mindfulness. It has four parts: body scan, breath scan, meditation, and mindfulness. First, we will practice mindfulness on the body and breathing, then on a meditation focus or inner sound called a mantra, and then a light. We end with mindfulness on outside sounds and stimuli that come and go. In all exercises we simply attend. We are quiet and neutral observers, effortlessly returning again and again after our minds wander, doing nothing to interfere.

BEGINNING

We are ready to begin.

Quietly sit up straight with your feet flat on the floor.
Make sure your hands are resting quietly in your lap.
Take a deep breath and relax.

Our first exercise is body/breath scanning meditation. Here we attend to each part of the body, note any tension, and let go. Do this quietly, effortlessly.

We start with a scanning-release image. Imagine tension flowing from the top of your head, through your body, and out through your toes. You may think of a warm stream of water flowing from head to toe. Or a soothing tension-dissolving beam of light moving down from your head. Or a soothing breeze moving down. Pick your way of imagining the release and flow of tension from your head to your toes.

PAUSE

BODY/BREATH SCANNING MEDITATION

Head: Eyes and Forehead

Attend to your eyes and forehead.

Your eyelids and the area around your eyes.

What do you feel?

With every outgoing breath, let sensations and tension dissolve and flow away.

Quietly attend. You are the quiet observer.

Head: Jaws and Mouth

Attend to your face.

Notice your jaws and mouth.

What do you feel?

Then, as you exhale, let sensations and tension dissolve away from your face.

Back of Neck

Attend to the back of your neck.

What do you feel?

With every outgoing breath, let sensations and tension dissolve and flow away.

Quietly attend. You are the quiet observer.

Front of Neck

The front of your neck.

What do you feel?

With every outgoing breath, let sensations and tension dissolve and flow away.

You are the quiet observer.

Shoulders

Attend to your shoulders.

What do you feel?

With every outgoing breath, let sensations and tension dissolve and flow away.

Arms

Attend to your arms.

What do you feel?

Note any tension.

Simply note and accept.

With every outgoing breath, let sensations and tension dissolve and flow out through your fingers.

Hands and fingers

Attend to your hands and fingers.

What do you feel?

Note any tension.

Simply note and accept.

With every outgoing breath, let sensation and tension dissolve and flow out through your fingers.

Abdomen

Your abdomen.

What do you feel?

With every outgoing breath, let sensations and tension dissolve and flow away.

Quietly attend.

You are the quiet observer.

Back

Your lower back.

What do you feel?

With every outgoing breath, let sensations and tension dissolve and flow away.

Glutes

Attend to your buttocks.

What do you feel?

With every outgoing breath, let sensations and tension dissolve and flow away.

Legs

Your legs.

What do you feel?

With every outgoing breath, let sensations and tension dissolve and flow away.

Attend and accept.

You are the quiet observer

Toes and Feet

Attend to your toes and feet.

What do you feel?

With every outgoing breath, let sensations and tension dissolve and flow away.

Whole Body Review

Quietly attend to your entire body.

There is no need to make yourself focus on any part.

If you happen to note any tension, let go.

Let the tension flow away with every breath.

[PAUSE 30 SECONDS]

BREATHING

We move on to another level of scanning.

Attend to how you are breathing.

Let your breathing be slow and even.
Note the air coming in through your nostrils,

Your throat,

Your chest,

Your belly.

Relax, and exhale.

Simply attend to the flow of breath.

Let your mind dwell on where ever you experience the effortless and easy flow of breath.

Your nostrils

Throat

Chest

Belly

[PAUSE 20 SECONDS]

FOCUSED ATTENTION MEDITATION

We move on to meditation. We will try several types. You pick what's best.

Rocking

The first is rocking meditation.

Let yourself gently rock.

Rock back and forth.

More and more quietly.

So gently no one would notice.

Attend to your rocking.

When your mind wanders, that's OK.

Gently return to attending to your quiet rocking.

[20 SECONDS]

Mantra Meditation

Next we try mantra meditation.

Select one of these words to repeat in your mind.

You can let the word "one" go over and over, on its own.

One . . . one . . . one

[PAUSE 5 SECONDS]

Or the word peace. . . Peace . . . Peace

[PAUSE 5 SECONDS]

Or the word faith. . . Faith . . . Faith

Pick a word: one, peace, or faith.

Let it easily go over and over in your mind.

All you do is attend, and return after every distraction.

[PAUSE 20 SECONDS]

Now let go of your word.

Spot of Light

Our third meditation is on an inner spot of light.

Attend to a simple spot of light in your mind.

Whenever your mind wanders, gently return.

[PAUSE 20 SECONDS]

Now let go of what you are attending to.

MINDFULNESS

We move on to mindfulness.

We will do two kinds of mindfulness.

With your eyes closed,

Sounds

Simply attend to the sounds.

Let them come and go.

Simply observe.

Whenever you find yourself thinking about anything,
let go.
You are the quiet observer.

[PAUSE 2 MINUTES]

Full Mindfulness

Attend to everything you see

Hear

Feel touching your skin

Think

Smell

You are the quiet observer.

Whenever you find yourself thinking about anything,
gently let go, and continue attending.

[PAUSE 3 MINUTES]

~ END OF SCRIPT ~

THE R/M TRACKER

WHAT DID YOU FEEL OR EXPERIENCE DURING **THE EYE OF MINDFULNESS EXERCISE?**
CLICK BOXES USING THIS KEY
(SKIP ITEMS YOU DON'T UNDERSTAND OR DIDN'T FEEL OR EXPERIENCE)

☒☐☐☐	☒☒☐☐	☒☒☒☐	☒☒☒☒
Felt this SLIGHTLY	Felt this MODERATELY	Felt this VERY MUCH	Felt this EXTREMELY (the most ever)

1. ***FAR AWAY*** *and distant from the troubles around me.*	☒☒☒☐
2. ***PHYSICALLY RELAXED****. Muscles relaxed, loose, limp, warm and heavy. Breathing slow, even, and easy.*	☒☒☐☐
3 ***AT EASE, AT PEACE.***	☒☒☐☐
4. ***REFRESHED.***	☒☐☐☐
5. ***PLEASANT MIND WANDERING****. Undirected, random positive thoughts.*	☒☐☐☐
6. *Lost in* **FANTASY** *and* **DAYDREAMING.**	☒☐☐☐
7. *Periods of sustained, continuous* **FOCUS. ABSORPTION.**	☒☒☒☐
8. ***CENTERED, GROUNDED.***	☒☒☐☐
9. ***QUIET.*** *Still, few thoughts. Little mind wandering.*	☒☒☐☐
10. ***UNBOTHERED.*** *Accepting. When I had a negative thought or feeling, I didn't get caught up in it. No judging, clinging, pushing away, figuring things out.*	☒☒☐☐
11. ***EASY, EFFORTLESS.*** *Effortless to let go, put thoughts aside, sustain focus.*	☒☐☐☐
12. *I felt like an* **OBSERVER** *standing aside and watching what happens.*	☒☒☐☐
13. ***CLEAR, AWAKE, AWARE.*** *I saw things as they really are.*	☒☐☐☐
14. ***INTERESTED, CURIOUS, FASCINATED.***	☒☐☐☐
15. *Things seemed* **BEAUTIFUL.**	☒☐☐☐
16. ***GOING DEEPER****. Things seemed unexpected, new, changing, opening up,being revealed. Felt like I was in a different place or space.*	☒☐☐☐
17. *Sense of* **SPACIOUSNESS, EXPANSIVENESS.**	☒☒☐☐
18. *I felt the* **SENSE OF SOMETHING GREATER** *than myself (God, a higher power, spirit, energy, love, or consciousness.); God is with me.*	☒☐☐☐
19. *A sense of* **MEANING, PURPOSE, DIRECTION.**	☒☐☐☐
20. *I felt* **REVERENT, PRAYERFUL.**	☒☐☐☐
21. ***AWE / WONDER, DEEP MYSTERY*** *of things beyond my understanding.*	☒☐☐☐
22. *I felt a profound personal meaningful* **"SPIRITUAL"** *or* **"MYSTICAL"** *experience -- sudden awakening or insight.* • *Felt an underlying hidden* **TRUTH.** • *Feeling* **AT ONE.** • *Feelings so profound they* **COULD NOT BE PUT INTO WORDS.**	☒☐☐☐
23. ***HAPPY, OPTIMISTIC, TRUSTING.***	☒☒☒☐
24. ***LOVING, CARING.***	☒☒☐☐
25. ***THANKFUL.*** *Grateful.*	☒☐☐☐

Stress & Coping
Eye of Mindfulness Journal

LESSON 3

PROBLEM-SOLVING

Chapter 13

© Ditty_about_summer/Shutterstock.com

Active Mindfulness, Singletasking, and Problem-Solving

For every task there is an optimum level of arousal. This, of course, is the Yerkes-Dodson law we discussed in Chapter 3 when we introduced stress arousal and the stress engine. We can be so aroused, so stirred up, that we do not perform well. Alternatively, low levels of energy can get in the way. Here we may be bored and uninterested.

If we explore the Yerkes-Dodson law further, we can see arousal as having two components, motivation and effort. You can want something so much, and try so hard, that you get in your way. You stumble over your words during that urgent job interview. You can't seem to think during the exam. Conversely, your motivation and effort may be so low your performance also fails. Every task has its optimum, its ideal level of motivation and effort.

As students of mindfulness, the notion of motivation translates to judgment, wanting to get or get rid of something, or not accepting things as they are. In addition, the mindful task, one of attending to a garden, breath, a mantra, or the present moment, is done with the minimum amount of effort, "less effort" or "effortless." The mindful optimum is: to sustain focus in a way that is accepting and effortless.

Active Mindfulness and Optimal Acceptance and Effort

I propose that we do any task in the spirit of mindfulness when we sustain simple focus with an optimal level of judgment/acceptance (i.e., motivation) and effort. Here we put aside too much, or too little judgment and effort as diversions from the task at hand. I call this *active mindfulness*. If we try too hard or try too little, we are not doing something mindfully. If we want or judge something too much or too little we are not being mindful.

In active life a degree of effort and a degree of judgment/motivation are called for. Otherwise we do too little or too much, try to little or too much, and we fail to perform our best. A few teachers of mindfulness are perhaps misguided when they advise us to embrace every task in life with the same utter calm and quiet one might experience in a meditation session. Let me give a blunt example. A student may be the victim of date rape. He could let this pass, detach or "defuse" himself from his feelings of anger and shame as "mere thoughts, not facts," and go on living. Reading this text, he might see this as dereification and meta-awareness (Chapter 10).

In contrast, our student could take charge, acknowledge and own his intense feelings, and march into the police station and take forceful, direct, and appropriate action.

There is a place for pure mindfulness. Once the urgent task of the moment is done, our student can mindfully put his upset aside, accept what has happened, and go on with life. He can choose to live in the moment no longer preoccupied with the judgmental and effortful thoughts of the past. He deploys the mindful skills of putting needless effort and judgment aside.

Victims of social injustice throughout the world—whether it be anti-Semitism, racism, homophobia, or the legion of other "isms" or "phobias" that plague our planet—have a mindful challenge. It is to engage in battle with honest, undistracted, and undistorted focus. It is to put aside battles when moments of deep quiet call and the need arises to come in touch with what really matters.

Multitasking

We started our journey by contrasting mindfulness with mind wandering. Actually, this is just partly true. Mindfulness is also the opposite of *multitasking*, the counterproductive attempt to do several things at once.

Students often think multitasking is a useful skill for work and school. As one student, Chen, describes:

> *"I multitask to get more things done. On my desk I have my textbook, which I am reading and summarizing in my notes. I also have a job application due the next day, and the forms are right next to my book. And I'm on the phone with a friend planning a vacation. I'll work on these simultaneously and finish my chores in record time!"*

© Kit8.net/Shutterstock.com

It is understandable that people think multitasking is some amazing superskill. Think of the fabled "power mom" (or "power dad"). She works, studies, and tends to a family, all while cooking dinner. We can imagine her sitting at a desk working on her accounting class assignment. She does this while dropping tomatoes into a pot of soup and talking on the phone about the latest shopping tasks. Meanwhile, there are letters to be written, vegetables to be chopped, and in the distance, a patient cat waiting to be fed. And then there's the kid.

But the unfortunate fact is that multitasking is myth. Not only does it not save time, it wastes time. How can this be? First, look at what your brain does when it multitasks. You switch attention from one task to another. You focus on your text, then your job application, then your phone call, and then back to your text. Each time you switch, the brain takes a few milliseconds to let go of what it's doing, to "put it on the shelf." Then it takes another few milliseconds to search for the next multiple task. And then a few addition milliseconds to orient to and refocus on the new task.

Multitasking is quite different from mindfulness in three important ways. The task at hand is not singular and simple (a garden, breath, a mantra, the present moment), but complex (doing several things at once). It is made complex partly because the degree of judgment and effort involved is not appropriate for the efficient task completion.

A certain type of inappropriate judgment and effort is characteristic of multitasking—the **multitasking observer stance**. Here you stand back and consider the task before you. In addition, tou take the stance that something unnamed is not right and demands your attention and effort. This thinking can take many forms. You may feel ambivalent and confused, wondering what to do next, how much time to spend on each task, when to switch, and so on. You might experience a millisecond of doubt, confusion, and indecision. You may have the uncanny feeling that something is unfinished. Something unnamed needs to be figured out. Something tells you it is time to switch again to a different task.

The multitasking observer task is inherently doomed to failure and leads to more multitasking. It actually stirs up more urgent thoughts and tasks that demand attention. Multitasking is something like a snowball rolling down a hill, collecting more snow and dirt the more it rolls.

The multitasking observer stance can be contrasted with the observer stance associated with simple mindfulness. Here one is truly a neutral, noninterfering observer, exerting only the most minimal effort to return attention to the target focus of breath, a mantra, or the present moment. In active meditation, the observer focuses efficiently on the task at hand.

Costs of Multitasking

Multitasking is costly. Milliseconds add up and waste time. With every shift in attention you introduce the possibility of making an error, of missing something, forgetting something, or getting something wrong. Think of it this way. In every task, like reading a book or filling out a job application, there's always the possibility of making some mistake. And the brief moments of switching are in themselves tasks, each with their own chance for error.

When we multitask, we are forcing the brain to work on several different things at once. This increases the possibility of task interference, of thoughts and skills related to one job getting in the way of another. For example, imagine you are multitasking by having a heated phone discussion with your boss over a poor review while simultaneously talking to your roommate about what to do this weekend. Unexpectedly, you start arguing with great force and passion with your roommate about whether to go to a Mexican or Chinese restaurant.

It is not surprising that multitasking correlates with poor productivity (Zack, 2015). The brain simply can't do two things at once (Miller & Buschman, 2014). Multitasking weakens one's ability to sustain focus and respond flexibly to new situations (Foerde et al., 2006). Some have even speculated that multitasking releases stress hormones (cortisol), reducing further information processing. The brain is impaired and shrinks (Ansell et al., 2012).

Continuous Partial Attention and Automatic Tasks

Before we proceed, it is important to distinguish multitasking with **continuous partial attention** (https://lindastone.net/). Here one attends to several things, but at a superficial level. By skimming the surface one picks the relevant data and moves on. You're paying partial attention and casting a wide net (but risking missing deep and important details) is can be a useful skill.

Also, there is another type of situation where multitasking can work. When two tasks call for different mental resources, one complex and one simple and automatic, it's OK to multitask. For example, talking to a friend on the phone while picking up clutter from a desk. Here different tasks do not compete. Also, work that requires no conscious effort or concentration, and can be done automatically, is less likely to interfere with complex tasks. Some automatic tasks include listening to music, housecleaning, making diner, doing simple crafts, fixing things.

However, even a simple task can rise to a multitasking distraction when an unexpected challenge emerges. If you are driving home down a familiar path, it may be relatively safe to talk on your cell phone. However, something unexpected happens, demanding your attention, for example it starts raining, you notice a rumbling noise in your engine, or you have to take an unexpected detour, then talking on a cell phone can be quite dangerous. This is why distracted driving and drunk driving are nearly equal as causes of deadly crashes (National Highway Traffic Safety Administration, 2010). Texting while walking can even be dangerous (Nasar & Troyer, 2013)

Singletasking and Mindfulness

The opposite of multitasking is singletasking. Singletasking is a variant of active mindfulness. One focuses on the *one task* at hand, with an optimum level of acceptance (nonjudgment) and effort. Instead of being mindful of a beautiful garden, one's breath, a mantra, or the flow of sensations that come and go, one directs attention to what one is doing. This becomes the task at hand, the task of the moment. And everything else becomes distraction, to calmly put aside with as little fuss as possible.

Unmindfulness–Mindfulness Cycles

It is quite likely impossible to be mindful 100 percent of the time. How might we consider those many times we are not mindful, when we find ourselves distracted, multitasking, overreacting, and the like? I like to think of the path of mindfulness as something of a never-ending cycle. Unmindfulness is like mind wandering. Simply accept it as natural, a part of life. It is OK, indeed sometimes desirable to be unmindful. But then there is a time to return home for mindful renewal.

Imagine you discover your house is on fire. Without thought you scream, thinking that this may be the end of everything. Pushing all aside you run outside and call the fire department. They arrive as you worry about what you might have lost. When the fire is extinguished, you sit, take a few deep breaths, collect your thoughts, and settle down.

You permit yourself a moment of mindfulness to recover. One might observe that your theatrical reaction to your burning house was perhaps a bit unmindful. But it got you out of the house! And perhaps it would not have been wise to practice a short mindfulness meditation before escaping. Mindful living is not sustaining quiet simple focus all the time. It, like the exercise itself, is returning again and again, without fuss, to mindfulness. There may be times in life when you need to be unmindful to get the job done.

Coping and Problem-Solving

Coping is active mindfulness and singletasking. In most general terms this can be stated as something of a philosophy: *Stress is a problem to be solved.* It is the perspective of this book that no matter how bad or how impossible things may seem, there is something that can be done about it. And often it is best to approach a problem mindfully.

Perhaps it's not the ideal solution. But this moment's answer may be the best you can expect. It may address only part of what's wrong. Rome was not built in a day. And from your efforts you may develop important skills for dealing with future problems.

An important part of solving a problem quickly and efficiently is coming up with a good definition of what's wrong. First, we will consider mistakes that are often made.

Vague, Overemotional, Distorted Definitions

Below are examples of various individuals under stress. In each example, the person knows there's a problem and is trying to define it clearly.

Bart has no girlfriend and is feeling lonely. He desperately wants to meet people. Here is how Bart defines his problem:

> *"Everyone keeps to themselves. No one likes to talk to people anymore. People are too selfish."*

Bart's definition doesn't get to what the real problem is, how to meet people. His definition is actually a distorted view of the world. It reflects a multitasking stance doomed to stir more rumination or worry. Why do people keep to themselves? How could I possibly deal with this? What should I do next?. . .

Realistically, it is just not true that everyone keeps to themselves or that no one likes to talk to people. His complaint that people are too selfish sounds too overemotional to be helpful.

Eloise has planned a month-long vacation with her boyfriend. Suddenly, her mother comes down with a serious illness, and Eloise must stay with her to help her recover. Here is how Eloise defines her problem:

> *"This is the worst thing that could ever happen to me. This is an absolute disaster. Everything's ruined. I give up."*

Notice how this definition reflects a multitasking observer status. Eloise's definition of her problem is so emotional she can barely figure out what her options are. And surely she is exaggerating and distorting things by seeing her predicament as an absolute disaster. And it is vague. It is easy to see how Eloise is setting herself up for substantial mind wandering and worry.

Abdul is a convenience store manager and is having a bad week. Food deliveries are late, there's not enough change in the cash register, his daughter is sick and needs attention, and he has supplied his store with too many eggs. Here is Abdul's problem definition:

> *"Everything is happening at once. I feel like a wall of rocks has just crumbled down on me and there's nothing I can do."*

This definition is also clouded with vague emotional outburst. When faced with a challenge, often our first reaction is emotional outburst. That can be very healthy and motivate us to get to work, communicate to potential helpers the seriousness of our predicament, and release tension. However, it is important to realize that our initial outburst is not the same as a good problem-definition. That may come next, once the air has cleared.

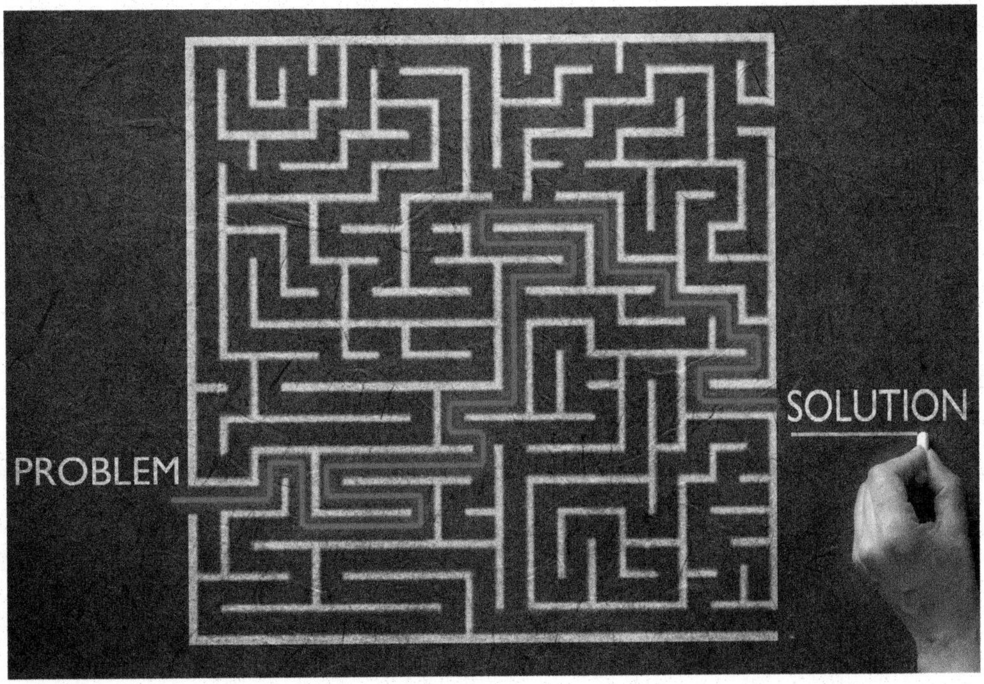

Fast-Track Problem Definitions

A fast-track problem-definition goes beyond one's initial emotional, vague, and distorted outburst. You select a stress situation and then focus simply on one task: How might you concretely answer these three questions?

1. What do you ideally want?
2. What part can you realistically get for now?
3. When and where can you start?

What do you ideally want? Think of what is causing stress in your life. Now, identify what you really want. Describe your ideal want in positive rather than negative terms, for example:

Negative want: "To get people to ignore me less."

Positive version: "To meet more people."

Negative want: "Be less poor."

Positive version: "To find ways of making money."

Negative want: "Stop messing up at school."

Positive version: "Improve my grades."

What Can You Realistically Get for Now?

Very often, when we think of a positive outcome we might want in a stress situation, we ask for too much. The following wants may be quite laudable and desirable, but none can be realistically achieved in a day or two.

"Find a job that really fits my needs and abilities in my neighborhood."

"Find a boyfriend who shares my interests in music and Chinese food."

"Get a passing grade in my math class."

"Work more efficiently, so I have fewer projects to take home."

"Get my two kids to stop fighting."

"Figure out how to balance the demands of work, school, and play."

"Get thin with nice muscle definition."

"Get enough money to pay for school and my car."

People sometimes fall into the trap of not identifying subgoals that must be achieved before seeking their identified stress-management goals. One step in identifying what you can realistically get for now is identifying any prerequisite subgoals. If there is a subgoal, make that your "goal for now." Let's illustrate this with one of the above examples, a student who has identified as her goal:

"Getting a passing grade in my math class. "

She quickly identified the immediate task that had to be confronted, what she could realistically try to get for now:

"Getting a better grade on my daily homework assignments."

And when our student focused on this realistic goal, she quickly realized she needed a subgoal:

"Finding a quiet place, conducive to study, where I can work on my homework an hour every evening."

What, when, and where can you start? It is easy to get stuck at the stage of identifying a specific, realistic goal. A useful sign that you are on the right track is if your goal is defined in terms of specific deeds or words you will do or say, in a specific time and place—what, when, and where. Our previous student has made real progress by defining her problem in terms of finding a study environment. She can fine-tune this definition by answering the "what, when, and where" questions.

"What? I want to sit in front of a desk with my book in front of me so I can read my assignment and complete the homework."

"When? I need to figure out how to study sometime every evening, preferably 7–9 PM."

"Where? The place has to be quiet, with few distractions."

Bart, Eloise, and Abdul—Problems Redefined

Let's return to the individuals we met at the start of this chapter, Bart, Eloise, and Abdul. Here is how they redefined their problems in terms of the concepts of this chapter. Can you see how each concept was applied?

Bart: "Eventually I want a girlfriend, but that can't happen overnight. I need to start socializing more, but that too takes time. I can at least figure out where I might meet people, for example, at the temple, the local coffee house, or in my dorm. Here's what I'll do. Before Friday I will make a point of introducing myself to at least three women, and ask at least one if they might be interested in having a coffee. That's a step."

Eloise: "My mother is sick and I have to stay home rather than go on my vacation with my boyfriend. Sure, that's frustration, even a downer. But it isn't the end of the world. My boyfriend will understand. I'll get together with him tonight and we can discuss this predicament. By putting our heads together we can come up with a solution."

Abdul: "It seems like everything is happening at once at the store I manage. Late deliveries, too many eggs on stock, and my sick daughter. I sure wish my problems wouldn't come all at once! Well, something has to be done. I need to start chipping away at this mess. I'll prioritize, figure out what has to be done now, and do one job at a time. I'll start now."

EXERCISES

The Mindfulness Exercise Challenge. Try practicing a five-minute version of your home mindfulness exercise before completing any chapter exercise.

13.1. How Do You Multitask?

Think of a time you multitasked. Did it work? What were the costs? Explain, using the concepts in this chapter.

13.2. Fixing Troubled Problem Definitions

Below are some examples of problem definitions. For each, identify what's wrong with the definition. Which of the following steps is missing?

1. What does the person ideally want?
2. What part can the person realistically get for now?
3. When and where can the person have a reasonable chance of getting it?

Then offer your suggestion of a better definition, and explain how it incorporates each of the above steps.

PROBLEM 1

I want the traffic situation not to be so bad when I'm going to work. There's so much traffic that I get really upset and tense. Sometimes I have to wait 20 minutes in a traffic jam going nowhere. This really upsets me for the entire day!

WHAT'S WRONG WITH THIS DEFINITION?
PROVIDE YOUR IMPROVED VERSION.

PROBLEM 2

Every time we have a weekly church meeting, I am voted to be the secretary. This upsets me, especially when I have other important things to do. My problem is this: I want people to respect me more and pay more attention to my needs.

WHAT'S WRONG WITH THIS DEFINITION?
PROVIDE YOUR IMPROVED VERSION.

PROBLEM 3

I'm just too lonely. This makes me feel blue. I feel like there's nothing that can be done. There are no options for me.

WHAT'S WRONG WITH THIS DEFINITION?
PROVIDE YOUR IMPROVED VERSION.

PROBLEM 4

I have a full-time job and am taking a full load of courses. This is just too much. I don't know where to begin. It just overwhelms me. I feel like giving up.

WHAT'S WRONG WITH THIS DEFINITION?
PROVIDE YOUR IMPROVED VERSION.

This week, identify some stressful situations or events. Then define each in terms of a problem. Describe the stressful situation or event.

1. What do you ideally want?
2. What part can you realistically get for now?
3. What, when, and where can you start?

Stress & Coping
Eye of Mindfulness Journal

Chapter 14

Brainstorming to Success

Harry has a specific stress management goal: How to get his supervisor to recognize his work accomplishments. One day during a coffee break it comes to him: "I'll list my accomplishments on a bright pink sticky note, which I will then affix to the monthly report I turn in. That's it!"

This may seem like a perfectly sensible solution to a problem. It is not particularly vague, overemotional, or distorted. It identifies a specific course of action. But there is a problem, one that limits the success of many attempts at stress management. Harry jumped on the first idea that came to mind, treated it as "The Answer," and proceeded to act. If you think about it, surely Harry could have thought of something better than pink sticky notes!

The chances for successful stress management increase when we maximize our choices. Quantity yields quality. This requires we pause, generate many options, and carefully weed out the good. In this chapter we consider and supplement Osborn's (1963) widely quoted problem-solving tool—brainstorming. Although brainstorming is often applied to team problem-solving, it appears not to be particularly effective for group tasks. We will consider individual brainstorming.

Brainstorming involves putting aside efforts to judge, criticize, and analyze. As we have seen earlier, this is in the spirit of mindful reduced judgment. Instead, you let the ideas flow, without censorship. Because you do this without censorship, you let all ideas come, the good, the bad, and the silly. Your goal is to uncork an "idea fountain." And this is a variant of mindful reduced effort. Then, after the flood, you apply critical thinking, evaluate your ideas, and come up with more. This is active mindfulness.

Start the Brainstorming Idea Fountain

It can be frustrating to start the brainwashing idea fountain. Imagine you are an executive employed at a large cardboard box factory. You're at a very important business meeting, sitting at a huge, heavy oak table. Everyone is in a nicely pressed suit facing each other. The agenda is long and tedious. After two hours, your group reaches agenda item number 9: how to increase sales. The problem is that more and more people are using plastic bags, resulting in a business decline for many types of boxes. One person suggests, "Lets brainstorm!" People agree that this is a good idea. Then for the next five minutes everyone sits like frogs on a log, staring into space. Cautiously, someone suggests, "Well, we could do better at advertising." Another comments, "Yes, and we could cut our cell phone use." Another idea: "Maybe we could work six days a week." Clearly, this is going nowhere. The idea fountain is stuck or clogged. The lesson is that brainstorming doesn't just happen; it needs proper preparation and the proper setting. Our corporate table isn't quite right. And the suits don't help. Here are some suggestions:

- Set a brainstorming time and place apart from one's usual work or study environment. Take away reminders to be critical and serious. Have fun!
- Prepare for brainstorming with a little relaxation, possibly deep breathing followed by imagery. This can help reduce interfering tension and foster a creative mindset.

Think Outside the Box

Give yourself the instructions, "Try to think of something others will not have considered. Think of something new and different." Sometimes deciding to break the mold helps enhance the generation of new ideas.

Enhance Variety

Although brainstorming calls for temporarily putting aside critical thinking, sometimes that isn't enough to ensure variety. Try these tools:

First brainstorm general categories of solutions. Then treat each category as a separate brainstorming task. For example, let's return to our cardboard box problem. Your task is to brainstorm unusual product uses for cardboard boxes. Variety can be increased by first brainstorming categories:

Structures
Toys
Tools
Wacky Ideas

One then brainstorms possibilities for each category:

> *Structures: a cardboard house, church, skyscraper, doghouse, fish tank, birdhouse*
>
> *Tools: a big cardboard shovel, a step, a torch, emergency clothing, cement shaper*
>
> *Toys: Mr. Squarepants, a toy dog, a square pumpkin face, a drawing board with four sides, something to kick in kickball, a target*
>
> *Wacky Ideas: An emergency outdoor bathtub, an unexpected place to hide valuables, wax it and make it a boat, a very thin box could be a hot-air balloon, a place to store laughs (?)*

Visualize a similar problem situation, one not exactly the same, that you have faced. Brainstorm for that situation. See if any of the applications suggest your original problem. For example, if you are having trouble thinking of uses for cardboard boxes, think of a similar problem, perhaps uses for string.

You may think of the following:

> *Tie pets together with string when outside. Weave into a loose pair of gloves to cover fingers. Wrap your hands so you can pick up hot objects without getting burned. Drape them over a pond to begin making a bridge. Mash them up, mix with water and glue, and make a paste for sculptures.*

Some of these same ideas can transfer to cardboard boxes:

> *Store pets in big boxes outside. Put small boxes over your fingers so you can pick up hot objects. Glue them over a pond to make a bridge. Mash them up, mix with water, and make a paste for sculptures.*

The Critical Pause

Osborn recommends avoiding critical thinking during brainstorming. Actually, this can be less than helpful. Periods of evaluation can enhance quantity and quality by prompting one to give up old lines of thinking, take on a new perspective, and try harder. I recommend taking pause and seriously engaging in critical evaluation of your list after generating options. See if this prompts you to think of more new ideas.

Making a Choice

After brainstorming, you need to make a selection. First, cross out all of the ideas that are very unrealistic. Then pick three to five ideas that are the best. For each, do a "cost-benefit" analysis. That is, for each idea list all the negatives or costs in one column, and all the positives or benefits in another. Then rank your best ideas.

EXERCISES

The Mindfulness Exercise Challenge. *Try practicing a five-minute version of your home mindfulness exercise before completing any chapter exercise.*

14.1 Brainstorming Practice

1. Imagine you own a business that manufactures plastic dolls. Your dolls are something like the popular "Barbie" product. One day your major factory goofed up and produced thousands of dolls with something of a defect. You see, the robotic hair-gluing machine accidentally glued hair to each doll's feet, and none to the top of their heads, resulting in thousands of inflatable bald dolls with hairy feet. Because of the upcoming holiday season, you simply do not have time to order a new set of dolls. And that would be far too expensive. Your only solution is creative marketing. How can you package these "defective" dolls so that they are actually "desirable"? This is your brainstorming task.

   If you are in a group, divide the group into two subgroups. Group 1 has this task:

   Brainstorm ways of packaging and marketing Blow-up Barb. However, do not use the "brainstorm categories" option.

   Group 2 has a slightly different task:

   First brainstorm categories of uses. Then for each category, brainstorm solutions. At the end of this exercise, groups compare their responses. Discuss the advantages and disadvantages of category brainstorming.

   If you are not in a group, try brainstorming first without categories. Then repeat the exercise using categories. Compare your responses.

14.2 Pick a Problem to Brainstorm

Select a problem you have faced in the past. Make it as specific and concrete as possible. Brainstorm possible solutions. Do a cost-benefit analysis of the five best options.

Stress & Coping
Eye of Mindfulness Journal

Chapter 15

Time Management and Priorities

© stas11/Shutterstock.com

One of the most general problems people face is finding time. A busy schedule, competing demands, and unexpected emergencies can add up to a chaotic day. You may not complete all you want, or leave important tasks half done. And in spite of your efforts, you may end the day frustrated and fatigued.

Alan Lakein (1973) and Harold Greenwald (1973) have offered useful time management ideas that are frequently cited in the literature. Here are some of their ideas.

A good step in managing time is to take time off and complete a day inventory. Such an inventory can pinpoint where are you spending too much time, and what tasks are getting shortchanged. It is a good way of identifying time-busters, unnecessary activities that can eat up minutes and hours.

Consider, for example, Greta, a college student. When asked how she spends her time, she suggested, "I think I spend too much time walking the dog and eating." We will show how Greta completed her day inventory task.

Your Current Schedule

How do you spend your day? Divide your day into half-hour periods and record your activities for each. Here is Greta's day:

GRETA'S DAY

8:30-9:00	Eat breakfast
9:00-9:30	Eat breakfast
9:30-10:00	Surf the internet
10:00-10:30	Accounting Class
10:30-11:00	Accounting Class
11:00-11:30	Class
11:30-12:00	Walk the dog
12:30-1:00	Listen to the radio
1:00-1:30	Snack
1:30-2:00	Watch TV
2:00-2:30	Part-time job
2:30-3:00	Part-time job
3:00-3:30	Part-time job
3:30-4:00	Part-time job
4:00-4:30	Take a walk
4:30-5:00	Read magazines
5:00-5:30	Study by self
5:30-6:00	Doing homework with friends
6:00-6:30	Dinner
6:30-7:00	Dinner
7:00-7:30	Play video
7:30-8:00	Watch TV
8:00-8:30	Call mom
8:30-9:00	Study
9:00-9:30	Talk with friends
9:30-10:00	Study
10:00-10-30	Watch the news
10:30-11:00	Get ready for bed

At first there may seem to be nothing unusual with this log. However, if we look at it with a microscope, some suspicious things emerge. This involves first sorting the day's activities into different categories. Create five to ten general categories that represent what you have been doing. Greta listed the following:

What Greta Does: Categories

Eating and snacking
Studying

Work
In class
Socializing on phone
Recreation (TV, radio, video games)
Chores
Getting ready for bed, dressing, etc.

Now, add up how much time you devote to each category of activity. Greta discovered she devoted her day to the following activities:

Time Greta Spends on Each Activity

2.5 hr	*Eating and snacking*
2 hr	*Studying*
2 hr	*Work*
1.5 hr	*In class*
1 hr	*Socializing on phone*
4 hr	*Recreation (TV, radio, video games)*
0.5 hr	*Chores*
0.5 hr	*Getting ready for bed, dressing, etc.*

By examining this summary chart, you can consider four important time management questions:

1. Are you spending too much time on some activities?
2. Have you organized your day in the most reasonable way?
3. Have you scheduled in times for fun and recreation? Put these after a challenging and difficult activities, to reward yourself and help recover completely.
4. Have you scheduled your most demanding mental tasks for when you are most awake, your "prime time."

Greta was surprised that she spent 4 hours a day in recreation, 2 hours eating and snacking, and only 0.5 hour on chores. She decided to cut down on her recreation, or at least put off some of these activities to the weekend. She also decided to put her "fun time" right after work or study, as a kind of reward. She gets more studying done if she studies in one block of time, rather than breaking it up, so she scheduled one large block of evening time for study.

Work Schedules versus Personal Schedules

In this age of personal data assistants and pocket-sized leather schedule books, making a schedule is easy. Or so it might seem. There is one reason why schedules often fail. Here's an example. Ray is an undergraduate studying math. He also works in the school cafeteria. This semester he is taking a full load of classes and is quite busy. He decided he needed to carefully complete a schedule, but it didn't work out. Here's his account:

"I have so much work to do! It seems overwhelming! Well, let's get down to business. I get up at 6, get ready, and arrive at my first class at 7. The class goes until 10. I study from 10 to 12 and then grab a quick lunch. At 12:30 I run off to work and clean dishes for two hours. My next class is at 3:30 and is over at 5:30. I grab some food and by 6 go off to the library to write some papers for English. And at 8 I begin reading my math assignment and from 10 to 11 do my math homework. Then I go to bed."

Can you see any problem with this schedule?

Here's Ray's account:

"Well, this schedule worked for two days, then it fell apart. I got so caught up in my obligations that I forgot to put in time for myself, God, my friends, and, most important, my friend Chris. I had created an all-work schedule. It might have worked for a robot, but not for me."

Ray's story illustrates a problem many face when creating schedules. Often we are prompted to write a schedule because of too much serious work. So when we write a schedule our minds are on our work, and we forget the rest of life. To avoid this problem, let me suggest an exercise: First create a work schedule, one that includes all the things you have to do—your job, school, personal hygiene, cleaning your room, and so on. Then create your personal schedule, one that includes all the things you do for yourself and do with friends and those close to you. Then compare your two schedules. Often you may have to make some compromises in both. Your final schedule contains both what you have to do and your personal schedule.

Priorities and Goals

Difficulties with managing time can be a symptom of unclear and conflicting goals and priorities. Alan Lakein (1973) and Harold Greenwald (1973) offer some useful ideas we will consider in this chapter. Different people value different things. Some may want a life of adventure, others money, others a good family, and still others artistic expression. Your goals reflect what truly matters and how you wish to spend your time. However, sometimes we get sidetracked and find ourselves wasting time on pursuits that do not meet our

© Bakhitar Zein/Shutterstock.com

goals. Sometimes we get in habitual daily patterns in which we waste time with tasks that do not fit our priorities. It is indeed mindful to focus on tasks that truly reflect one's priorities and goals.

Long-Term Goals

First, what are your long-term goals? Try thinking at three levels: lifetime goals, five-year goals, and six-month goals. Here are some examples of each:

Lifetime goals
To get married, have children, no more than 6.
To get a stable and enjoyable job.
To find a place to settle down on the coast.

Five-year goals
To start and finish college
To try at least two jobs
To get married

Six-month goals
To get into a good college.
To take dating more seriously, look for a mate

Identify Six-Month Subgoals and Tasks

Your six-month goals are ones you need to start working on right away, Consider each, and ask what important subgoals are involved. What tasks have to be completed? For example, the six-month goals can be broken down like this:

Getting into a good college
Study for college exams
Keep my grades up
Look for people to write letters of recommendation

Taking dating more seriously
Look over my list of friends and ask if any are potentials for dating
Review my socializing "hangouts" and identify any that are not good places to meet people to date
Think of some quality time activities I could spend with my date.

Identify Activities That May Be Interfering with Your Goals

Can you think of any activities that are reducing your chances of completing your goals? Be realistic. Obviously, everything you do can't be goal oriented. You need some unscheduled fun time. However, if your goal is to get into college, habitually missing class can get in the way. If you want to increase your chances of finding a spouse, spending all your time alone isn't helping.

Identify Goals and Activities for This Week. . . then Today

Lakein suggests first thinking of your week, and then today, as filing cabinets with three drawers. In your "top drawer" put your most important priorities and goals, those that absolutely, positively, must be done this week or today. In the "middle drawer" include activities it would be nice to complete, but can be temporarily postponed until you complete your top drawer activities. Bottom drawer priorities can be put off until last, until you have extra time. To this filing cabinet, lets add a waste basket, or using today's computer lingo, a "recycle bin." In your recycle bin put activities you need to cut down on or cease, because they are just a waste.

Here's an example:

This Week's Filing Cabinet

Top Drawer
Getting an A on my exams and homework
Spending at least some good time with my date

Middle Drawer
Having fun playing basketball
Writing letters

Bottom Drawer
Perfecting my video game

Recycle Bin
Looking for and test driving a new car, even though I can't buy one

Today's filing cabinet

<u>Top Drawer</u>
Finish English assignment; ask my English Major friend to read it for errors

<u>Middle Drawer</u>
Schedule my date

<u>Bottom Drawer</u>
Write my Mom
Recycle Bin
Going through ads for new cars

The "80/20 Rule"

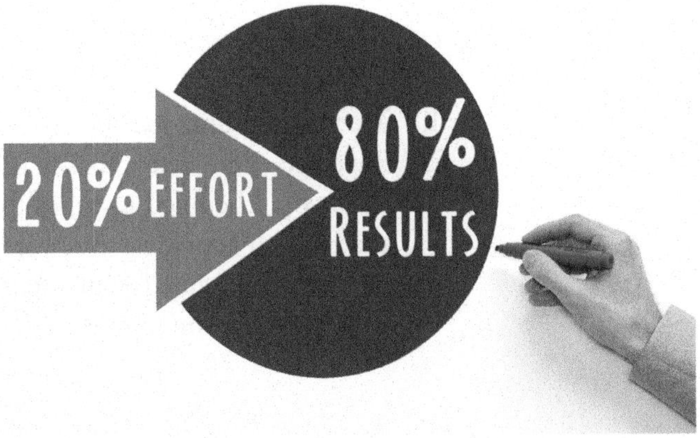

© astephan / Shutterstock.com

Consider your to-do lists and the relative payoff of each job. Which will yield the greatest gain? Which will yield smaller payoffs? Now consider the amount of time required for each task. Management consultant Joseph Juran (1988) has suggested using this information to select which tasks to complete first, and which to put off for later. The "80/20 rule" or "Pareto Principle" claims that for many tasks, 80% of effects come for 20% of causes. Applied here, 80% of important problem-solving comes from 20% of problem-solving tasks. Which tasks on your to-do list might yield the greatest payoffs? Do those first.

What Makes You Really Happy and Satisfied

Now that you have done some structured review of your goals and activities, it is time to sit back and give them one more review. This time simply ask yourself the Big Question: What do you really want in life? Imagine you are in a time machine and go many years, even decades, into the future. From this special perspective you can see all that you have done. Then ask, "What might I have done differently? What is really important to me?"

EXERCISES

The Mindfulness Exercise Challenge. *Try practicing a five-minute version of your home mindfulness exercise before completing any chapter exercise.*

15.1 How You Spend Your Time

Complete a time schedule, using the instructions in this chapter. When your schedule is complete, identify any activities that may be taking up too much time.

15.2 Analyze Your Time

Look at your response to Exercise 15.1.

Consider these questions:

1. Are you spending too much time on some activities?
2. Have you organized your day in the most reasonable way?
3. Have you scheduled in times for fun and recreation? Put these after challenging and difficult activities, to reward yourself and help you recover completely.
4. Have you scheduled your most demanding mental tasks for when you are most awake, your "prime time"?

15.3 Your Work, Personal, and Compromise Schedules

Work schedule. First, list all of the things you have to do today, your work obligations. This includes your job and school as well as the necessities of taking care of yourself like eating, brushing your teeth, cleaning your room, and so on. Put these activities in a "work schedule."

Personal schedule. Now, put your work schedule aside. Forget about it for a minute. Then list the personal and people-related activities you want to do today. Put them in your "personal schedule."

Compromise schedule. Finally, look at both your work and personal schedules. Where do they conflict? Where can you compromise?

What was the most difficult challenge in creating a compromise schedule?

15.4 Defining Goals

What are your long-term goals?

What are your six-month goals?

What might interfere with your goals?

Identify, for this week, the following:

Top Drawer Priorities and Goals

Middle Drawer Priorities and Goals

Bottom Drawer Priorities and Goals

Recycle Bin

Identify, for today, the following:

Top Drawer Priorities and Goals

Middle Drawer Priorities and Goals

Bottom Drawer Priorities and Goals

Recycle Bin

Apply the "80/20" rule. List those tasks that give the most bang for the buck. Which yield the greatest payoff for the least effort? Now list those that give you the least payoff for the most effort.

What makes you really happy and satisfied? Which goals contribute to this?

Stress & Coping
Eye of Mindfulness Journal

Chapter 16

Procrastination

© Brian A Jackson/Shutterstock.com

The best schedule is worthless if you procrastinate. Procrastination is avoiding tasks you have chosen to do. People sometimes avoid activities they actually enjoy; however, it is more common to procrastinate with tasks that may have a long-term or delayed payoff. Procrastination is especially likely when there is possible payoff to avoidance or delay.

Procrastination has its costs. The procrastinator experiences a special type of stress—avoiding a task he or she has chosen to do. It interferes with school performance. And it creates more procrastination (Jaffe, 2013). The causes of procrastination are relatively simple to identify, and readily suggest coping solutions.

Short-Term Delay Tricks

Sometimes we procrastinate through delay tricks, by focusing on short-term payoffs while ignoring long-term benefits. Simply identifying your delay tricks can clarify your choices: Are the immediate rewards worth putting long-term rewards in jeopardy? Some short-term delay tricks include:

- Maybe someone else will do the task.
- It feels good to avoid potential failure.
- Maybe the problem will just solve itself.
- Maybe it will be easier to do the task later.
- Putting off a task is a way of "getting even," or showing others indirectly how you feel.

Which fit you? Which are unrealistic? Can you identify specific times and places you use these delay tricks?

Procrastination Triggers and Environments

We are more likely to procrastinate when in a setting that encourages putting things off. If you are living with three party-going roommates, you might find it difficult to get serious work done because of the constant temptation to go partying.

If you work next to the coffee machine, you might be tempted to put tasks off in order to take another coffee break. In identifying procrastination triggers, you need to specify:

1. What didn't get done.
2. What distracted you.

Sometimes one's environment is simply not conducive to the task at hand, and is more conducive to some other activity. Examples include:

Filing out tax forms in the TV room (rather than a quiet, serious study room)
Writing a serious letter while in a restaurant
Planning a family budget at lunch

The following questions can help you consider whether the environment is contributing to procrastination.

1. What didn't you get done?
2. Where were you procrastinating?
3. How was this environment conducive to another, competing activity?

Difficult Jobs

Sometimes people procrastinate when confronting a task that is seen as too big or challenging. Burns (1990) emphasizes making a job easy, either by breaking it down into logical steps or completing work in "small spurts." Here one commits to doing, say, 15 or 30 minutes of a task (no more) a day, until it is done. The advantage of the small spurt approach is that it frees one from worrying about how a task when viewed as a whole might be overwhelming. Another approach is to simply break a job down into component parts, and take on one part at a time.

Distorted Thoughts

Ferrari, Johnson, and McCown (1995) suggest a number of types of distorted thinking about a task that can lead to procrastination:

- Overestimating the amount of time or work required for a task
- Overestimating future motivational states ("I'll feel like doing this later")

- Assuming that success at a task requires one be in a positive task-oriented mood and "feel smart, motivated, awake, and calm" (and that this mood will change in the near future)
- Assuming that unproductivity is the result of lack of such states
- Assuming one must be perfect
- Thinking everything one does should go easily and without effort
- Believing that if it's not done right, it's not worth doing at all
- Assuming there is one right answer, and one should wait until they find it

Tuckman et al. (2008) has extended this list of procrastination rationalizations to a list of 15:

- Ignorance: "I didn't know I was supposed to do that."
- Skill deficiency: "I don't know how to do it."
- Apathy (1): "I really don't want to do this."
- Apathy (2): "It really doesn't make any difference if I put this off."
- Apathy (3): "No one really cares whether I do this or not."
- Apathy (4): "I need to be in the mood. I'm not."
- Fixed habits (1): "But I've always done it this way and it's hard to change."
- Fixed habits (2): "I know I can pull this out at the last minute."
- Fixed habits (3): "I work better under pressure."
- Inertia: "I just can't seem to get started."
- Frail memory: "I just forgot."
- Physical problems: "I couldn't do it; I was sick."
- "Appropriate" delays (1): "I'm just waiting for the best time to do it."
- "Appropriate" delays (2): "I need time to think this through."
- "Appropriate" delays (3): "This other opportunity will never come again, so I can't pass it up."

Yes, we come up with many reasons to put things off. All of these rationalizations contribute to a vicious cycle, a procrastination doom loop. Putting off a task evokes negative feelings such as anxiety and guilt. These feelings in turn sap the motivation and energy to do work, making us more prone to procrastinate. The cycle continues: Procrastination – negative emotion – less likely to initiate tasks – more procrastination.

Aaron Beck (1993) has invented a useful and popular tool for dealing with such procrastinating thoughts. He calls it the "TIC-TOC Technique." First you identify *t*ask-*i*nterfering *c*ognitions (TICs), perhaps among those listed above. Then think of improved replacement thoughts, or *t*ask-*o*riented *c*ognitions (TOCs). Here are some TIC-TOCs:

> ***TIC***: *"I can't begin this work until I am sure I will do it to near perfection."*
> ***TOC***: *"I can't tell how this work will go until I begin. Once I'm into it, I can decide what more needs to be done."*
>
> ***TIC***: *"This problem will solve itself if I just wait."*
> ***TOC***: *"Realistically, the problem won't go away, and it may get worse."*

TIC: *"I shouldn't be doing this task until I am in the right mood."*
TOC: *"Sometimes everyone has to complete chores that are less than pleasant. There is no reason why I should be different."*

EXERCISES

The Mindfulness Exercise Challenge. *Try practicing a five-minute version of your home mindfulness exercise before completing any chapter exercise.*

16.1 Short-Term Rewards and Delay Tricks

List some specific tasks you put off this week. Specify exactly what the task was, and when and where you attempted to complete it.

What possible short-term rewards and delay tricks contributed to your procrastination for the above activities?

16.2 Procrastination Triggers and Environments

Describe your favorite procrastination triggers. What environments are most likely to foster procrastination for you?

16.3 TIC-TOC

Select a task you have been putting off. What are your TICS (task-interfering cognitions)? What are your TOCS (task-oriented cognitions)?

Procrastination Incident	TICS	TOCS

Procrastination Incident	TICS	TOCS

Procrastination Incident	TICS	TOCS

Stress & Coping
Eye of Mindfulness Journal

Chapter 17

Yoga Stretches and Postures

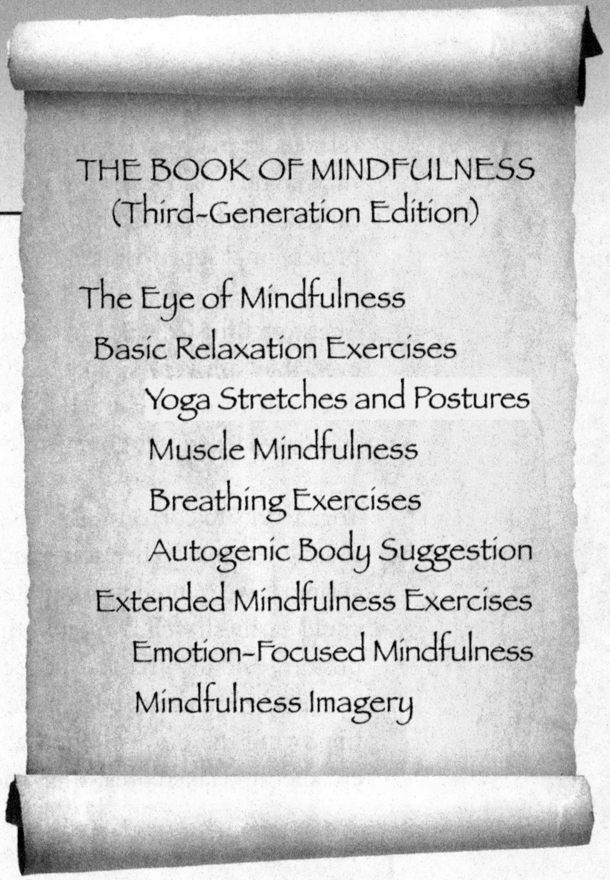

Yoga originated in India over 5,000 years ago. Thousands of exercises and hundreds of systems of techniques and thoughts have evolved. To say you "practice yoga" says little about what you actually do, like claiming that you're "into health" or "politics." Systems include: hatha yoga, prana yoga, kundlini yoga, bhakti yoga, raja yoga, kriya yoga, and tantric yoga. Every year, new yoga systems emerge, not unlike the routine invention of popular diet fads.

A YOGA SAMPLER

Ashtanga yoga is a physically demanding system tying breath to postural flow.

Bhakti yoga resembles devotional religion and includes prayer and worship in group settings not unlike one might find in a Western church, temple, or mosque.

Bikram yoga involves practicing in a hot setting to induce sweat and loosen joints and muscles.

Hatha yoga focuses primarily on slow stretching and maintaining certain postures (like the cross-legged "lotus" position, or more advanced posture of standing on one's head and shoulders); secondary supportive breathing exercises are included.

Iyengar yoga is a precise and popular system focusing on body alignment and holding postures, sometimes using blocks and straps to improve positioning.

Karma Yoga focuses on social action and service to others.

Kundlini yoga teaches meditation on nonmaterial spiritual energy centers in the body called "chakras."

Prana yoga emphasizes focuses on breathing or training the flow of breath or "prana," the nonmaterial energy of spirit.

Raja yoga is the yoga of philosophy.

Sivananda yoga focuses on yoga postures and stretches as well as maintaining a vegetarian diet.

Tantra yoga focuses on sexual energies.

Of these, the most popular are hatha yoga and prana yoga. Hatha yoga focuses primarily on maintaining postures, stretching, and to some extent, breathing in a way that is relaxed. Prana yoga is primarily breathing. Yoga is associated with Eastern religion and may involve restrictions in diet and other activities. Hatha yoga can involve rigorous, difficult, and potentially dangerous positions and should be practiced under qualified professional supervision.

The stretching exercises in this chapter are similar to those found in hatha yoga. However, they are very simple, easy, and not associated with any religion or philosophy. They can readily be practiced with audio or book instructions. Collectively, they are *chair yoga*, exercises done while sitting in a chair rather than standing or lying down.

Yoga works to correct self-stressing postures and positions, and to gently "stretch out" muscle tension. When tense, our muscles and joints are like a tightly bent and coiled spring. If we wanted to straighten out and loosen the spring and reduce its stiffness, we could easily stretch it out and then release the stretch. A yoga stretch corrects stressful posture, and also reduces muscle tension and fatigue, and increases energy. A multitude of somewhat speculative physical effects are often claimed for yoga, including improving the flow of blood and waist removing lymphatic fluid, stimulating joints, enhancing relaxed breathing, and even stimulating critical glands.

The biggest problem beginners have with yoga stretching is that they tend to rush through the exercises, to get the effects as fast as possible. Unfortunately, yoga stretching can't be sped up. First, it takes time to untense a muscle by stretching it out. If you stretch quickly, it simply may not work. Second, if you stretch quickly, you might trigger what is called the "stretch reflex" in which the muscles automatically tense up. Our muscles are wired in such a way that if they are stretched too quickly, they instinctively tense up to prevent possible overstretching. So stretch very slowly, smoothly, and gently. It doesn't matter how far you stretch. You don't have to look like a master yoga practitioner tied up in knots! And it is OK if your stretching feels a little jumpy or jerky, like a rusty door that needs to be oiled. Just do the exercise as slowly, smoothly, and gently as you can. As you gain practice, your stretches will smooth out.

Finally, some yoga exercises can be dangerous. This is important to note given that yoga is often presented as a completely innocuous strategy. Avoid exercises that involve:

- Bouncing or jumping
- Twisting joints
- Extreme flexing of joints beyond what might experience in everyday life
- Be careful with exercises that place stress on the neck, shoulder joints, elbows, wrists, lower back, knees, ankles, and toes.

Here are some popular yoga poses that are potentially dangerous and illustrate the risks we have noted.

Full Lotus (stresses knees, ankles)

© Veronika Surovtseva/Shutterstock.com

Downward Facing Dog (stresses wrists, elbows, ankles)

© Comaniciu Dan/Shutterstock.com

Camel Pose (stresses knees, back, neck, shoulders)

Head Stand (stresses neck, shoulders)

Bridge (stresses neck, lower back)

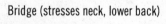

Triangle (stresses back, knees)

I recommend 11 stretching exercises, the same number of muscle groups targeted for another exercise we will try, progressive muscle relaxation. This is also the "head to toe" sequence we use in the Eye of Mindfulness. This selection was designed to be safe and easy and should be practiced in a chair.

1. Face Stretch (jaw and mouth, eyes, forehead)
2. Back of Neck Stretch
3. Front of Neck Stretch
4. Shoulder Stretch
5. Arm and Side Stretch
6. Hand Stretch
7. Stomach and Chest Stretch
8. Back Stretch
9. Leg and Glute Stretch
10. Leg Stretch
11. Foot Stretch

To do them, first find a comfortable chair in which you can sit upright, with your back firmly supported and your feet flat on the floor. When you can complete the entire sequence, take the R/M Tracker at the end of this chapter. Remember to continue practicing your version of The Eye of Mindfulness, your home exercise.

YOGA AS MINDFULNESS

Yoga can be practiced as a mindfulness exercise. The objective is to sustain focus on the stretch, making it as slow, smooth, and graceful as possible. And when you have achieved a full stretch or posture, simply sustain attention on the stretch sensation or the posture. As usual, whenever your mind wanders or you are distracted (for example, by thoughts that the exercise is boring or too simplistic), gently return to your sustained focus.

Unmindful yoga is a mechanical and unfocused fitness chore. Mindful yoga is focused.

Time: 30 minutes.

YOGA STRETCHING
(Do every day. After one session fill out an R/M Tracker)

MAKING YOUR OWN RECORDING: Read very slowly and calmly. Stretch out your vowels, as if you were stretching while reading. Your voice should be clear and alert, but very gentle and unforced. Pause between each sentence. Beginners often make the mistake of speaking to quickly and not introducing enough pauses. If your recording is shorter than 30 minutes, you spoke too quickly and your pauses were too short.

Orientation

In this exercise we relax by slowly, smoothly, and gently moving and stretching various muscle groups. Each exercise has three parts. We slowly move. We stretch. We relax, and attend to the good feelings of tension release and the flow of blood. When your mind is distracted or wanders, that's perfectly fine, and indeed has to happen for the exercise to work. When it happens, move back to the exercise as easily and with as little thought or disruption as possible.

First make sure you are seated upright in a comfortable position. Place your feet flat on the floor. Close your eyes.

1. Face Stretch

Eyes and Forehead

We begin with our eyes and forehead.

Open your eyes and forehead, all the way.

[REPEAT]

Feel the stretch.

[REPEAT]

Hold the stretch.

[REPEAT]

Slowly release the stretch, bit by bit.

[REPEAT]

And enjoy the feelings of unstretching.

Now close your eyes.

Jaws and Mouth

Slowly, smoothly, and gently open your jaws, mouth. Focus on doing this as slowly and smoothly as possible.

[PAUSE]

Open wide, very slowly.

[PAUSE]

Feel every muscle of your jaws and mouth stretch more and more.

[PAUSE]

When you feel a good comfortable stretch, hold it. Attend to the good feelings.

[PAUSE]

Then gently and easily release the stretch.

[PAUSE]

Very slowly. Bit by bit.

[PAUSE]

Let your face settle into a comfortable position.

[REPEAT]

And enjoy the release of tension.

And the flow of blood.

And now attend to your eyes and forehead.

[REPEAT]

2. Back of Neck Stretch

Attend to the back of your neck.

[PAUSE]

Let your head begin to tilt forward, and as slowly and smoothly as possible.

[PAUSE]

Bit by bit, let go and let the head move.

[PAUSE]

Notice the good feelings of stretching in the back of your neck.

[PAUSE]

When your mind wanders, return to attending to the good feelings of stretching.

[PAUSE]

When you are ready . . .

[PAUSE]

Gently and easily lift your head.

[PAUSE]

Lift it until it is again comfortably upright.

[PAUSE]

Relax.

[PAUSE]

Focus on the good feelings of tension release.

[PAUSE]

Focus on the blood flowing to your muscles.

[REPEAT]

3. Front of Neck Stretch

Very very slowly, bit by bit let gravity pull your head back, but not too far, just enough to feel the stretch.

[PAUSE]

Attend quietly to the stretch, without effort.

Do not force your head back.

[PAUSE]

Let gravity do the work for you as it pulls the heavy weight of your head back, farther and farther.

[PAUSE]

Gently and slightly open your mouth, and let your head relax and fall back.

[PAUSE]

When you have a good stretch, simply attend to the good feelings.

Savor and enjoy them.

[PAUSE]

Then gently and easily lift your head.

[PAUSE]

Very slowly, attend to the movement. Gradually return it to upright position.

[PAUSE]

When your head is upright, attend to the release of tension and the flow of blood.

[REPEAT]

4. Shoulder Stretch

Attend to your arms and shoulders.

[PAUSE]

Now very slowly lift both arms straight ahead in front of you and let your fingers touch.

[PAUSE]

Let the motion be as slow and smooth as possible. See how slow you can make it.

[PAUSE]

Slowly, smoothly, and gently circle your arms around together, as if you were squeezing a big pillow.

[PAUSE]

Very slowly, let your hands cross, pointing in opposite directions.

[PAUSE]

Continue until you feel a good stretch in your shoulders.

[PAUSE]

Hold and attend to the good feelings of stretching

[PAUSE]

And gently release the stretch.

[PAUSE]

Gradually return your arms to your sides.

[PAUSE]

Attend to the slow and graceful movement.

[PAUSE]

Let your arms relax.

[PAUSE]

Attend to the release of tension and the flow of blood.

[REPEAT]

5. Arm and Side Stretch

Now let both your arms fall limply to your sides.
[PAUSE]

Slowly, smoothly, and gently circle your right arm and hand up and away from your body like the wing of a butterfly.

[PAUSE]

Move very slowly and gracefully, inch by inch.

[PAUSE]

Let your arm circle to the sky. Focus on the slow movement. Make your movement as slow and easy as possible.

[PAUSE]

And then circle your arm over your head so your hand points to the other side . . . and arch your body as you reach and point farther and farther.

[PAUSE]

Hold the stretch. Attend to the good invigorating sensations. When your mind wanders, return it to attending to the stretching sensations.

[PAUSE]

Now gently and easily . . .

[PAUSE]

Circle your arm back over your head . . . to your side . . .

[PAUSE]

Attend to how slow and gentle the movement is.

[PAUSE]

And return to the resting position.
Let your arm hang.

[REPEAT]

Attend to the good sensations of tension release and the flow of blood.

[REPEAT ONCE FOR RIGHT ARM AND SIDE AND TWICE FOR LEFT ARM AND SIDE]

Let tension flow out through your fingers.

6. Hand Stretch

Slowly, smoothly, and gently open your fingers and easily stretch them back and apart.

[PAUSE]

Move very slowly and smoothly, as if a butterfly were resting on your fingers.

[PAUSE]

Focus on the good feelings of stretching.

[PAUSE]

Take your time.

[PAUSE]

Stretch every muscle fully.

[PAUSE]

Then hold the stretch.

[PAUSE]

And slowly, smoothly, and gently
release the stretch.

[PAUSE]

Release as slowly as possible.

[PAUSE]

Very smoothly and gently.

[PAUSE]

And rest your hand. Notice the pleasing sensations as tension releases and blood flows into your fingers.

Let tension flow out through your fingers.

[REPEAT ONCE WITH RIGHT HAND, TWICE
WITH LEFT HAND]

7. Stomach and Chest Stretch

Now attend to the front of your body, your chest and abdomen.

[PAUSE]

Slowly, smoothly, and gently arch your stomach and chest out.

[PAUSE]

Do this slowly and gently. Very easily. Just enough to be comfortable.

[PAUSE]

Feel the stretch along your torso . . .

[PAUSE]

Attend to the enjoyable stretch.

[PAUSE]

Then gently and easily release the stretch . . . very slowly.

[PAUSE]

Slowly and easily return to an upright position.

[PAUSE]

And enjoy the release of tension and the flow of blood.

Take your time. There is no reason to hurry.

[REPEAT]

8. Back Stretch

Now focus your attention on your back, below your shoulders.

[PAUSE]

Slowly, smoothly, and gently begin to bow over.

[PAUSE]

Let your arms hang limply.

[PAUSE]

Let your head fall forward, as you bow forward farther and farther in your chair.

[PAUSE]

Do not force yourself to bow over . . . let gravity pull your body toward your knees . . . farther and farther. It's OK to take a short breath if you need to.

[PAUSE]

Attend to the slow movement. . . inch by inch.

[PAUSE]

When you feel a nice stretch along your back, pause and attend to the stretch.

[PAUSE]

Then gently and slowly sit up.

[PAUSE]

Attend to the movement.

[PAUSE]

Until you are seated comfortably in an upright position.

[REPEAT]

And relax. Attend to the release of tension and the flow of blood.

9. Leg and Glutes Stretch

Now again focus your attention on your right leg. Focus on the upper leg, the glutes.

[PAUSE]

Move your foot forward a little so it is comfortably resting on the heel.

[PAUSE]

Slowly and easily glide the foot ahead, easily reaching your leg in front of you.

[PAUSE]

Just enough to feel a comfortable stretching of your glutes..

[PAUSE]

Do this easily and gently.

[PAUSE]
Feel a good energizing stretch all along your glutes.

[PAUSE]

Slowly unstretch, gliding your foot back.

[PAUSE]

Move slowly and gently.

[PAUSE]

Slowly let your leg return to its original resting position.

[PAUSE]

Enjoy the release of tension and flow of blood.

[REPEAT ONCE FOR EACH LEG]

Let tension flow out through your toes.

10. Leg Stretch

Now focus your attention on your right leg.

[PAUSE]

Move your foot forward a little so it is comfortably resting on the heel.

[PAUSE]

Slowly and easily glide the foot ahead, easily reaching your leg in front of you.

[PAUSE]

Just enough to feel a comfortable stretch.

[PAUSE]
Do this easily and gently.

[PAUSE]

Feel a good energizing stretch all along your leg.

[PAUSE]

Slowly unstretch, gliding your foot back.

[PAUSE]

Move slowly and gently.

[PAUSE]

Slowly let your leg return to its original resting position.

[PAUSE]

Enjoy the release of tension and flow of blood.

Let tension flow out through your toes.

[REPEAT ONCE FOR EACH LEG]

11. Foot Stretch

Now focus your attention on your right foot.

[PAUSE]

While resting your heel on the floor, gently begin to pull your toes and foot up, as if they are being pulled by strings.

[PAUSE]

Very very slowly, attend to the movement.

[PAUSE]

Feel the full and comfortable stretch.

[PAUSE]

Hold and attend to the stretch.

[PAUSE]

Now easily and gently release the stretch.

[PAUSE]

Slowly move the foot back, bit by bit.

[PAUSE]

Inch by inch, let the foot return.

[PAUSE]

And rest your foot. Enjoy the release of tension and the flow of blood.

Let tension flow out through your toes.

[REPEAT ONCE FOR RIGHT FOOT AND TWICE FOR LEFT FOOT]

Let go of what you are attending to. Slowly open your eyes all the way. Take a deep breath and stretch. This completes our exercise.

~ END OF SCRIPT ~

EYE OF MINDFULNESS
BRIEF SCRIPT
(Practice this until you select your home exercise)
Do every day. After one session fill out an R/M Tracker

BODY/BREATH SCANNING

Imagine tension flowing from your body with every outgoing breath. Flowing from the top of your head to your toes. Flowing from your head, neck, shoulders, arms, hands, back, abdomen, legs, and feet.

[PAUSE 60 SECONDS]

Attend to the easy flow of breathing, in and out through your nose, throat, chest, and belly.

[PAUSE 60 SECONDS]

FOCUSED ATTENTION MEDITATION

Select your preferred meditation focus, perhaps the word "One. . . one . . . one" slowing going over and over in your mind like an echo.

Attend to it for the next few minutes.

Whenever your mind wanders, that's OK. You can change if you want.

You are always the quiet observer. Accept what comes and goes. Return to your focus again and again.

[PAUSE 6 MINUTES]

MINDFULNESS

And now we move on to mindfulness meditation. Simply attend to sounds as they come and go. Or open your eyes halfway and attend to all stimuli that come and go. Or do both.

If you slip into centered focus meditation, that's ok.

Return to mindfulness.

You are the quiet observer.

[PAUSE 6 MINUTES]

Gently let go of what you are attending to.

~ END OF SCRIPT ~

THE R/M TRACKER

WHAT DID YOU FEEL OR EXPERIENCE DURING **YOGA STRETCHING**?
CLICK BOXES USING THIS KEY
(SKIP ITEMS YOU DON'T UNDERSTAND OR DIDN'T FEEL OR EXPERIENCE)

☒☐☐☐	☒☒☐☐	☒☒☒☐	☒☒☒☒
Felt this SLIGHTLY	Felt this MODERATELY	Felt this VERY MUCH	Felt this EXTREMELY (the most ever)

1. ***FAR AWAY*** *and distant from the troubles around me.*	☐☐☐☐
2. ***PHYSICALLY RELAXED***. *Muscles relaxed, loose, limp, warm and heavy. Breathing slow, even, and easy.*	☐☐☐☐
3 AT EASE, AT PEACE.	☐☐☐☐
4. REFRESHED.	☐☐☐☐
5. ***PLEASANT MIND WANDERING***. *Undirected, random positive thoughts.*	☐☐☐☐
6. *Lost in* ***FANTASY*** *and* ***DAYDREAMING.***	☐☐☐☐
7. *Periods of sustained, continuous* ***FOCUS. ABSORPTION.***	☐☐☐☐
8. CENTERED, GROUNDED.	☐☐☐☐
9. ***QUIET.*** *Still, few thoughts. Little mind wandering.*	☐☐☐☐
10. ***UNBOTHERED.*** *Accepting. When I had a negative thought or feeling, I didn't get caught up in it. No judging, clinging, pushing away, figuring things out.*	☐☐☐☐
11. ***EASY, EFFORTLESS.*** *Effortless to let go, put thoughts aside, sustain focus.*	☐☐☐☐
12. *I felt like an* ***OBSERVER*** *standing aside and watching what happens.*	☐☐☐☐
13. ***CLEAR, AWAKE, AWARE.*** *I saw things as they really are.*	☐☐☐☐
14. INTERESTED, CURIOUS, FASCINATED.	☐☐☐☐
15. *Things seemed* ***BEAUTIFUL.***	☐☐☐☐
16. ***GOING DEEPER***. *Things seemed unexpected, new, changing, opening up,being revealed. Felt like I was in a different place or space.*	☐☐☐☐
17. *Sense of* ***SPACIOUSNESS, EXPANSIVENESS.***	☐☐☐☐
18. *I felt the* ***SENSE OF SOMETHING GREATER*** *than myself (God, a higher power, spirit, energy, love, or consciousness.); God is with me.*	☐☐☐☐
19. *A sense of* ***MEANING, PURPOSE, DIRECTION.***	☐☐☐☐
20. *I felt* ***REVERENT, PRAYERFUL.***	☐☐☐☐
21. ***AWE / WONDER, DEEP MYSTERY*** *of things beyond my understanding.*	☐☐☐☐
22. *I felt a profound personal meaningful "****SPIRITUAL****" or "****MYSTICAL****" experience -- sudden awakening or insight.* • *Felt an underlying hidden* ***TRUTH.*** • *Feeling* ***AT ONE.*** • *Feelings so profound they* ***COULD NOT BE PUT INTO WORDS.***	☐☐☐☐
23. HAPPY, OPTIMISTIC, TRUSTING.	☐☐☐☐
24. LOVING, CARING.	☐☐☐☐
25. ***THANKFUL.*** *Grateful.*	☐☐☐☐

Stress & Coping
Eye of Mindfulness Journal

LESSON 4

THINKING REALISTICALLY

Chapter 18

Hidden Stress-Producing Thoughts

© ImageFlow/Shutterstock.com

I just don't see how my thinking contributes to stress. It seems so obvious. I get a flat tire. I get upset, and that's it. My daughter doesn't return my car on time, and that makes me angry. My doctor says I have a condition, and I get depressed. Bad things cause me to get stressed out.

When something goes wrong our first impulse is often to look for an outside culprit. Yet our thoughts, our cognitions, can play a crucial role. Sometimes this is clear when we compare two versions of the same problem:

Todd has just broken up with his girlfriend of two years. He is taking it very hard. He finds it hard to sleep each night and feels depressed and anxious. He is bothered by stomach distress. When discussing his breakup, he complains, "This was my only chance to make a relationship work. This breakup proves that I don't have what it takes to find a girl. I'm a loser."

Ted has also broken up with his girlfriend of two years. However, he isn't taking it so hard. He sleeps just fine, and goes on with his day. When discussing his breakup, he explains, "Sure, the breakup was a disappointment. But it wasn't the end of the world. Life goes on. You learn from your mistakes."

Tod and Ted have experienced a breakup, but Tod is distressed, whereas Ted is mildly upset. The reason for the difference is obvious. Tod is worrying unnecessarily. He is taking things too hard. He is making an unfortunate situation worse. In other words, he is thinking himself into stress.

Whatever stress situation you may be experiencing, imagine that somewhere there is a Ted (or Tina) in the same predicament. However, they are not as upset. The difference is that Ted / Tina is not thinking stressful thoughts.

One popular way of uncovering hidden thoughts or cognitions is through a technique called cartoon captioning (Beck, 1993). There are four parts of any cartoon: the figure doing the action or talking, what they are saying, what they are thinking, and what they are feeling. Speech can be indicated very simply with words coming out of the figure's mouth. Thoughts are placed in a "thought balloon" over the figure's head. And feelings, especially negative feelings, by something of a cloud over the figure's head.

This is illustrated below. My young friend, Rod, just broke up with his girl and was taking it rather badly. He decided to draw a cartoon of his predicament attempting to use his new computer drawing software. Yes, the drawing will not make it into any art show or even a tabloid newspaper. But it does show that a good captioned cartoon can make a point without being artistically perfect.

LOST MY
GIRLFRIEND!

Mindful Dereification

A student of mindfulness might recognize cartoon captioning as an example of dereification (not treating simple thoughts literally as if they were objective fact; gaining perspective). *make something abstract more concrete or real*

One experiences a reified thought as (Hayes, Strosahl, & Wilson, 2003):
- "The absolute truth"
- "A command or rule that must be met"
- "A threat that absolutely must be removed"
- "Immediately urgent"
- "Something you can't stop, even though it isn't doing you any good whatsoever"

Meta-awareness and the Mindful Observer

Cartoon captioning also suggests to a stance of acceptance toward distraction, one in which you are just the quiet observer, noting thoughts and stimuli that come and go while doing nothing to interfere. We have noted this earlier as meta-awareness.

This involves taking on a certain role, a **mindful identity.** One can affirm this identity at the onset of practice, in step 1 ("ORIENTING TO PRACTICE") of our Core Mindfulness Cycle (Chapter 12). A mindful identity can be affirmed in a few words (Hayes, Strosahl, & Wilson, 2003):

- "I am the quiet observer."
- "I simply note what comes and goes."
- "I am the witness of the world."
- "I am simply the screen of consciousness on which the 'movie' of life plays."
- "I see what happens. None of this defines me."

Active Approaches to Dereification

Cognitive stress management takes a direct approach, one that involves seeking a deeper understanding of one's stressful thinking and actively challenging it. We consider these approaches in the following chapters.

EXERCISES

The Mindfulness Exercise Challenge. *Try practicing a five-minute version of your home mindfulness exercise before completing any chapter exercise.*

18.1 Create Your Own Cartoon

Think of a recent stress situation or event. For this to work the situation needs to be specific, one where you can identify WHO was there, WHAT was done and said, WHERE you were, and WHEN it happened. In your cartoon, indicate:

- What you were doing (or what was happening)
- What you said, if anything
- What you were thinking—your beliefs and expectations
- Your negative feelings—probably some variation of sadness, anxiety, or anger.

18.2 Create a Cartoon About Someone

Think of a person you have met or know. Can you recall a time this person created stress through his or her thinking? Describe this as a cartoon here.

18.3 Mindfulness, Dereification, the Observer

Some mindfulness trainers (Hayes, Strosahl, & Wilson, 2003) suggest a variety of game exercises to cultivate a more mindful attitude.

Creating a distraction metaphor. What distractions come to mind when you meditate? What diverting thoughts interfere with effective coping? In this exercise create a metaphor or story that labels your distraction. Examples:

- My distracting thoughts are like a radio spouting babble
- My distracting thoughts are like a child's temper tantrum or whining
- My distracting thoughts are like a factory chimney that spouts smoke in the forms of judgments and excuses
- My distracting thoughts are like an inner dog barking as it wanders aimlessly around.

Carding. Take a stack of blank cards. On each, write a thought that might emerge in mediation. Mix the cards up. Then slowly pick up one card at a time. Attend to each about five seconds before going on to the next.

The Observer. Imagine you are a poet, journalist, or astronaut landing on a new land for the first time. You are to provide an accurate overall description of everything you see, without judgment or elaboration. You even put aside attempts to analyze or interpret, leaving this work to the experts. All you have to do is provide an initial picture, an overview of the landscape. Your words become something of a camera. You simply report, just the facts, like this: "A brown rock . . . dust on my boots . . . stars in the distance . . . three mountains. . . a small creature with four legs . . . the moon . . . a brick building . . . a tree with no leaves."

Acquiring the role of mindful observer transforms or defines what is observed. The coming and going stimuli become temporary, not permanent. They become objective, not self-defining. It can be helpful to think of metaphors that reflect this view. For one with a mindful identity, stimuli may be viewed as:

- Cars passing by on a freeway
- Clouds drifting in the sky
- People walking by on the other side of the street
- Bubbles rising in a pond
- Waves washing up on a beach
- Birds flying across the sky

Each metaphor recognizes the futility of "getting rid" of the stimuli we note. Each calls for deliteralizing and taking perspective. And each calls for acceptance of what comes and goes. Hundreds of metaphors can serve the purpose. Invent one observer role that fits you and describe what you observe.

© iunewind / Shutterstock.com

Chapter 19

The Distorted Thoughts Film Festival

© Mmaxer/Shutterstock.com

Events don't automatically cause distress. Two people can react quite differently to the same stressful event. Sometimes the source of stress can be traced to a simple mistaken perception or a misunderstanding. For example:

> *"Last night I was frightened silly by the sound of someone in the basement – until I realized it was a cat, not a burglar."*
>
> *"I was really upset that my boss was going to fire me until I found out she was actually going to give me a raise."*
>
> *"When my boyfriend frowned at me, I thought he didn't like my hair style. Then he explained the reason – an upset stomach."*

However, our concerns are not with everyday mistakes or misunderstandings that can be cleared up with a simple question or two. Our focus is on more subtle and persistent ways we aggravate the impact of life's stressors through our thoughts.

Distorted versus Realistic Thoughts

Our thoughts, specifically our beliefs and expectations, are often the deciding factor in creating or setting up stress. Two psychologists, Albert Ellis and Aaron Beck, are famous for clarifying the toxic ingredient in thoughts, just what makes some beliefs and expectations more stress producing than others. (Ellis focused more on what we think, while Beck was more interested in how we think unrealistically.) Put simply, distorted thoughts are potentially stress producing.

Realistic thoughts are more likely to be associated with less stress. Here's a quick test to determine if your thought is distorted: Ask if it is:

- Contrary to what the facts are
- Illogical or doesn't make good sense, and
- A waste of time to think (Why even think it if it doesn't get you anywhere?)

Here are some examples:

> *"I must be perfect in everything I do, like my dad. I just can't accept myself if I am anything less."*

- This can't possibly be factual. No one has ever been completely perfect.
- This is illogical. No one can be perfect at absolutely everything. Sometimes one has to compromise and set up priorities.
- This is a waste of time. You waste time trying to be perfect at things that don't particularly matter. Devote your efforts to what is really important.

> *"I can't stand being alone! I can't go on living without a boyfriend. I must have love to survive! I'm so lonely I can't bear it any more."*

- Probably not factual. How do you know for sure you can't live being alone? Not proven.
- Illogical. Many people live alone. It doesn't make sense to think that you are somehow different than the rest of the world.
- Wasted thinking. This complaining isn't getting you anywhere.

Learning to Distance Yourself from Stress

In this chapter we will consider one way of distancing ourselves from stress, a way of becoming a mindful observer and dereifying problems. Often stress feels serious because we are so "caught up" in it. We are so stuck in our problems that we can't see things objectively. We get carried away by stressful emotions like anger, fear, anxiety, and depression. Stress becomes like a tunnel, and we have climbed so deep into it that we can't see out.

Distancing yourself from stress involves mindfully standing back and taking perspective. It involves recognizing when our thinking may be distorted, that is, not factual, illogical, and simply a waste of time. Two powerful tricks for doing this involve labeling and humor. When we put a label on our problem or our negative thinking, we automat-

© Oksana Mizina / Shutterstock.com

ically have to stand back a bit. When we laugh at our problems, we take one step toward distancing ourselves from them.

I remember a silly cartoon of a frustrated young man standing with his nose and face pressed against a very high brick wall. The caption read something like, "Damn! I'm lost! There's no where to go! I'm trapped!" The only reason he felt trapped was that his face was so tightly stuck against the wall that he couldn't see anything but bricks. If he simply took a step back, he would see all sorts of paths, walks, parks, trees around him. Indeed, we could trick him to do this by giving him a poster that reads "THIS IS A WALL, NOT A BOX" and asking him to glue it to the wall. He would have to stand back in order to paste the label on the wall. Perhaps he would recognize the absurdity of the label, and chuckle. Then he might see that he was not so trapped.

We will try a dereification observer tool that uses the power of humor. We will label our stress-creating distortions as if they were silly B-grade movies. Movie reviewers might observe our personal soap operas and give them "two thumbs down" for being "not factual," "illogical," or simply a "waste."

Movies can be organized into various types or "genres"—for example, love stories, adventure, and fantasy. Similarly, there are at least four genres of internal stressful dramas in the multiplex theaters of our lives. They are listed here as four series of B movies in "The Distorted Thoughts Film Festival."

Each movie series names a type of distorted thinking. Each is a category of "stress movie" featuring how we live parts of our lives.

The Desperate Desire Series

This is the unrealistic and exaggerated feeling that you absolutely, positively MUST have something in order to be happy, go on living, be successful, and so on. Desperate desires also include exaggerated expectations and bloated beliefs. Examples of sensible alternatives to desperate desires include:

> *"It would be nice if I could be rich, but not a desperate necessity."*
> *"I am looking for a wife, but not frantically seeking one."*
> *"Of course, it would be desirable if I received a raise."*

Here are some Desperate Desire movies in our festival:

1. *Musts, Oughts, and Shoulds.* Turning simple honest desires and wants into absolute musts, oughts, and shoulds. "*I must be a success,*" rather than, "*It sure would be nice to be successful, but that may or may not happen.*" Or: "*I should be more likable (or hard-working, relaxed, rich, religious, etc.),*" rather than "*I would like to be more likable.*"
2. *Special Privilege.* Acting as if you have a special privilege or entitlement because you are somehow more important or deserving than others. "*People should always treat me nicely.*" "*I should get what I want.*" "*I truly deserve and must get favorable treatment.*"

3. *Childhood Fantasy.* Assuming (as children may do) that everything should go your way. *"Everyone should be nice and love each other." "Problems should have happy endings." "We should all get what we want in life."*
4. *Needless Perfectionism.* Picking an unfairly high standard for yourself and others, even though practically no one has ever been able to achieve it. *"I should never do dumb things." "I have to be better than others."*
5. *Desperate Need for Love and Caring.* Thinking that your needs for love and caring are so important (or strong) that no one can or will ever meet them. *"The kind of love I need no one can provide." "I am nothing without friends or lovers."*

The Foolish Frustration Series

Here the distorted thought is that a desperate desire isn't going to be, or has not been, met; and that it is absolutely terrible, the end of the world, rather than just a frustration or disappointment. Realistic examples of alternatives include:

> *"Sure, I will be disappointed if I don't get an A. But that will not be the end of the world."*
> *"I'll be irritated if he stands me up again, but I'll deal with it."*
> *"I would like to get out of the hospital in a week, and will feel blue if I have to stay longer. But worse things could happen."*

Some Foolish Frustration B movies include:

1. *Catastrophizing.* Turning simple frustrations, irritations, and disappointments into unbearable disasters and catastrophes. *"I didn't get that raise (good grade, date, etc.); therefore it is the end of the world for me." "Things didn't turn out like I wanted; this is a disaster."*
2. *Preoccupation on Regretting the Past.* Focusing on past wrongs, frustrations, and mistakes, rather than what you have or can do now. *"So many things have gone wrong in my life." "The past is filled with frustration."*
3. *Negative Fortune Telling.* Consistently predicting the future negatively, typically thinking that things will only get worse. *"I'll fail that exam or won't get the job." "I will never be really contented."*
4. *Negative Spin.* Arbitrarily and pessimistically putting a negative interpretation on events, even though they may be neutral or positive. *"This is not what I really want." "I always look at the dark side of things."*

The Horrible Helplessness Series

If a desperate desire isn't met, leaving you feeling foolishly frustrated, what could be worse? Unrealistically believing there is absolutely nothing you can do about this predicament. Then you are stuck in the rut of horrible helplessness. Here are some realistic alternatives:

"I'm not sure what to do about this problem. I'll brainstorm some possibilities."
"Getting the flat tire was just bad luck. It can be fixed."
"Sometimes it seems like others just ignore me."
"I'll have to be more assertive."

Here are some movies in the Horrible Helplessness Series:

1. *Hyper-neediness.* Believing you can't cope by yourself and need much help from others. *"I just deal with things by myself." "I always need help on important problems."*
2. *Fatalism.* Believing that the uncontrollable powers of fate, your "genes," or even the Divine Supreme Being, determine the present, and that there is little we can do about it. *"No use in trying to make things better; it's all been fated to happen this way." "It's my lot in life (my social background, genes, family) to have these problems, and there's not much I can do to change that."*
3. *Imperfections = Unlovability.* Feeling that you are basically defective and flawed—unlovable to others if they find out. *"If people knew what I am really like, they would never like me." "I have flaws that will always keep people from accepting me."*
4. *Unrealistic Isolation.* Feeling that you are isolated from the rest of the world, different from other people, and are not, or cannot be part of any group or community. This terrible fact prevents you from doing anything about your frustrations. *"I just don't belong." "I'm different from others."*
5. *Needless Self-Blaming.* Needlessly blaming yourself for negative events, and failing to see that some events have other, complex causes. *"The only reason my marriage ended is because I failed." "I broke my leg because God is punishing me."*
6. *Needless Other-Blaming.* Looking for someone else to blame when things don't go right. *"My husband is to blame for the way I feel." "Mother caused my problems."*
7. *Task Exaggeration.* Treating simple barriers or challenges as overwhelming or insurmountable. *"I don't break a problem down into manageable parts. I see the whole thing as overwhelming. If I can't immediately solve it all, why try?"*

THE DENIAL-DECEPTION-DELUSION SERIES IN GLORIOUS 3D!

So far our Distorted Thoughts Film Festival features a rather scary, sad, and upsetting fare. Our final series is a bit different. The Denial-Deception-Delusion Series is based on the idea of pretending the problem isn't there. You might simply deny it isn't so, deceive others into believing there isn't a problem, or perceive your problem in such an unrealistic way that you are engaging in delusion. Alternatives might include:

"Sure, I'd rather hide from my problem, but I might as well face up to it."
"I get nowhere putting on a happy face and lying to others that everything is OK."
"It's time to get out of my fantasy world and see facts as they really are, rather than see my wishes as realities."

Movie listing:

1. *Denial.* Ignoring what is true. "*This isn't a problem for me. It isn't an issue.*"
2. *Deception.* Lying to others. "*I'm actually very good at expressing my feelings*" (when you aren't).
3. *Delusion.* Lying to yourself. "*I don't care what others think. I'm very good at expressing my feelings.*"

Stress & Coping
Eye of Mindfulness Journal

Chapter 20

Changing Your Stressful Thinking

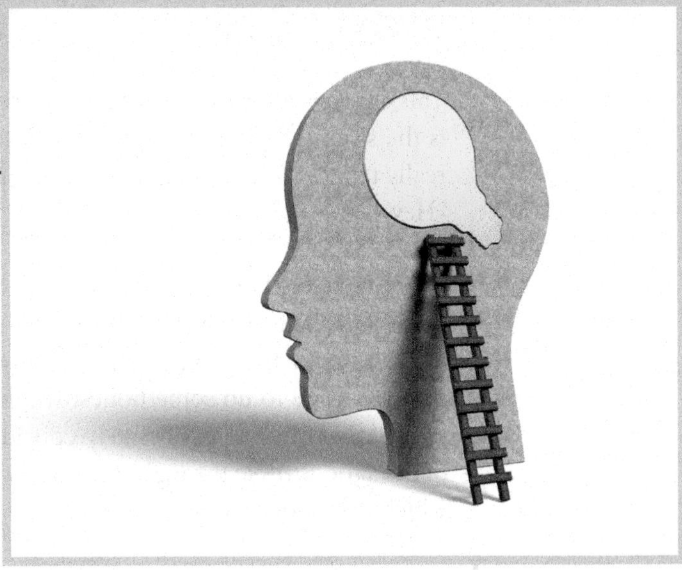

© CHW/Shutterstock.com

Distorted stressful thoughts have a way of lingering. They are notorious triggers for unmindful mind wandering. You may know very well that you make things worse by catastrophizing, overpersonalizing, or thinking in a perfectionistic way. Simply having this understanding may not be enough.

Changing stressful thinking habits can be like changing any habit. It takes time and practice. I recommend trying many tools again and again. Eventually you may find which fit you best and use them automatically at the first sign of stressful thinking.

The first step is to identify which of your beliefs and expectations are creating stress. Complete the "thought balloon" exercise in the previous chapter. Select a type of distorted thinking.

Then do a **reality check**. Challenge the distortion. Think it through. Decide on a replacement thought that is more realistic. Reality checking is not a quick fix. It is a skill, like swimming or dancing. You have to practice over and over before it begins to sink in. Important skills involve creating real changes in the brain, and this doesn't happen overnight.

The goal of this chapter is to give you extensive practice in making reality checks. We make this job a little easier by considering the process of reality checking from various perspectives.

You might wonder "How is reality checking mindful? It seems to involve effort, judgment, and activity that may be anything but simple." There are several ways of thinking about this. A reality check can simplify a needlessly complicated situation or worry. It can remove troublesome concerns that prompt needless mind wandering. It can jar one from a multitasking observer stance. It can reflect single-tasking, or mindfully focused work.

Reality Checking Tools

This chapter offers four types of reality checks you might consider. The **basic smell test** is the simplest and fastest check. You simply examine a thought and ask "Hey, is this really true?" It's like going to a market, picking up a piece of fish, sniffing it, and asking "Hey, is this fish OK?"

The **quick check** is something like checking yourself in the mirror in the morning to see if your hair, tie, lipstick, teeth, etc. are OK. You check a specific idea or feeling to see if it passes the reality test. More involved is the process of **self-analysis**. Here you set time aside to do some honest thinking as part of your reality check. The **positive alternative** involves deliberately considering realistically hopeful and optimistic lines of thought. Browse through this library. Try those that seem to catch your interest. See which ones work.

The Basic Smell Test

Simply look at what you are thinking. Can you find a thought that is obviously distorted? Obviously out of touch with the facts? An unprovable guess? Just plain silly and illogical? A pointless waste of time? If so the thought doesn't pass the "basic smell test." Toss it out.

The Quick Check

- Are you using words that are vague, global, and judgmental? *"I am a complete failure."* Just what is a complete failure? *"I got an F on my first exam." "She is evil."* Define evil. *"She didn't return my call."*

- Are you unfairly evaluating persons rather than behaviors? *"I failed as a person"* versus *"I failed the midterm." "I am a terrible husband"* versus *"I made a mistake."*
- Are you distinguishing unrealistic desires and expectations from simple preferences? *"I feel like I must get that promotion, or I could never live with myself"* versus *"I want a promotion."*
- Are you distinguishing certainties from possibilities? *"I will get nervous during the interview and forget everything"* versus *"I will probably get a bit nervous during the interview, but it is very unlikely I will forget everything."*
- Is your thinking needlessly rigid, one-sided, or inflexible? *"I think in all-or-nothing terms"* versus *"I recognize there are shades of gray."* Or *"It's this way, and there's no other way of looking at it"* versus *"Maybe there are alternative perspectives I haven't considered."*
- Are you exaggerating simple feelings, or letting one feeling color your whole world? *"Everyone is so irritating"* versus *"So I'm angry; I don't have to wear a dark pair of glasses that colors and distorts the whole world according to my mood."* Or *"I'm a bit anxious over the speech I have to give; that's not good"* versus *"It's normal to feel a bit nervous."*
- Are you mind-reading? *"She looked at me. That must mean she doesn't like me"* versus *"She looked at me. What does that mean?" "You're trying to analyze me. I can see it in your smile"* versus *"You're smiling at me, and I don't know what you're thinking. That makes me a bit uncomfortable."*
- Are you setting up impossible expectations? *"I want to be perfect in everything and never give up a task."* Trying to be perfect at many tasks means you have to be less than perfect at others (to have enough time to be perfect).

Self-Analysis

- Weigh evidence for and against a thought. *"People think that I don't know what I am talking about when I'm having a discussion."* Let's list all the times you had clear evidence that people thought you did not know what you were talking about, and all the times when you had evidence people thought you did know what you were talking about. Evidence for: *"People tell me I'm stupid; people walking away; people telling other people that they think I don't know things. I have no evidence any of this has happened."* Evidence against: *"People continuing to talk with me, people ask me questions—I must know some-*

thing. This happened about six times this week."

© racorn / Shutterstock.com

- Consider full chain of consequences, and evaluate. *"I didn't get the raise, and that's the end of the world."* What's the consequence of not getting the raise? *"I won't be able to fix the car."* What's the consequence of that? *"My car will be less comfortable and more noisy when I drive."* What's the consequence, is that so bad? *"I'll still get places in my car, I'll still be able to entertain."*
- Test the thought with an experiment. *"When I talk to my friends, they really don't want to talk with me and want to be somewhere else."* Let's design an experiment to test this out. *"The next 10 friends and acquaintances I start to talk to, I could suggest, 'I know you might be a bit busy, would you rather continue this later sometime?' Record when someone agrees and walks away."*
- Examine if past worries or predictions haven't come true or are no longer important. *"I know I'll mess up this date. I'm always worrying about how things will go wrong."* Let's look at past things you might have worried about. Let's see which have actually come true? Which are no longer important?
- Apply the same standard to everyone else. *"I am a weak person because I can't immediately calm down whenever I'm in a stressful situation."* Is it reasonable to call everyone weak when they can't immediately calm down in stressful situations? Why or why not? *"I do not have a wife; therefore I must be unlovable."* Is everyone who does not have a wife unlovable? Be fair to yourself.
- Question how others might evaluate the quality of your evidence and thinking. *"I'm just no good at work."* Why is that? *"Yesterday I was five minutes late, last week I couldn't find my report, and today I forgot to make a phone call."*
- Imagine you are (name a friend you can trust). Realistically how would this person rate you if he or she knew these facts about your work?

The Positive Alternative

- Look for mitigating circumstances. Are you being too hard on yourself? Are there certain circumstances, people, or past events that should be taken into account?
- Anticipate realistic possible futures that put things in perspective. *"Yes, we've talked about this for quite some time. My employer is going out of business and I won't have a job next month."*

Let's stand back and think about a year, two years, even five years from now. What kinds of things might happen that would cause you to look back at today and say, "That wasn't so bad after all"? *"I hope I'll be married. I certainly will have another job, hopefully one that is stable."*

© Brian A Jackson / Shutterstock.com

- What is the possible "silver lining" in this cloud? What possible good could come from this? *"My illness will get me to pay more attention to my health, something I need to do." "I lost out on this interview. At least it taught me some good things about interviewing." "Sometime it's important to learn to accept things that cannot change, and go on living." "I am learning how to forgive."*
- Examine what might be worse, or others who might be worse off. *"I was turned down for that promotion yesterday. I understand how that might be frustrating, but it's not the worst thing that could happen. Yes, I could have been fired, demoted, put in a smaller office, or given a bad review. Think of all of the people who have been fired from work this year."*
- Consider what is possibly funny about this situation. *"I was at the grocery with a full cart. I turned the corner and collided into another cart. Mine turned over and spilled everything. I felt so embarrassed."* Anything amusing about this situation?

© dedMazay / Shutterstock.com

Hidden Distortions: Digging up the Dirt

One distorted thought can be the tip of deeper hidden distorted thoughts. For example, a gardener may discover a strange blue wire sticking up out of the lawn. She asks, "*Why is that there?*" Then she digs it up and discovers a child's toy that had been buried years ago. When it comes to distorted thinking, we are all gardeners. The shovel we use to uncover hidden weeds and distorted thinking is the "Why question."

You simply note a negative thought, and ask, "*Why is this important to me? So what?*" Whatever answer then emerges, ask again, "*Why is this important to me? So what?*" When asked repeatedly, the "Why question" can unearth deeper distorted beliefs. Here's an example:

> *"Joan criticized me at work and I got upset. Why is that important to me? Because I don't want Joan to criticize me at work, and I don't want to get upset. Why is this important to me? So what? Why don't I want Joan to criticize me at work? Actually, I don't want anyone at work to criticize me. Why is it important that people at work don't criticize you? It is important to me that I be liked by everyone."*

Once you have identified what appears to be a deeper and more general distortion ("*I need to be liked*"), you can do a reality check. There is a payoff to identifying deep and general distortions. Imagine you are trying to teach your young child not to play in mud puddles in the street. You discover your child playing with her Barbie doll in the mud. You reply, "*Please do not play with your doll in the mud, you will get its hair dirty.*" Then you discover your child playing with a toy car in the mud. You say, "*Please do not play with your toy car in the mud. You will get it all clogged up with dirt.*"

Once again you catch the child playing, this time with a stuffed animal in the mud. You ask yourself, "*Why is this important to me? Because I don't want my child and her toys to get covered with unhealthy dirt.*" You then explain to the child, "*Please do not play in the mud. Playing in the mud is dirty and can make you sick.*"

In this example, your first confronted specific problems, just as one might confront specific distorted thoughts. You then decided to address the more general problem, dirt. This is similar to confronting a more general distorted belief. The payoff of confronting a general problem is that you automatically deal with all specific types of this problem—playing in the dirty mud includes everything, playing with dolls, toy cars, stuffed animals, food, makeup, boats, etc.

Here are some example of deep general distortions and specific examples. Remember, we unearth deep general distortions by asking the "Why question":

- Specific Distorted Thoughts. *"I must be perfect at my job. I must be the perfect husband. I must have the perfect car. Why is this important to me?"*
- Deep General Distortion: *" I must be perfect in all things in order to accept myself."*
- Specific Distorted Thoughts*: "My friends lie to me. My coworkers make up stories. I can't believe my kids anymore. Why is this important to me?"*
- Deep General Distortion*: "I want people always to tell the truth. You can't trust anyone."*

EXERCISES

> ***The Mindfulness Exercise Challenge.*** *Try practicing a five-minute version of your home mindfulness exercise before completing any chapter exercise.*

20.1 Favorite Distortions

What are your three favorite types of distorted thinking from the previous chapter? (Use the Distorted Thinking Checklist at the end of this chapter.) Challenge and replace each in the space provided.

20.2 Challenging Distorted Thinking Examples

Below are some examples of distorted thinking. For each, describe

- The type of distortion (Use the Distorted Thinking Checklist at the end of this chapter.)
- How you might challenge it effectively

Jim is a college student who just interviewed for a part-time job at the school cafeteria. He didn't get it. Here's his worry: "I'm just a no good slob. Nobody wants me."

- Type of distortion
- How you might challenge it effectively

Freeda has just discovered a problem. She promised her mosque that she would help with their weekend cleaning project. She forgot and didn't show up. Instead, she went to the zoo. "I'm just a terrible person. How could I possibly do such a thing? I've disappointed and hurt so many people. Unforgivable!"

- Type of distortion
- How you might challenge it effectively

Josh has had his eye on a young classmate, Gretchen. Finally he musters up the courage to ask her out for a coffee. She says she's too busy. "I feel terrible! I'm so depressed. Women just don't like me. What's wrong with me?"

- Type of distortion
- How you might challenge it effectively

Brittany has been studying her Bible very hard for church school. She has been doing a lot of thinking about her life and wonders if some changes might be in order. "I must love everyone all of the time. I must love people for who they are, accept them 'as is,' without judgment." But how can I love people I don't know? And honestly, I just don't like some people, like murderers.

- Type of distortion
- How you might challenge it effectively

Bud was walking down the sidewalk with his books and a full cup of Starbuck's coffee. A group of four teens were walking in his direction. They were completely absorbed in laughing and talking about something they saw on TV. As they passed, one teen gently bumped Bud's left arm, causing him to spill his coffee all over his new Nike shoes. Bud stopped, looked down to assess the damage, and realized they would have to be cleaned. When he looked up, the teens were several feet away, still laughing and talking. "People should always think about how their actions might affect others. Everyone is so damn inconsiderate!" He spent the rest of the day thinking about this.

- Type of distortion
- How you might challenge it effectively

Shelah has to give a talk in class. She is very nervous. "I will forget everything and everyone will think that I did not prepare or that I'm stupid or on drugs."

- Type of distortion
- How you might challenge it effectively

George has a drinking problem. He has been drinking every day and night. Finally, he had enough and decided to stop. He went to the library instead to study for class. There he met some of his drinking buddies who invited him out for a drink. He went along, and felt very very guilty. "Nothing's ever going to change. I just don't have what it takes to resist what my friends want."

- Type of distortion
- How you might challenge it effectively

Berto is trying to lose weight. For the past two months he has been off his diet, tempted by the pizza restaurant next to where he lives. When his doctor asked him about his diet, he says, "Things are just too stressful. I can't focus on my diet with all this homework."

- Type of distortion
- How you might challenge it effectively

20.3 Your Distorted Thinking

Think of a recent stressful situation made worse by distorted thinking. What type of thinking was it? (Use the Distorted Thinking Checklist at the end of this chapter.) How would you challenge and replace it?

20.4 Mindfulness

How do the ideas of this chapter reflect mindful dereification and meta-awareness? How might you incorporate mindfulness in coping with stressful negative thinking, and replacing negative stressful thoughts?

THE DISTORTED THINKING CHECKLIST

The Desperate Desire Series

☐ 1. *"Musts, oughts, and shoulds."* Turning simple honest desires and wants into absolute musts, oughts, and shoulds.
☐ 2. *Special privilege.* Acting as if you have a special privilege or entitlement because you are somehow more important or deserving than others.
☐ 3. *Childhood fantasy.* Assuming (as children may do) that everything should go your way.
☐ 4. *Needless perfectionism.* Picking an unfairly high standard for yourself and others, even though practically no one has ever been able to achieve it.
☐ 5. *Desperate need for love and caring.* Thinking that your need for love and caring are so important (or strong) that no one can or will ever meet them.

The Foolish Frustration Series

☐ 1. *Catastrophizing.* Turning simple frustrations, irritations, and disappointments into unbearable disasters and catastrophes.
☐ 2. *Preoccupation on regretting the past.* Focusing on past wrongs, frustrations, and mistakes, rather than what you have or can do now.
☐ 3. *Negative fortunetelling.* Consistently predicting the future negatively, typically thinking that things will only get worse.
☐ 4. *Negative spin.* Arbitrarily and pessimistically putting a negative interpretation on events, even though they may be neutral or positive.

The Horrible Helplessness Series

☐ 1. *Hyper-neediness.* Believing you can't cope by yourself and need much help from others.
☐ 2. *Fatalism.* Believing that the uncontrollable powers of fate, your "genes," or even the Divine Supreme Being, determine the present, and that there is little we can do about it.
☐ 3. *Imperfections = unlovability.* Feeling that you are basically defective and flawed and unlovable to others if they find out.
☐ 4. *Unrealistic isolation.* Feeling that you are isolated from the rest of the world, different from other people, and are not or cannot be part of any group or community. This terrible fact prevents you from doing anything about your frustrations.
☐ 5. *Needless self-blaming.* Needlessly blaming yourself for negative events, and failing to see that some events have other, complex causes.
☐ 6. *Needless other-blaming.* Looking for someone else to blame when things don't go right.
☐ 7. *Task exaggeration.* Treating simple barriers or challenges as overwhelming or insurmountable.

THE DENIAL-DECEPTION-DELUSION SERIES—IN GLORIOUS 3D!

☐ 1. *Denial.* Ignoring what is logical, factual, or workable/unworkable.
☐ 2. *Deception.* Lying to others.
☐ 3. *Delusion.* Lying to yourself.

© iunewind / Shutterstock.com

Chapter 21

The Four Deep Questions

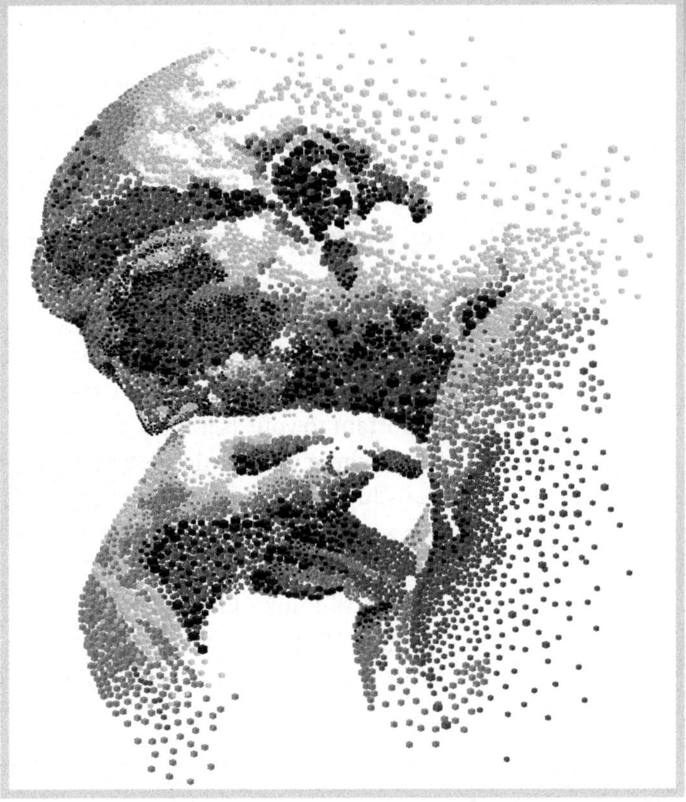

© Davi Sales Batista/Shutterstock.com

Four categories of distorted thinking can create stress: Desperate Desire, Foolish Frustration, Horrible Helplessness, and Denial-Deception-Delusion.

We may desperately desire things that are unrealistic or impossible, such as:

> *"I want to be perfect in all things."*
> *"I want to be loved by everyone."*

We may exaggerate the frustration of not getting what we want:

> *"Not getting what I want is the end of the world."*
> *"This is a terrible catastrophe."*

We may feel utterly and unrealistically helpless:

> *"I guess I am just fated to be unhappy. There's nothing I can do about it."*
> *"Everyone's out to get me. There's no way I can succeed when no one wants to help."*

And we may avoid our problems through denial, deception, or delusion:

> *"No, I'm not frustrated. My low grades are of no concern to me."*
> *"I did poorly on my exam because my instructor is out to get me."*
> *"The instructor will eventually see the error of her ways and change my grade."*

We conclude with four philosophical questions that can play an important role in reducing stress. These deep questions are profound and positive versions of our four types of distorted thinking. They reflect meta-cognition.

QUESTION 1

What Is Truly Important in Your Life?
What's your direction and purpose?

All desperate desires can be seen as misplaced or confused priorities. Consider a person who says, "I desperately want to be perfect in all things." Is this really what's most important to you? Is it more important than health, love, or happiness? Surely there are times where you would be willing to give up a chance at winning in order to achieve some higher goal. A student may want to earn an A in every class, but have to take a few weeks off to care for a sick mother. He accepts a lower grade in order to offer help.

We can all think of instances that force us to put our everyday wants and goals in perspective. We pause and consider the question, What is the most important thing in life? What is a top drawer goal? Happiness? Health? Family? Friends? One's country? God?

QUESTION 2

What's It Worth?
What meaningful sacrifices and potential frustrations are called for? How might you have to delay gratification?

What frustrations can you accept when working toward your most important goal? What immediate satisfactions are you willing to put off and delay? Your answer to the first question puts all frustrations into perspective.

QUESTION 3

What Are Your Positive Choices?
What are you going to do about it?

We have defined horrible helplessness as the belief that one is helpless, perhaps because of blaming oneself and others, feeling defective or imperfect, or simply because of bad fate or genes.

When considering the four deep questions, horrible helplessness is not an option. If you have picked a goal or concern that is truly of commanding importance, then you have committed yourself to accept the temporary frustrations of taking risks, exploring, and trying. You have committed yourself to try, learn from setbacks, and try again. You have a reason to act, even on a piece of the problem.

QUESTION 4

Have You Faced Reality?
What's real? What's possible?

Once you have looked at what is important, what it's worth, and what your choices are, stand back, take a deep breath, and do a reality check. What can actually be done? What are the facts? How much of your thinking is wishful thinking, making things up, or lying to yourself?

Here's a summary of the four deep questions:

DISTORTED THINKING	DEEP THINKING
• Desperate Desire	• Direction and Purpose
• Foolish Frustration	• Meaningful Sacrifice Delayed Gratification
• Horrible Helplessness	• Positive Choices
• Denial-Deception-Delusion	• Facing Reality

DEREIFICATION, METACOGNITION, AND YOU AS THE OBJECTIVE OBSERVER

We conclude our discussion of distorted thinking where we began, by standing back and being mindful. In your most effective meditation, how might you as an objective observer view your distorted thoughts? As an objective observer how might you take a stance or perspective that puts you "above" or "apart" from troublesome thoughts?

EXERCISE

> ***The Mindfulness Exercise Challenge.*** *Try practicing a five-minute version of your home mindfulness exercise before completing any chapter exercise.*

21.1 Your Answers to the Four Deep Questions

What are your answers to each of the four deep questions considered in this chapter?

QUESTION 1

What Is Truly Important in Your Life?
What's your direction and purpose?

QUESTION 2

What's It Worth?
What meaningful sacrifices and potential frustrations are called for? How might you have to delay gratification?

QUESTION 3

What Are Your Positive Choices?
What are you going to do about it?

QUESTION 4

Have You Faced Reality?
What's real? What's possible?

Stress & Coping
Eye of Mindfulness Journal

Chapter 22

Muscle Mindfulness (Progressive Muscle Relaxation)

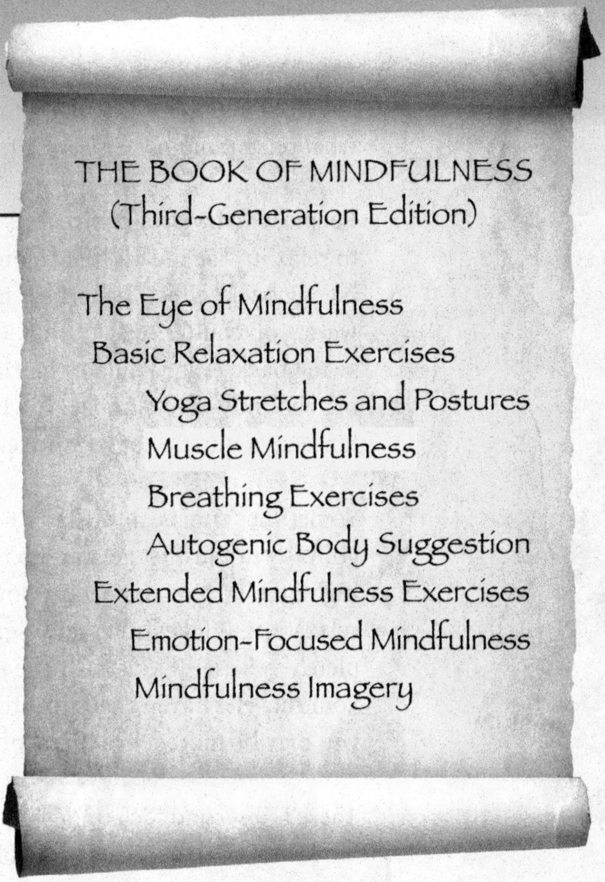

© Vadim Sadovski / Shutterstock.com

Progressive muscle relaxation is an approach to relaxation very popular among health professionals. In the late 1920s, Chicago physician, Edmund Jacobson, was looking for a way to help his anxious patients reduce their anxiety. He noted that our thoughts are often reflected in our bodies. For example, if you were to think about running away from a wild dog, your legs might actually tighten up a bit during the fantasy. While imagining the act of smiling, you might automatically smile a bit. In other words, certain thoughts lead to tension in certain muscles. Jacobson figured out a way to reverse this process. In his progressive muscle relaxation, relaxing muscles leads to a more relaxed mind. So he taught his patients the subtle (and mindful) skill of identifying and letting go of muscle tension (Jacobson, 1929). Interestingly, Jacobson observed that his muscle relaxation students often described a condition of "mental emptiness" in which the mind is blank (Jacobson, 1932). Even though Jacobson had little appreciation of meditative disciplines, his patients were likely experiencing mindfulness. Today, progressive muscle relaxation is rarely, if ever, taught in mindfulness programs. This is unfortunate. Jacobson's approach has many mindful features.

Later, psychologists perfected this approach into what we currently call progressive muscle relaxation. The idea is simple, like squeezing a squishy "stress ball" and then letting your fingers go completely limp. More formally, begin by tightening up a specific muscle while the rest of the body remains relaxed. Notice how the tension feels. Then go completely limp. Let go for about 20 seconds, and attend to the feelings of relaxation.

You can try this right now with your shoulders. Attend to your shoulder muscles. While keeping the rest of your body nice and relaxed, shrug your shoulders now. Create a good shrug. Feel the sensations of shrugging. Then let go and go completely limp. Imagine your shoulders have been held up by strings (like a puppet), and the strings have been cut. Your shoulders then fall limp. Let them stay limp as you slowly count to 20. Notice what relaxation in the shoulders feels like.

People who try progressive muscle relaxation often ask, Why tense up a muscle in order to relax it? The idea is that tightening up first sets the stage for a relaxation rebound or "swing back" effect. Imagine a small child is sitting on a swing. To move the swing forward, you could slowly push it ahead. However, what you would probably do is pull the swing back, let go, and let the child swing forward on his own. This is the "swing back" or rebound effect similar to what happens in progressive muscle relaxation. You first tense up a muscle, let go, and let your muscles "fall" or "swing" into deeper relaxation.

Sometimes sports enthusiasts wonder why it is important to count to 20 while letting go. Why not just let go, and go right on to the next exercise, like doing isometrics. This highlights a very important point. You cannot rush the effects of progressive muscle relaxation. It takes at least 20 seconds for the muscle tension you have created to completely release. If you rush the exercise and start tensing up again before 20 seconds, your muscles haven't had time to relax, and will remain tense. At the end of the exercise, you may be more tense than you were before.

There is a second idea underlying progressive muscle relaxation. If you are reading this book indoors, there are probably many sources of potential noise you simply do not notice. Perhaps you are unaware of the constant drone of the air conditioner, heater, or outside traffic. The brain has a way of simply tuning out potential background nuisances. In a similar way, we grow numb to continuous muscle tension. We are simply less aware of how our muscles may be tightening up.

To elaborate on this idea, imagine you are watching a very long and frightening mystery movie. Your mind is completely absorbed in the scary plot. Every minute you are sitting on the edge of your seat grasping your can of cola. At the end of the movie, you sigh. Then you notice that your cola can has been crushed and that your fingers ache. You realize, "Gosh, I must have been holding on real tight! I wasn't even aware of it!" For hours your hands were very very tense. However, the tension was a continuous background stimulus, which the brain has a way of automatically tuning out.

Psychotherapists sometimes see patients who have a lot of muscle tension. In a way, the lives of these patients are something like continuous stressful movies. If you talk these tense patients, they may well describe all the problems in their lives; but if you ask them how their muscles feel, often they will say "my muscles feel fine." If you look carefully, you may notice they are clenching their teeth, making a fist, and furrowing up their brow. You may see how they are actually tightening up. Yet they may be unaware that they are actually straining as much as a weight lifter! Our brain tunes out continuous feelings of muscle tension.

Nearly everyone has some tuned-out or numbed-out muscle tension. One of the major goals of progressive muscle relaxation is to teach you to detect hidden sources of tension. This is a type of introspection (Chapter 10). When you learn this skill, you have acquired a powerful new ability —you can begin to deeply let go of tension. With progressive muscle relaxation you learn to detect muscle tension, and then release it.

We will target 11 muscle groups, the same areas targeted by yoga stretching presented earlier. By targeting the same areas you can more readily compare the effects of yoga and muscle relaxation. This is also the "head to toe" sequence we used in the Eye of Mindfulness.

1. Face Squeeze (jaw and mouth, eyes and forehead)
2. Back of Neck Squeeze
3. Front of Neck Squeeze
4. Shoulder Squeeze
5. Arm and Side Squeeze
6. Hand Squeeze
7. Stomach and Chest Squeeze
8. Back Squeeze
9. Leg and Glute Squeeze
10. Leg Squeeze
11. Foot Squeeze

DOING IT MINDFULLY

When you practice progressive muscle relaxation mindfully it becomes *muscle mindfulness.* You focus on detecting muscle tension that may be hidden, the feelings of gently letting go, gently returning your attention to muscle sensations.

MUSCLE MINDFULNESS (PROGRESSIVE MUSCLE RELAXATION)

MAKING YOUR OWN RECORDING: Be very generous with pauses. Pause at least 20 seconds after each "tense up" instruction. "Tense up" words should be louder than "let go" words, as if you were a coach encouraging an exerciser to tighten muscles. Instructions to "let go" should be read with a sense of "letting go," or relief. "Let go" instructions should be very soft, slow, and monotonous. Remember that the person listening to your instructions is relaxing, and you don't want to disturb them. If you are recording and finish before 30 minutes, you spoke too quickly and did not pause long enough between exercises.

(Do every day. After one session fill out an R/M Tracker)

Orientation

In this exercise we relax by tensing up and letting go of various muscle groups. By doing this we will let tension flow from our body.

We will do this mindfully, by directing our attention to the feelings of tension we may notice, letting go of them, and returning our attention to feelings of relaxation.

First make sure you are seated upright in a comfortable position. Place your feet flat on the floor. Close your eyes.

1. Face Squeeze

Eyes and Forehead

Begin by focusing on the muscles around your eyes, and your forehead.

Close your eyes tightly.

Scrunch up your forehead now.

Let the tension grow.

Notice the feelings of tension.

And let go.

Let your eyes and forehead relax.

Let the tension flow away.

Let the tightness smooth out.

As your eyes and forehead become more and more relaxed.

[REPEAT]

Jaws and Lips

Now focus on your jaws and lips.

Squeeze them together, now.

Press your lips tightly together.

Close your jaw tightly.

And let go.

Let your jaw and lips relax.

Let the tension flow away from your jaw and lips.

Let the tension smooth out.

As the muscles become more and more relaxed.

[REPEAT]

2. Back of Neck Squeeze

Focus on the muscles in the back of the neck.

Gently tilt your head back and gently press the back of your head against your neck, now.

Tighten up the muscles.

Squeeze the muscles more and more.

And let go.

Let the muscles become more deeply relaxed.

Let your entire body become loose and limp.

Let yourself sink deeper and deeper into relaxation. . . Far away from the world.

[REPEAT]

3. Front of Neck Squeeze

Focus on the muscles of the neck.

Bow your head and gently press your chin down to your chest, now.

Tighten up the muscles.

Let the tension grow.

And let go.

Let tension begin to melt into liquid.

Let the rest of your body remain relaxed.

Let yourself sink deeper and deeper into relaxation. . . Like a tight wad of paper, slowly opening up.

4. Shoulder Squeeze

This time, focus on your shoulder muscles.

Squeeze your shoulders, now.

Create a nice good shrug. Let the feelings of tightness grow.

And let go.

Let the tension flow out.

Let your tension begin to unwind.

Let the muscles begin to smooth out.

Let the muscles become more deeply relaxed.

[REPEAT]

5. Arm Squeeze

This time, focus on your right arm.

Squeeze your lower and upper arm together. . . Touching your wrist to your shoulder.

Do this now.

Press tighter and tighter.

Notice the feelings of tension.

And let go.

Let the tension go.

Let the rest of your body remain relaxed.

The tension melts away.

Let the muscles become more deeply relaxed.

[REPEAT ONCE FOR RIGHT ARM AND TWICE FOR LEFT ARM]

6. Hand Squeeze

Focus on the right hand. Squeeze the fingers together by making a fist, now.

Tighten up the muscles.

Let the tension grow.

And let go.

Release the tension.

Let your muscles begin to go limp.

Let the tension begin to flow out . . . As your hand sinks into relaxation.

[REPEAT ONCE FOR RIGHT HAND AND TWICE FOR LEFT HAND]

7. Stomach and Chest Squeeze

Focus on the muscles of your stomach and chest.

Tighten them up, now.

Tense your stomach and chest in whatever way feels best . . .

By pulling your stomach in . . . pushing it out . . .

Or tightening it up.

Let the muscles get nice and hard.

And let go.

Feelings of tension dissolve. Let yourself feel more detached.

Tension begins to melt into liquid.

Far away from the world.

[REPEAT]

8. Back Squeeze

This time focus your attention on the back muscles that are below the shoulders.

Tense up your lower back, now.

Let the tension build.

Let the muscles get nice and hard.

And let go.

Let the tension go.

Feelings of tightness melt and flow away.

Let yourself feel more relaxed.

Let feelings of tightness go.

[REPEAT]

9. Leg and Glutes Squeeze

Focus on the muscles of your glutes.

Tighten them up, now.

Tense your glutes, pressing them together,

Tighten them up.

Then release the tension

Let the tension slowly dissolve

Let the tension melt away.
As your muscles become more and more relaxed.

[REPEAT]

10. Leg Squeeze

Focus on your right leg.

Tense up the muscles in whatever way feels best.

By pushing down, or pulling against your chair.

Do this now.

Let the tension grow.

Then let go.

Let the tension flow away.

Notice the feelings of tension dissolving.

As your leg becomes more and more relaxed.

[REPEAT ONCE FOR RIGHT LEG AND TWICE FOR LEFT LEG]

11. Foot Squeeze

Focus on your right foot.

Tense up the muscles of the right foot and toes, now.

Curl your toes into the floor while pushing down.

Tighten up the muscles.

Tense up only the muscles of your right foot.

And let go.

Let the tension flow out.
And you become more completely
relaxed, at ease.

Completely passive and indifferent.

Far away from the world.

[REPEAT ONCE FOR RIGHT FOOT AND TWICE FOR LEFT FOOT]

~ END OF SCRIPT ~

EYE OF MINDFULNESS
BRIEF SCRIPT

(Practice this until you select your home exercise)
Do every day. After one session fill out an R/M Tracker

BODY/BREATH SCANNING

Imagine tension flowing from your body with every outgoing breath. Flowing from the top of your head to your toes. Flowing from your head, neck, shoulders, arms, hands, back, abdomen, legs, and feet.

[PAUSE 60 SECONDS]

Attend to the easy flow of breath, in and out through your nose, throat, chest, and belly.

[PAUSE 60 SECONDS]

FOCUSED ATTENTION MEDITATION

Select your preferred meditation focus, perhaps the word "One. . . one . . . one" slowing going over and over in your mind like an echo.
Attend to it for the next few minutes.

Whenever your mind wanders, that's OK. You can change if you want.
You are always the quiet observer. Accept what comes and goes. Return to your focus again and again.

[PAUSE 6 MINUTES]

MINDFULNESS

And now we move on to mindfulness meditation. Simply attend to sounds that come and go. Or open your eyes halfway and attend to all stimuli that come and go. Or do both.

If you slip into body/breath work, that's ok.

If you slip into centered focus meditation, that's ok.

Return to mindfulness.

You are the quiet observer.

[PAUSE 6 MINUTES]

Gently let go of what you are attending to.

~ END OF SCRIPT ~

THE R/M TRACKER

WHAT DID YOU FEEL OR EXPERIENCE DURING **MUSCLE MINDFULNESS?**

CLICK BOXES USING THIS KEY

(SKIP ITEMS YOU DON'T UNDERSTAND OR DIDN'T FEEL OR EXPERIENCE)

☒❑❑❑	☒☒❑❑	☒☒☒❑	☒☒☒☒
Felt this SLIGHTLY	Felt this MODERATELY	Felt this VERY MUCH	Felt this EXTREMELY (the most ever)

1. *FAR AWAY* *and distant from the troubles around me.*	❑❑❑❑
2. *PHYSICALLY RELAXED*. *Muscles relaxed, loose, limp, warm and heavy. Breathing slow, even, and easy.*	❑❑❑❑
3 *AT EASE, AT PEACE*.	❑❑❑❑
4. *REFRESHED*.	❑❑❑❑
5. *PLEASANT MIND WANDERING*. *Undirected, random positive thoughts.*	❑❑❑❑
6. *Lost in* ***FANTASY*** *and* ***DAYDREAMING.***	❑❑❑❑
7. *Periods of sustained, continuous* ***FOCUS. ABSORPTION.***	❑❑❑❑
8. *CENTERED, GROUNDED.*	❑❑❑❑
9. *QUIET.* *Still, few thoughts. Little mind wandering.*	❑❑❑❑
10. UNBOTHERED. *Accepting. When I had a negative thought or feeling, I didn't get caught up in it. No judging, clinging, pushing away, figuring things out.*	❑❑❑❑
11. *EASY, EFFORTLESS.* *Effortless to let go, put thoughts aside, sustain focus.*	❑❑❑❑
12. *I felt like an* ***OBSERVER*** *standing aside and watching what happens.*	❑❑❑❑
13. *CLEAR, AWAKE, AWARE.* *I saw things as they really are.*	❑❑❑❑
14. *INTERESTED, CURIOUS, FASCINATED.*	❑❑❑❑
15. *Things seemed* ***BEAUTIFUL.***	❑❑❑❑
16. *GOING DEEPER*. *Things seemed unexpected, new, changing, opening up,being revealed. Felt like I was in a different place or space.*	❑❑❑❑
17. *Sense of* ***SPACIOUSNESS, EXPANSIVENESS.***	❑❑❑❑
18. *I felt the* ***SENSE OF SOMETHING GREATER*** *than myself (God, a higher power, spirit, energy, love, or consciousness.); God is with me.*	❑❑❑❑
19. *A sense of* ***MEANING, PURPOSE, DIRECTION.***	❑❑❑❑
20. *I felt* ***REVERENT, PRAYERFUL.***	❑❑❑❑
21. *AWE / WONDER, DEEP MYSTERY* *of things beyond my understanding.*	❑❑❑❑
22. *I felt a profound personal meaningful "****SPIRITUAL****" or "****MYSTICAL****" experience -- sudden awakening or insight.* • *Felt an underlying hidden* ***TRUTH.*** • *Feeling* ***AT ONE.*** • *Feelings so profound they* ***COULD NOT BE PUT INTO WORDS.***	❑❑❑❑
23. *HAPPY, OPTIMISTIC, TRUSTING.*	❑❑❑❑
24. *LOVING, CARING.*	❑❑❑❑
25. *THANKFUL.* *Grateful.*	❑❑❑❑

Stress & Coping

Eye of Mindfulness Journal

LESSON 5

DESENSITIZATION AND RELAPSE

Chapter 23

Desensitization

© Lindsay Snow/Shutterstock.com

Stress is a problem waiting to be solved. Our past solution was to mindfully pick a manageable piece of the problem, something that can be done here and now (Chapter 13). But what if the problem makes you so uncomfortable, anxious, or even bored, that you avoid it altogether? Here you never get to work with the problem in the first place. You confront the great problem of ultimate procrastination in which you say "I'll never do this!" or "I'll put this off." Your problem remains unsolved. It is a mountain too high, an ocean to wide, a wall too tall. We can call these special problems "roadblocks" or "barriers." Here are some examples:

- Going to a doctor or dentist
- Going to a funeral
- Fear of flying
- Fear of public speaking
- Fear of going on a date with that "special person"
- Fear of bringing up a threatening topic with a teacher, parent, boss, or spouse

© Lightspring/Shutterstock.com

Psychologists have developed a very powerful strategy for overcoming such barrier problems. It is called **desensitization** and it is based on a very simple idea, illustrated in the following example:

> *Bruce is only 9 years old and is very afraid of the water. When the rest of his family goes swimming, he screams and complains, and wants to stay home. One summer, the family decided to spend a month at a*

cabin. A few hundred feet away was a small lake, perfect for swimming. On the first day, the entire family had a picnic on the beach, a few dozen feet from the lake. This was relaxing and fun. Bruce at first felt a little nervous, but quickly adjusted. The next day the family built sand castles on the beach, just a few feet from the lake. Again, Bruce was initially a little uptight, but he quickly got involved in play and forgot about the water. On the third day, the family again built castles in the sand, this time surrounding them with a moat. To fill the moat with water, a small trench had to be dug a few feet to the lake. This made Bruce a bit uncomfortable, but he recovered. On the fourth day the family sat in a shallow part of the pond and splashed each other with water. The next day they waded in a few more feet, and tossed the beach ball around. Eventually, the entire family, including Bruce, was playing and swimming.

Bruce overcame his fear of water through desensitization. We desensitize to a fear by first getting very relaxed (with relaxation or mindfulness), and then approaching a non-threatening version of the fear. Once we can do this without anxiety, we increase the stakes, and repeat the process, this time on a slightly more threatening version. When we can confront this version without getting upset, we introduce a slightly more serious variation of the stressor.

Eventually, we condition ourselves to remain relaxed even when doing the thing that initially made us upset.

Learning to Relax and Be Mindful

First, you must master an approach to relaxation/mindfulness. Do not continue until you can achieve the relaxation or mindfulness response, and feel deeply at ease and relaxed, in a relatively short period of time. You will have to use your quick relaxation/mindfulness procedure again and again in desensitization, otherwise it won't work.

Build a Hierarchy

First, select a topic, a situation, or activity that creates so much anxiety or distress that you either avoid it or have difficulty engaging in it. Then, create 10 versions of your topic, ranging from very easy to very challenging. In your "Top 10 List," item number 1 should evoke very little or no tension. If it creates tension, then it is too severe and perhaps should be placed higher on your hierarchy. Item 10 should be the most severe version of your selected theme. It should create sufficient distress that you almost certainly avoid it or have difficulty when confronting it. The remaining items, 2 to 9, should be increasingly severe.

Make sure your items are realistic, under your control, and do not risk your health or well-being. So, for this exercise, avoid topics like "racing my car on the streets," "lighting a huge firecracker indoors," "approaching a live bear in the wild," or "swimming alone in a quarry at night." Here is a simple hierarchy for asking for a raise.

The Boss on My Mind

10. *Meeting with my boss alone and asking for a raise*
9. *Phoning my boss and asking for a raise*
8. *Meeting with my boss to review my performance*
7. *Emailing my boss to inform him that the office workers would like a new water cooler*
6. *Having lunch with my boss and others*
5. *Riding home with my boss on the subway*
4. *Meeting my boss unexpectedly in the grocery store*
3. *Talking about my boss to coworkers at work*
2. *Talking about my boss to my family at home*
1. *Looking at a photo of my boss on my work desk*

This was a very simple hierarchy of loosely related events. You may want each item in a hierarchy to reflect an actual step you are taking, with each step bringing you closer to a situation or event that creates anxiety. We see this in the following hierarchy for fear of flying. Note that this fear is not based on any fact, but it prevents the person from flying.

Fear of Flying

10. *I am safely on the airplane, and we hit a little turbulence.*
9. *I am safely on the airplane, and I can see the ground far below.*
8. *We are taking off.*
7. *I am sitting on the plane waiting to take off.*
6. *I am boarding the plane.*
5. *I am waiting at the airport for the plane to arrive.*
4. *I am being checked at the airport.*
3. *I am arriving at the airport in the bus.*
2. *I am driving to the bus that goes to the airport.*
1. *I am packing my gear for the flight today.*

Create Detailed Fantasies of Each Item

Once you have created your hierarchy, the next step is to create a detailed description of each item. Each description should be as vivid and as realistic as possible. Include *who* is there, *when* it is happening, *where* it is happening, and *what* is happening. In addition, describe the thoughts and feelings you have. Here is an example of item 1 for Fear of Flying:

THEME: Fear of Flying
ITEM 1: I am packing my gear for the flight today.

> *"Today I take my first flight in over five years. It has me really uptight! I've put off packing until the last moment, but now it has to be done. I think about what size of bag I will need. Will they want to open the bag? I shouldn't carry on a bag that is too big. And I have to avoid anything that looks sharp, otherwise the metal detector will go off. I feel myself starting to sweat as I think about the flight and what I will have to do to get ready. What if they turn me away? What if the flight is cancelled? What if they lose my luggage? I better take along stuff that isn't too valuable. And I don't want anyone taking my bag by mistake, so I'll make sure my bag is clearly identified. It should have a lock so no one gets in. I slowly put my shirts and pants into the bag, along with toothpaste. What if the drop in air pressure causes my toothpaste to burst? I better put it in a bag. Will I have enough time to get to the plane and get on?"*

Desensitization Protocol

Once you have your 10 detailed descriptions, you are ready to begin desensitization. Here's the process:

1. Select the lowest hierarchy item. Practice your preferred relaxation technique until you are deeply relaxed.
2. Begin fantasizing about the item you have selected.

You may read what you have in your description, adding details as they come to mind. Or imagine you are describing the item to a friend, including as much detail as possible. **The instant you experience the slightest anxiety, STOP. Relax. Then start over with the same item**. Keep repeating this cycle: fantasizing about or describing the item – relaxing – fantasizing or describing the item – relaxing until you are able to fantasize or describe every detail. When you can do this and your level of anxiety is no more than half what it was initially, you're done with that item. Next session, continue with Item 2 on your hierarchy.

EXERCISES

> *The Mindfulness Exercise Challenge. Try practicing a five-minute version of your home mindfulness exercise before completing any chapter exercise.*

23.1 What's Wrong with This Hierarchy?

Making a desensitization hierarchy is more difficult than it may seem. The following hierarchies have many mistakes. Can you find them?

THEME: Going to the dentist to have my teeth worked on.

10. Having the dentist replace an entire tooth
9. Breaking my arm
8. Having to stay home a week because of stomach flu
7. Having a tooth pulled
6. The dentist telling me he has to pull a tooth
5. Talking to my minister about something I did wrong.
4. Having to stay overnight with my girlfriend's mother
3. Having my teeth cleaned
2. At a party, introducing myself to a person I want to meet
1. Walking home, thinking about the dentist

THEME: Test anxiety

10. I am now in the middle of taking a very important and difficult test.
9. I have just started taking a very important and difficult test.
8. The professor is starting to distribute the very important and difficult test.
7. I am studying at home freaking out about my very important and difficult test.
6. I am studying the wrong textbook.
5. I spent the weekend partying rather than studying.
4. I told my roommate that my exam would be very easy and important.
3. I avoided studying for a week.
2. I couldn't relax.
1. I realized I have to take additional courses in math.

23.2 Creating Hierarchy Descriptions

First assemble 10 blank cards (or sheets of paper). Then create a detailed description for each item on your hierarchy, one per card (or sheet). Remember: (1) Keep it realistic (you are not writing a fantastic horror script!). (2) Make it very vivid, including specific and concrete details.

23.3 Mindful Desensitization

In this exercise we practice a special type of mindfulness. First, select a specific stressor in your life, something that causes worry. Then deliberately spend about 5 minutes fantasizing about it. Then start a session of yoga or muscle mindfulness. Practice a complete session. Next, practice mindfulness. Whenever thoughts about your stressor come up, simply put them aside (meta-awareness and dereification).

Stress & Coping
Eye of Mindfulness Journal

Chapter 24

Relapse Prevention

© comussu/Shutterstock.com

Often the tools of stress management are most effective when one plans ahead. One very useful way of planning ahead involves considering the possibilities of setback and failure. This is the idea underlying relapse prevention.

Marlatt and Gordon (1984) describe a relapse as a special type of stressor, one in which your attempted coping efforts unexpectedly do not work and you face failure and setback. You may forget your lines while giving a lecture. You may get a grade of D instead of the expected A in a course. Perhaps your boss rejects your request for a modest raise.

Such unexpected failures or setbacks can lead to stress-producing distorted thinking. You may believe you are helpless, or have to worry constantly to solve your problems.

Relapse prevention treats the possibility of failure and setback as a stressor in itself. It is a way of insuring yourself against failure or setback. You anticipate possible setbacks, and develop "Plan Bs" or alternative backup coping strategies. There are two types of relapse strategies: comebacks and fallbacks.

Comeback Strategies (Your Plan B)

A **comeback strategy** is a very simple alternative plan, one you put into effect once it becomes clear your plans are not working. For example:

> *"Tomorrow I will take my defective radio back to the store and ask for my money back. Even though I don't have the receipt, I did buy the radio yesterday and know the clerk. If I chicken out and don't go to the store, my backup plan is to practice relaxation for half an hour and assertively return the piece of de-*

fective merchandise tomorrow and ask for my money back. That will give me a chance to practice my relapse prevention skills."

Fallback Strategies (Your Safety Net)

What do you do when coping and comeback fail to work? A **fallback strategy** is your coping option of last resort, one you use when all else fails. A fallback strategy is something like the safety net circus performers use when they swing high over the crowd. If the rope breaks, at least they will be caught by the net. A fallback strategy is like the extra stash of cash you may have tucked away for a rainy day. Sometimes the best fallback strategies are positive, realistic, and supportive things we say to ourselves, such as (Meichenbaum, 1985):

> *"Well, life goes on."*
>
> *"Everyone makes mistakes."*
>
> *"I still love myself (or have a loving family) in spite of my problems."*
>
> *"Let's look at things in perspective. Life is too short to make too much of this problem."*
>
> *"I'll treat this as water under the bridge."*
>
> *"Maybe I'll learn somehow from this."*

Phases of Stress

One effective way of anticipating relapse is to divide an upcoming stress event into stages. I find it useful to think of four phases: pre-stress, onset-stress, mid-stress, and post-stress. Then, consider comeback and fallback strategies for each.

The pre-stress phase refers to the time before a stress event. Onset-stress is the moment the event begins. Mid-stress is the actual stress event. And post-stress is the time after the event is over. For example, imagine you are about to interview for a job. Here are the phases:

> ***Pre-stress.*** *The day before the interview. You are thinking about and planning for the interview.*
>
> ***Onset-Stress.*** *You arrive at the setting of the interview, walk in the office, and shake hands with the interviewer.*

Mid-stress. *The interview starts, continues, and ends.*

Post-stress. *It's over. You return home.*

Preparing Your Relapse Strategies

Preparing your relapse prevention strategies involves three steps:

1. Identify the four phases of your stress event.
2. Identify what might go wrong in each stress.
3. Create a comeback and fallback strategy for each. This may include specific actions or thoughts.

Meichenbaum (1985) and others provide a number of examples of comeback and fall-back thoughts for each phase of stress.

Pre-stress

"It's a good idea to practice problem-solving, regardless of the outcome."
"Most people get a little tense before a stressful encounter."
"Stress energy can actually help me do better."
"I'll do my best, and that is all I can reasonably expect of myself."
"I will just keep my mind on what I'm doing, rather than on worrying."

Onset-Stress

"Things are starting. Stress is normal."
"Stay with the plan. Keep organized."
"Let's try a quickie relaxation. Just breathe slowly, out of the lips."
"Soon this whole thing will be over."
"Most people don't notice when you get cold hands or feel nervous."

Mid-stress

"Keep on going. I'm practicing using my coping skills."
"Think realistically."
"Take it easy; don't try to do it all at once."
"Makes no sense to take setbacks personally."
"Remember to take a positive, problem-solving perspective."
"Let's not catastrophize."
"Don't focus on the stress, just the job."

Post-stress

"Let's analyze objectively what went right and where there is room for improvement."
"This is a learning opportunity."
"Remember to recognize what went right."
"No one's perfect."
"I've learned what to do differently the next time."
"Time to relax!"

EXERCISES

> ***The Mindfulness Exercise Challenge.*** *Try practicing a five-minute version of your home mindfulness exercise before completing any chapter exercise.*

24.1 Phases of a Stressor

Identify a stressor in your life in which relapse is possible. In the spaces provided, describe pre-stress, onset-stress, mid-stress, and post-stress phases. Be as concrete and specific as possible.

PRE-STRESS

ONSET-STRESS

MID-STRESS

POST-STRESS

24.2 What Could Go Wrong?

For each phase of the stressors you described in Exercise 24.1, identify one or two things that might go wrong, one or two coping failures or setbacks you might experience. Then, think of a comeback and fallback strategy (actions / thoughts) for each.

PRE-STRESS

Relapse Possibilities

Comeback/Fallback

ONSET-STRESS

Relapse Possibilities

Comeback/Fallback

MID-STRESS

Relapse Possibilities

Comeback/Fallback

POST-STRESS

Relapse Possibilities

Comeback/Fallback

© iunewind / Shutterstock.com

Chapter 25

Breathing Exercises

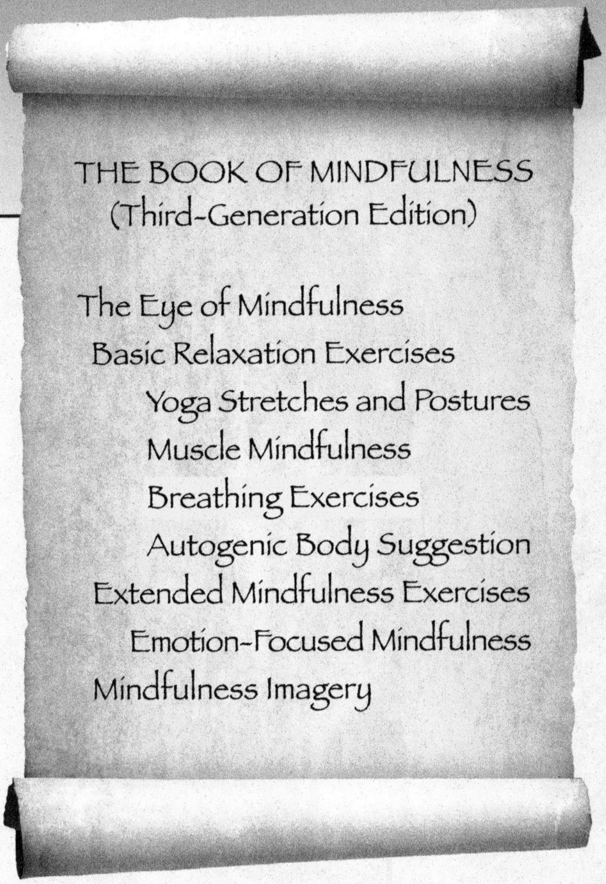

© Vadim Sadovski / Shutterstock.com

Breathing exercises have a special place in mindfulness training, both as a warmup and as an actual focus of attention. Outside of mindfulness, breathing exercises are typically woven into other approaches and often are presented alone as unified strategy. Given their importance, we will devote additional time to this important and complex component of relaxation and mindfulness.

Orientation

We breathe to bring in air and oxygen, and, more importantly, to expel waste gas or carbon dioxide. Overall the goal is to maintain a proper balance of oxygen and carbon dioxide.

Breathing is normally involuntary. However, we can deliberately modulate the pace of our breathing. Stressed breathing maintains arousal and can continue as a source of distraction. To understand, we need to explore the mechanics of breathing.

The process of breathing is complex and involves more than simply breathing in and out. First, at least three groups of muscles are involved. The **trapezius** muscle is shaped like a trapezoid, "trapezium," or square triangle. Generally, it can be referred to as the "shoulder muscle." During stressed breathing the upper and middle trapezius muscles rise and fall, drawing air in and out of the lungs.

Intercostal Muscles

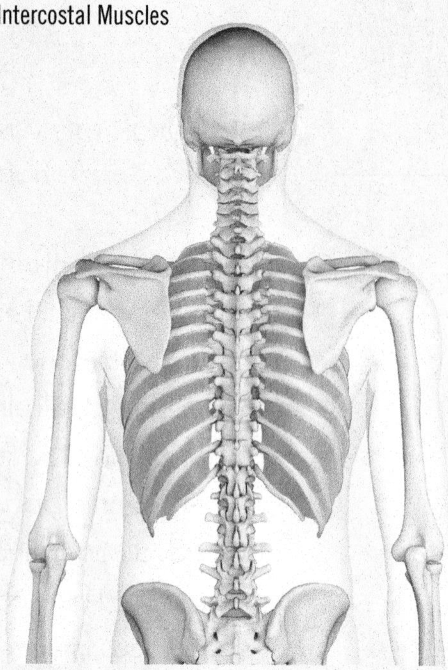

Trapezius Muscles

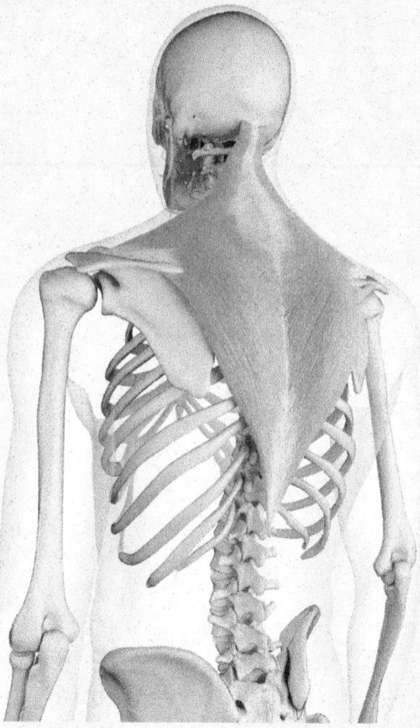

Diaphragm

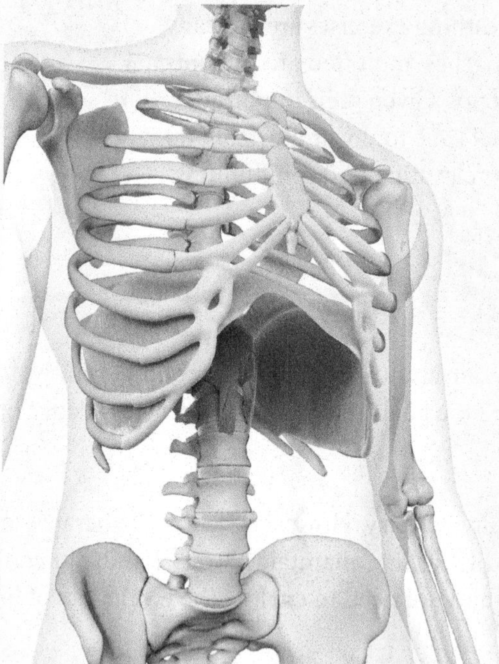

The **intercostal** muscles surround the ribs and form the chest wall. They expand and shrink the chest as we breathe in and out.

The **diaphragm** is like the skin of a kettle drum, and separates the stomach from the lungs. When we inhale, the diaphragm pulls down, like a piston, and the lungs expand with air. When we exhale, the diaphragm muscles relax inward, move up, and force air out.

Movement of Diaphragm During Breathing

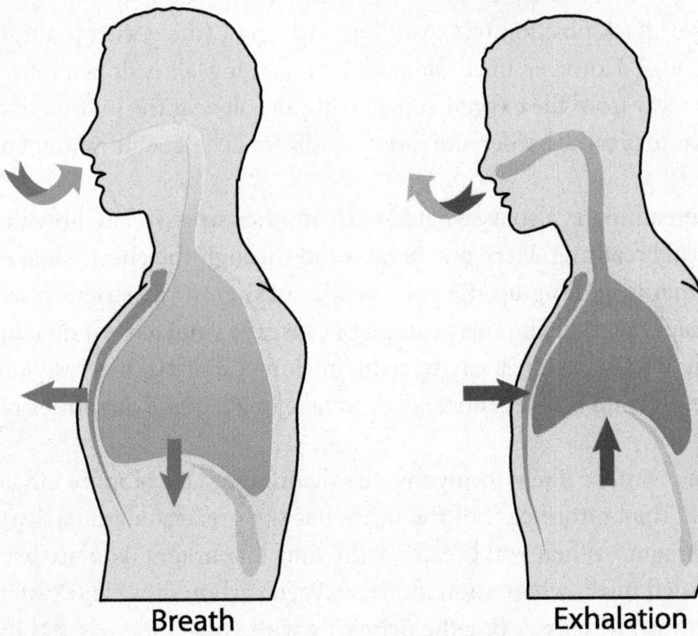

When we breathe in, oxygen-rich air enters the lungs, and life-giving oxygen transfers to the bloodstream. The "exhaust" gas, carbon dioxide (CO2), is transferred from the blood to the air in the lungs and exhaled is transfer of oxygen takes place in tiny air sacks (bubbles) of tissue called **alveoli**, near the bottom of the lungs, closest to the diaphragm. Overall, the flow of air into the lung follows this path: Nose – Ethmoid sinuses – Pharynx – Trachea – Bronchial tubes – Diaphragm. It is useful to understand this path because some breathing exercises involve attending to the flow of air through it.

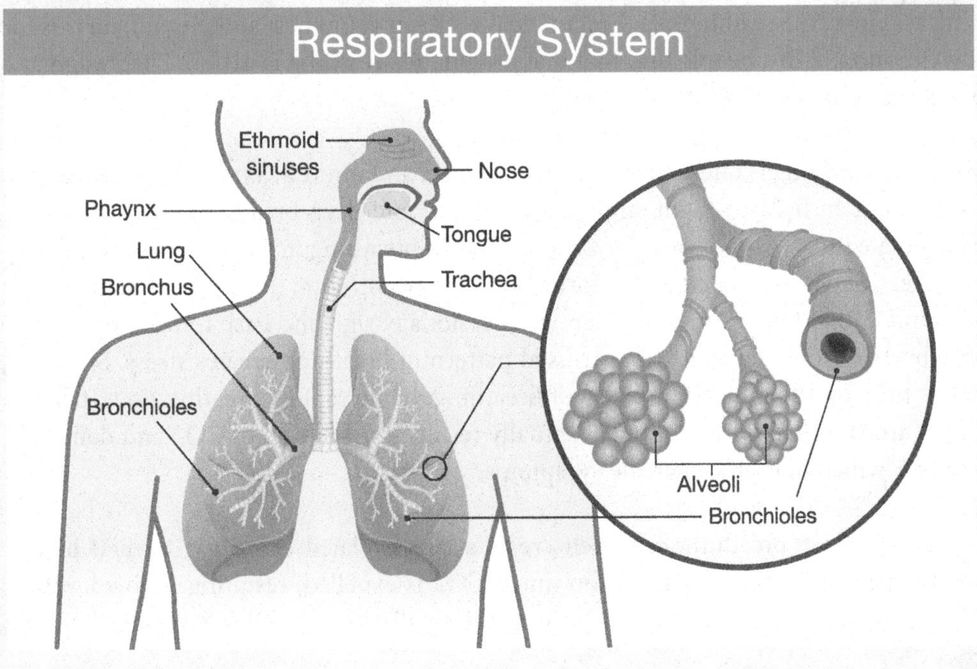

Stressed breathing is more likely to incorporate the intercostal and trapezius muscles. Note the defensive attack position of expanding one's chest (the gorilla pounding his or her pumped up chest). However, in chest/shoulder breathing, air is drawn into the upper part of the lungs, away from the oxygen-transferring alveoli near the bottom of the lungs. As a result, one has to breathe harder and more rapidly for an adequate amount of oxygen.

Chest/shoulder breathing is also associated with another stress-related breathing condition, paradoxical breathing. Here one breathes in through the chest while pulling in one's abdomen, that is, puffing up the chest while sucking in the stomach. Note what happens to the diaphragm during this process: Because the stomach is pulled in, it pushes the diaphragm up into the chest cavity, reducing lung capacity. As a result, breathing is even more stressful and it takes more effort to take in adequate quantities of air.

Relaxed breathing is more likely to involve the diaphragm and is more efficient. The reason is simple. The bottom part of the lungs has the greatest air capacity and rests next to the diaphragm. When you breathe with your diaphragm, you are bringing air to where it is needed most, where more of the oxygen carbon dioxide transfer is likely to occur. In contrast, when you breathe primarily with your trapezius and intercostal muscles, by raising and lowering your shoulders or heaving in and out with your chest, you bring air where it does less good, the midsection and upper part of the lungs.

It is easy to demonstrate the efficiency of diaphragmatic breathing. Simply sit in a comfortable position. Rest your hands over your abdomen. When you breathe in, your abdomen will extend out. When you exhale, your abdomen will pull in. Now, attempt to breathe only through your chest, not your diaphragm. That is, keep your abdomen perfectly still as you chest breathe. Do this for two minutes. Now relax, and while placing your hands over your abdomen, breathe in and out through your stomach. This will involve breathing diaphragmatically. Keep your chest still. Again, do this for two minutes. Most people find that diaphragmatic breathing is easier. Diaphragmatic breathing is more efficient.

Stressed breathing is often rapid, shallow or deep, and uneven, a pattern that may have some value in fight-or-flight emergencies. Rapid and deep breathing can bring in an immediate infusion of oxygen for action. Shallow breathing makes us less noticeable to attackers, and is associated with effortful active concentration (on a potential threat, for example). Breathing is uneven when we occasionally sigh and gasp to take in an overdue breath. However, in time, a stressed pattern of breathing creates stress. Spending more time on the inhalation phase of breathing, while rapidly breathing out, triggers stress arousal. Shallow breathing eventually results in a buildup of CO_2 and deficits in oxygen, which in itself can create symptoms.

Rapid and deep breathing can itself create a stress-related condition termed **hyperventilation.** In hyperventilation too much CO_2 is expelled, resulting in low levels of CO_2 in the blood. Low blood CO_2 causes the small blood vessels leading to the brain and spinal cord to constrict, reducing blood flow to the central nervous system. This is termed **hypocapnia,** a condition associated with anxiety-related symptoms, panic, dizziness, and eventually unconsciousness.

In sum, stressed breathing is likely to be rapid, uneven, and shallow or deep. It is more likely to involve the chest and shoulder muscles. All of these may persist as after-effects and interfere with recovery and relaxation.

Relaxed breathing is more likely to involve the diaphragm and has a pace that is slow and even, and at times deep or shallow (depending on whether one is vigorous or inactive). Such breathing is diaphragmatic and is less likely to involve the trapezius or intercostal muscles. During inhalation, the diaphragm muscle moves down, drawing air into the lungs and pushing the stomach out. During exhalation, the diaphragm relaxes and moves up drawing the abdomen in. Diaphragmatic breathing is relaxed because it is most efficient. Most of the lung's alveoli, those tiny air sacks through which oxygen is transferred to the blood, are near the bottom of the lungs, close to the diaphragm. When we breathe diaphragmatically, we draw air down to the highest concentration of alveoli, where the "work" of oxygen-transfer takes place. Thus, diaphragmatic breathing uses the least amount of energy.

In addition, relaxed breathing has a special rhythm. Exhalation is slow and even. Initially it may be deep, and later (when one is relaxed and needs less oxygen) effortlessly shallow. Although muscle tension is generated during inhalation, the chest muscles and diaphragm relax while air is quietly expelled. When air has been exhaled, there is a pause until the need for oxygen prompts an automatic and relaxed inhalation. The inhalation phase occurs quietly and easily. Generally relaxed exhalation takes twice as long (6 seconds) as inhalation (3 seconds).

Slow, shallow breathing, may contribute to relaxation by increasing blood CO2 levels. Moderate CO2 elevation can lower heart rate, dilate peripheral blood vessels, depress arousing cortical brain activity, and evoke a general sense of mild somnolence (Lichstein, 1988). Indeed, early stages of sleep, when one moves from wakefulness to drowsiness, are associated, in part, with increments of CO2.

Instructions

There are thousands of breathing exercises. I have selected eight that are safe, easy, and can be presented without visual demonstration. They represent three general categories of breathing exercises available: (1) active deep breathing exercises in which breathing is woven into a stretch or other vigorous physical activity, (2) diaphragmatic breathing exercises, and (3) passive exercises. These can be presented as a stand-alone sequence or incorporated into a mindfulness protocol replacing the body/breath segment of the Eye of Mindfulness.

We start with three active deep breathing exercises, that generally involve pacing simple movement with the flow of breath. *Slight Bowing Forward Breathing* involves exhaling while slightly bowing forward, and inhaling while sitting up. *Leaning Back Breathing* involves inhaling while slightly leaning back, and exhaling while sitting up. With *Occasional Deep Breaths,* one deliberately and slowly breathes in deeply, pauses, and breathes out. Each of these exercises is very easy and gentle with little risk. Under proper yoga supervision, the movement for each can be extended for a more prolonged stretch.

The next four exercises focus on the diaphragm. *Stomach count* breathing starts by gently placing your hands over your abdomen. Breathe naturally. Slowly count as you breathe in, and again as you breathe out. If you count more while breathing in, exhale more slowly until your count for inhalation and exhalation are the same. Eventually exhalation should last twice as long as inhalation. Continue with this pattern. After five inhalations, increase your exhalation count until it takes twice as long as for inhalation. This increases the amount of carbon dioxide in the blood and is soothing.

For *Stomach Squeeze Breathing*, one spreads one's hands over the abdomen, with fingers touching the bottom of the ribs. Gently squeeze in as you exhale. Relax the fingers as you inhale. In *Stomach Touch Breathing* do not squeeze in. Simply feel the movement of the abdomen as you inhale and exhale. *Book Breathing* is a way of overcoming paradoxical breathing (sucking the abdomen in while breathing in). Rest a book or notebook with a stiff back on the abdomen. If sitting up, you can balance the lower edge of the book on your lap. Adjust the book so it moves noticeably as you inhale and exhale. Once adjusted, simply observe the book and breathe such a way that the book extends in the air as you inhale, indicating extension of your abdomen (and diaphragmatic breathing).

The final breathing exercises introduce a pace that is slow and even. These exercises are more likely to correct the balance of $CO2$ in the blood (combating hyperventilation). *Sniffing in through Nose* involves breathing in with a rapid succession of short breaths. Each inhalation is a sequence of short sniffs, that might be thought of as the ticking of a clock or water dripping from a faucet. One then exhales normally through the nose. *Exhaling through the Lips* involves opening the mouth slightly and exhaling through the lips smoothly and easily. One inhales naturally through the nose. Alternatively you can *curl your tongue*, making a tube and breathe out through your tongue. Breathe in through your nose. *Focused Breathing* involves simply attending the breathing process, and air as it flows in through the nose, breathing passages in the throat, and the lungs (see figure of respiratory system).

Our breathing exercises are easily practiced with minimal external guidance. In this sense they are portable. In addition, they are modular. Specific exercises can be practiced from the entire sequence. All are to be practiced in a chair. Today, sitting is the modern human stress position—sitting in a car during a traffic jam, sitting at a work desk, sitting by the phone. It makes sense to learn relaxation and mindfulness exercises in a position where they will be used. Second, by practicing all exercises in our program in the same seated position, we standardize the position. Any detected differences between exercises can be attributed to the exercise itself rather than whether or not one was lying down, seated, or standing. For example, if a practitioner performed breathing exercises while standing, and progressive muscle relaxation while lying down, any differences between the effects of techniques would be confounded by the practice position. ("Was muscle relaxation relaxing because I did it while lying down, or because the exercise itself worked for me?")

Here is a summary of our traditional breathing exercises:

ACTIVE DEEP BREATHING

- Slight Bowing Forward Breathing
- Leaning Back Breathing
- Occasional Deep Breaths

DIAPHRAGMATIC BREATHING

- Stomach Count Breathing
- Stomach Squeeze Breathing
- Stomach Touch Breathing
- Book Breathing

PASSIVE BREATHING

- Sniffing in through nose
- Exhaling through Lips
- Tongue Tube Breathing
- Focused Breathing

DOING IT MINDFULLY

There are several ways of turning a breathing exercise into mindful meditation.

Each breath can be your meditation. Focus on where the breath is. Attend to it in your nose – sinuses – pharynx – trachea (throat) – bronchial tubes – lungs – in and out of your "abdomen."

Focus on making your breath as slow, smooth, and gentle as possible.

Focus on the sensations associated with breathing. How does it feel? What does the pause between each breath feel like?

Simply be the mindful observer. Watch the breath come and go on its own, without trying to force it to occur in any way.

ACTIVE DEEP BREATHING SCRIPT

MAKING YOUR OWN RECORDING: Read very slowly and calmly. Your voice should be fresh and alert. Try to pace your voice with your own breathing. Emphasize your own breathing out as you read instructions to breathe out. Breathe slowly, smoothly, and evenly while reading. The person listening to your recording should notice how relaxed your breathing is.

Time: 10 minutes for active, 10 minutes for diaphragmatic, and 10 minutes for passive.

(Do every day. After one session fill out an R/M Tracker)

Orientation

In this exercise we relax by breathing in a way that is slow, deep, and even.

We will do so in a way that involves greater use of the abdomen or diaphragm.

First make sure you are seated upright in a comfortable position. Place your feet flat on the floor. Close your eyes.

1. Slight Bowing Breathing

In this exercise we relax by breathing in a way that is full and deep and even.

For each exercise that follows, I will first explain how it's done, and then you can practice.

Begin by making sure you are seated in an upright position.

Place your feet flat on the floor.

And close your eyes.

[PAUSE 3 SECONDS]

Let the tensions of the day flow away.

[PAUSE 3 SECONDS]

Let yourself breathe in a natural and easy way.

In and out, let your breathing become more relaxed.

Let yourself breathe in a natural and easy way.

[PAUSE 3 SECONDS]

We are ready to begin.

Now, let your arms hang by your sides.

[PAUSE 3 SECONDS]

Make sure you are seated in an upright position.

[PAUSE 3 SECONDS]

Here is how we will do our first exercise.

Gently exhale as you bow forward a few inches.

[PAUSE]

And then gently inhale as you slowly sit up.

Make your movements smooth and effortless.

Let's begin, take in a deep breath.

And bow forward a few inches while breathing out.

Pause, then breathe in.

Do this at your own pace a few times for the next minute or so.

[PAUSE 15 SECONDS]

Slowly and smoothly.

[PAUSE 15 SECONDS]

Take your time.

[PAUSE 15 SECONDS]

Do not force yourself.

[PAUSE 15 SECONDS]

And when you are ready, resume sitting up for the next exercise.

Let both arms hang by your sides.

[PAUSE 5 SECONDS]

2. Leaning Back Breathing

Let your arms hang by your sides.

Then lean back while taking in a slow, full breath.

Slowly sit up while breathing out.

[PAUSE]

We can begin.

Slowly, smoothly, and gently, lean back and breathe in, and gently sit up while breathing out.

Continue breathing this way for about a minute.

[PAUSE 15 SECONDS]

Let the air flow very smoothly and gently.

[PAUSE 15 SECONDS]

Take your time.

[PAUSE 15 SECONDS]

There is no need to hurry.

[PAUSE 15 SECONDS]

And gently return to an upright position for the next exercise.

Let your arms hang by your sides.

[PAUSE 10 SECONDS]

3. Occasional Deep Breaths

Let yourself breathe easily and naturally.

[PAUSE]

In our next exercise, simply take in a full deep breath, filling your lungs and abdomen with good, refreshing air.

Do this now.

[PAUSE]

And when you are ready, relax.

[PAUSE]

And slowly let the air flow out, very smoothly and gently.

[PAUSE]

And now, just continue breathing normally for a while, without taking in deep breaths.

[PAUSE]

Do not attempt to force yourself to breathe in any particular way.

[PAUSE]

Just let the air come in and out on its own.

[PAUSE 10 SECONDS]

And again, when you are ready, take in another full deep breath, filling your lungs with good, energizing air.

Feel the calm and strength it brings.

[PAUSE]

And, when ready, gently and smoothly exhale.

[PAUSE]

Then resume breathing in a normal way, easily in and out.

[PAUSE 10 SECONDS]

And again, when you are ready, take in a full deep breath, filling your lungs with good, energizing air.

Feel the calm and strength it brings.

[PAUSE]

And, when ready, gently and smoothly exhale.

[PAUSE]

Then resume breathing in a normal way, easily in and out.

[PAUSE 10 SECONDS]

DIAPHRAGMATIC BREATHING SCRIPT

4. Stomach Count Breathing

Sit up in your chair and open your hands and fingers and place them over your stomach.

[PAUSE 3 SECONDS]

Spread your fingers comfortably apart so they cover your entire stomach, then with your thumbs touch the bottom part of your chest.

Begin counting as you breathe in.

Start counting again as you breathe out.

[PAUSE 15 SECONDS]

If your inhalation is slower than your exhalation, gently breathe out a bit more slowly until the count is the same for breathing in and breathing out.

[PAUSE 15 SECONDS]

Slow your breathing out until the count is twice what it is for breathing in.

[PAUSE 15 SECONDS]

5. Stomach Squeeze Breathing

In this exercise gently press your fingers into your stomach as you breathe out, and release your fingers as you breathe in.

[PAUSE]

Now, very easily, take a full breath, filling your stomach and chest completely.

And when you are ready to exhale, firmly press in with your hands and fingers, squeezing in as if you were squeezing the air out of your stomach.

[PAUSE 3 SECONDS]

And when you are ready to inhale, gradually release your fingers and let your stomach relax and breathe in as if your stomach were filling with air.

[PAUSE 3 SECONDS]

Breathe easily and completely.

[PAUSE 3 SECONDS]

Now continue breathing this way, squeezing your stomach as you are breathing out, and relaxing your fingers as you breathe in.

[PAUSE 3 SECONDS]

Do not force yourself to breathe at a hurried pace.

[PAUSE 3 SECONDS]

Take your time.

[PAUSE 3 SECONDS]

Breathe very gently and very easily.

[PAUSE 3 SECONDS]

Focus on what it feels like to breathe completely and fully. Notice the awareness breathing brings.

[PAUSE 3 SECONDS]

At your own pace, continue breathing evenly in and evenly out. Do not hurry. Take your time.

[PAUSE 3 SECONDS]

Focus on the even flow of air as it rushes in and out of your lungs.

[PAUSE 3 SECONDS]

Now, when you are ready, exhale and relax your fingers.

6. Stomach Touch Breathing

Sit up in your chair and make sure your hands and fingers are placed over your stomach.

[PAUSE]

This time, let your hands and fingers remain relaxed.

Do not press in. And gently breathe in, as if you were filling your stomach with air, and exhale, so you can feel the rise and fall of your stomach.

[PAUSE]

We are ready to begin.
As you breathe in, let the air come in on its own, as if it were filling your stomach.

[PAUSE]

Feel the stomach filling, like a large, soft balloon, filling completely.

[PAUSE]

And when you are ready to exhale, keep your fingers and hands relaxed. Let the air flow out on its own, gently and slowly.

[PAUSE]

When you have breathed out, pull your stomach in gently toward your backbone.

[PAUSE]

Continue breathing this way, slowly and easily.
Notice your stomach filling and emptying with air.

[PAUSE]

Notice the air coming in and out.

[PAUSE 5 SECONDS]

Very smoothly and easily.

[PAUSE 5 SECONDS]

7. Book Breathing

This exercise is optional.
You can skip it if you desire.
And you might want to practice this exercise while lying on your back on the floor.
And you need a book.

[PAUSE 5 SECONDS]

And now gently place a book over your abdomen.
Adjust your book so it does not fall off.

[PAUSE]
And let yourself breathe easily and naturally.

[PAUSE]

In and out.

[PAUSE]

There is no hurry to breathe in any particular way.

[PAUSE]

Very smoothly and easily.

[PAUSE]

And now, very gently breathe in, filling your abdomen with air.

Breathe in such a way that you can notice the movement of the book resting on your abdomen.

You may adjust your book so you can see its movement more clearly.

[PAUSE]

The up and down movement of your book shows if you are breathing using your abdomen.

[PAUSE]

And when you have taken a full breath of air, gently and slowly exhale.

[PAUSE]
Let the air flow out very slowly and smoothly.

[PAUSE]

See if you can notice the movement of the book.

[PAUSE]

And when you are ready, try this again.

[PAUSE]

If you need to, adjust the position of your book.

[PAUSE]

Keep your chest still. Try not to fill your chest.

[PAUSE]

And let air flow into your abdomen, so you notice it moving.

[PAUSE]

Slowly and gently.

[PAUSE]

And when you have inhaled all the way, pause, and exhale.

[PAUSE]

Continue breathing this way for about a minute.

[PAUSE]

See if you can breathe in such a way that you can move your book when breathing in and out.

[PAUSE 30 SECONDS]

And now, gently let go of what you are attending to. We have completed our exercise.

~ END OF SCRIPT ~

PASSIVE BREATHING

8. Sniffing in through Nose

Rest your hands comfortably in your lap.

[PAUSE]

Let yourself relax.

[PAUSE]

As you breathe in, imagine you are sniffing a very delicate flower.
Breathe in slowly with many gentle little sniffs. We can begin.

[PAUSE]

Let the sniffing flow of breath into your nose be as smooth and gentle as possible, so you barely rustle a petal.

Take a full breath.

[PAUSE]

And when ready, relax, letting yourself breathe out slowly and naturally, without effort.

[PAUSE]

Continue breathing this way, breathing in and evenly at your own pace.

[PAUSE]

Calmly focus on the clear inner calm that breathes in a way that is slow, full, and even.

[PAUSE]

Notice the refreshing and energizing rush quietly move in and out of your lungs.

[PAUSE]

See how far you can follow the inward flow of air.
Can you feel it move past your nostrils?
Can you feel the air in the passages of your nose?
Take your time.

[PAUSE]

Breathe easily and fully.

[PAUSE]

Let yourself be fully aware of your breathing.

[PAUSE 10 SECONDS]

9. Exhaling through Lips

Take a slow deep breath and pause.

[PAUSE]

In our next exercise, breathe out slowly though your lips, as if you were blowing at a candle flame just enough to make it flicker, but not go out. Breathe in through your nose.

[PAUSE]

Start by taking a deep breath.
And when you are ready, gently exhale, making the stream of air that passes through your lips as you exhale as smooth and gentle as possible.

[PAUSE]

Let tension flow out with every breath.

[PAUSE 4 SECONDS]

Let the gentle movement of air dissolve any feelings of tension you might have.

[PAUSE 5 SECONDS]

Focus on the easy flow of air in as it refreshes and renews.

[PAUSE 5 SECONDS]

Let each breath fill you with peace and calm energy.

[PAUSE 5 SECONDS]

Let yourself breathe fully and evenly.

[PAUSE 10 SECONDS]

10. Tongue Tube Breathing

Curl your tongue into a tube.
And breathe out through your tongue.

[PAUSE 5 SECONDS]

Breathe in through your nose.

[PAUSE 5 SECONDS]

Out through tongue, in through nose.

[PAUSE 15 SECONDS]

Focused Breathing
Relax your tongue.
Simply breathe in a relaxed manner, in and out through your nose.

[PAUSE]

Try not to force your breathing.

[PAUSE]

Become fully aware of the air as it rushes in and out, flowing into and out of your lungs.

[PAUSE]

Filling your body with refreshing and renewing air.

[PAUSE]

Calmly focus on the unhurried rhythm of your breathing.
Let yourself breathe effortlessly, without strain.

[PAUSE 10 SECONDS]

Focus on the even flow of air as it moves in and out of your lungs through your nose.

[PAUSE 10 SECONDS]

Notice how the easy flow of air energizes and relaxes you.

[PAUSE 5 SECONDS]

The flow of air brings peace and inner strength.

[PAUSE 5 SECONDS]

11. Focused Breathing

Simply breathe in a relaxed manner, in and out through your nose.

[PAUSE]

Try not to force your breathing.

[PAUSE]

Become fully aware of the air as it rushes in and out, flowing into and out of your lungs.

[PAUSE]

Filling your body with refreshing and renewing air.

[PAUSE]

Calmly focus on the unhurried rhythm of your breathing.
Let yourself breathe effortlessly, without strain.

[PAUSE 10 SECONDS]

Focus on the even flow of air as it moves in and out of your lungs through your nose.

[PAUSE 10 SECONDS]

Notice how the easy flow of air energizes and relaxes you.

[PAUSE 5 SECONDS]

The flow of air brings peace and inner strength.

[PAUSE 5 SECONDS]

Let go of what you are attending to.
Slowly open your eyes all the way.
Take a deep breath and stretch. This completes our exercise.

~ END OF SCRIPT ~

EYE OF MINDFULNESS
BRIEF SCRIPT
(Practice this until you select your home exercise)
Do every day. After one session fill out an R/M Tracker

BODY/BREATH SCANNING

Imagine tension flowing from your body with every outgoing breath. Flowing from the top of your head to your toes. Flowing from your head, neck, shoulders, arms, hands, back, abdomen, legs, and feet.

[PAUSE 60 SECONDS]

Attend to the easy flow of breath, in and out through your nose, throat, chest, and belly.

[PAUSE 60 SECONDS]

FOCUSED ATTENTION MEDITATION

Select your preferred meditation focus, perhaps the word "One. . . one . . . one" slowing going over and over in your mind like an echo.
Attend to it for the next few minutes.

Whenever your mind wanders, that's OK. You can change if you want.
You are always the quiet observer. Accept what comes and goes. Return to your focus again and again.

[PAUSE 6 MINUTES]

MINDFULNESS

And now we move on to mindfulness meditation. Simply attend to sounds that come and go. Or open your eyes halfway and attend to all stimuli that come and go. Or do both.

If you slip into body/breath work, that's ok.

If you slip into centered focus meditation, that's ok.

Return to mindfulness.

You are the quiet observer.

[PAUSE 6 MINUTES]

Gently let go of what you are attending to.

~ END OF SCRIPT ~

THE R/M TRACKER

WHAT DID YOU FEEL OR EXPERIENCE DURING THESE **BREATHING EXERCISES:** _______?

CLICK BOXES USING THIS KEY

(SKIP ITEMS YOU DON'T UNDERSTAND OR DIDN'T FEEL OR EXPERIENCE)

☒❑❑❑	☒☒❑❑	☒☒☒❑	☒☒☒☒
Felt this SLIGHTLY	Felt this MODERATELY	Felt this VERY MUCH	Felt this EXTREMELY (the most ever)

1. ***FAR AWAY*** *and distant from the troubles around me.*	❑❑❑❑
2. ***PHYSICALLY RELAXED.*** *Muscles relaxed, loose, limp, warm and heavy. Breathing slow, even, and easy.*	❑❑❑❑
3 ***AT EASE, AT PEACE.***	❑❑❑❑
4. ***REFRESHED.***	❑❑❑❑
5. ***PLEASANT MIND WANDERING.*** *Undirected, random positive thoughts.*	❑❑❑❑
6. *Lost in* ***FANTASY*** *and* ***DAYDREAMING.***	❑❑❑❑
7. *Periods of sustained, continuous* ***FOCUS. ABSORPTION.***	❑❑❑❑
8. ***CENTERED, GROUNDED.***	❑❑❑❑
9. ***QUIET.*** *Still, few thoughts. Little mind wandering.*	❑❑❑❑
10. ***UNBOTHERED.*** *Accepting. When I had a negative thought or feeling, I didn't get caught up in it. No judging, clinging, pushing away, figuring things out.*	❑❑❑❑
11. ***EASY, EFFORTLESS.*** *Effortless to let go, put thoughts aside, sustain focus.*	❑❑❑❑
12. *I felt like an* ***OBSERVER*** *standing aside and watching what happens.*	❑❑❑❑
13. ***CLEAR, AWAKE, AWARE.*** *I saw things as they really are.*	❑❑❑❑
14. ***INTERESTED, CURIOUS, FASCINATED.***	❑❑❑❑
15. *Things seemed* ***BEAUTIFUL.***	❑❑❑❑
16. ***GOING DEEPER.*** *Things seemed unexpected, new, changing, opening up,being revealed. Felt like I was in a different place or space.*	❑❑❑❑
17. *Sense of* ***SPACIOUSNESS, EXPANSIVENESS.***	❑❑❑❑
18. *I felt the* ***SENSE OF SOMETHING GREATER*** *than myself (God, a higher power, spirit, energy, love, or consciousness.); God is with me.*	❑❑❑❑
19. *A sense of* ***MEANING, PURPOSE, DIRECTION.***	❑❑❑❑
20. *I felt* ***REVERENT, PRAYERFUL.***	❑❑❑❑
21. ***AWE / WONDER, DEEP MYSTERY*** *of things beyond my understanding.*	❑❑❑❑
22. *I felt a profound personal meaningful* ***"SPIRITUAL"*** *or* ***"MYSTICAL"*** *experience -- sudden awakening or insight.* • *Felt an underlying hidden* ***TRUTH.*** • *Feeling* ***AT ONE.*** • *Feelings so profound they* ***COULD NOT BE PUT INTO WORDS.***	❑❑❑❑
23. ***HAPPY, OPTIMISTIC, TRUSTING.***	❑❑❑❑
24. ***LOVING, CARING.***	❑❑❑❑
25. ***THANKFUL.*** *Grateful.*	❑❑❑❑

Stress & Coping
Eye of Mindfulness Journal

LESSON 6

BASICS OF ASSERTIVENESS

Chapter 26

Assertiveness

© Dewald Kirsten/Shutterstock.com

To be assertive is to honestly and effectively say what you want, think, and feel, while respecting the wants, thoughts, and feelings of others.

Assertiveness training is a standard part of most stress management programs. It is usually contrasted with passivity, aggressiveness, and at times, passive-aggressiveness.

Passive people do not say what they want, think, or feel. They keep to themselves, unheard and unrecognized. Problems are left unresolved, and wants unfulfilled.

Aggressive people may well say what's on their mind, but without respecting the wants, thoughts, and feelings of others.

Passive-aggressive people passively do not directly and effectively say what's on their minds. However, they express aggression in a variety of indirect ways, such as getting even, being dishonest, or pouting.

Examples

People often think they are assertive, when if fact they're not. We can see this in the following:

Housecleaning

Sue and Jane are roommates. They have agreed to divide their chores each week. Sue has not done her chores for a week. Jane decides to say something.

Assertive: "Sue, I thought we agreed we would split the chores of cleaning house. This week was your turn, and you haven't vacuumed or dusted. I know this work isn't fun. But I'm frustrated and feel like I'm doing more than my share. I would feel better if we could come to an agreement we both stick to."

Aggressive: "Sue, you are just a lazy pig.

Passive: "Sue, you know, I wonder if we could help each other out a little more. There would be a lot less tension, you know."

Passive-Aggressive: "Gosh, you know what's happened? I just won't have the time to clean the apartment next month. We're having guests over, I'm sure you won't mind if I put our junk in your bedroom."

Requesting a New Computer at Work

Jerome has been working as an accountant for over a year at a big downtown business. The policy is that anyone who has worked for over six month gets a new computer, rather than use the old common computer. Jerome is overdue. Business has been very good, and others have received their computers. He decides to talk to his supervisor.

Assertive: "When I started work, you promised I would get a new computer after six months. It has been a year, others have their new computers, and I still use the communal computer. I would like to talk about what is going on, and if I can expect a new computer."

Aggressive: "I feel you are not honoring our contract or respecting your workers. You don't give a darn about any of us! I find it difficult to work under these conditions, and feel slighted."

Passive: "Gosh, it's getting more and more difficult to complete all my work on the communal computer. I have to wait in line for my turn, and work doesn't get done."

Passive-Aggressive: "Actually, I have no problem using the communal computer, even though I was promised my own new computer. I enjoy working with others. And waiting my turn gives me extra time to catch up on local gossip with my coworkers."

Assertiveness and Distorted Thinking

Let's return to our chapters on distorted thinking. Actually, passive, aggressive, and passive-aggressive choices can be a consequence of distorted thinking. Here is a summary of three of the types of distorted thoughts we have considered. Can you see how each might contribute to nonassertiveness?

Desperate Desires

1. *"Musts, oughts, and shoulds."* Turning simple honest desires and wants into absolute musts, oughts, and shoulds. *"I must be a success."* (Rather than *"It sure would be nice to be successful, but that may or may not happen.") Or, "I should be more likable (hard-working, relaxed, rich, religious, etc.)."* (Rather than *"I would like to be more likable.")*

   Application: *"My boyfriend must pay attention to me. If he talks to another guy, I get jealous."*

2. *Special privilege.* Acting as if you have a special privilege or entitlement because you are somehow more important or deserving than others. *"People should always treat me nicely." "I should get what I want." "I truly deserve and must get favorable treatment."*

   Application: *"That lady standing in front me in line doesn't have anything to do. She's just a housewife. I'm a student and have to get to class right away. So I'll just slip in line in front of her, and give her a dirty threatening look."*

3. *Childhood fantasy.* Assuming (as children may do) that everything should go your way. *"Everyone should be nice and love each other." "Problems should have happy endings." "We should all get what we want in life."*

   Application: *"I just went to this church social. No one talked to me. Jeez, this is a church, people should be nice to each other and talk to strangers. Isn't that what church is all about. Well, I'll show them. I'm going to stick my pinkie in their punch bowl."*

4. *Needless perfectionism.* Picking an unfairly high standard for yourself and others, even though practically no one has ever been able to achieve it. *"I should never do dumb things." "I have to be better than others."*

   Application: *"The professor wants someone to volunteer an answer to his next question. I haven't been participating in class discussion so it would be a good idea to do so for my grade. But what if I freeze? What if I get the wrong answer? I'm just going to sit here."*

5. *Desperate need for love and caring.* Thinking that your need for love and caring are so important (or strong) that no one can or will ever meet them. *"The kind of love I need no one can provide." "I am nothing without friends or lovers."*

   Application: *"So, my roommate didn't pick me up and drive me home from school like she promised. I guess I'm not that important in her life. Next time I see her, I won't even bring it up, especially when she has that attitude toward me."*

Foolish Frustrations

6. *Catastrophizing.* Turning simple frustrations, irritations, and disappointments into unbearable disasters and catastrophes. *"I didn't get that raise (good grade, date, etc.); therefore it is the end of the world for me." "Things didn't turn out like I wanted; this is a disaster."*

   Application: *"I feel so stupid. I got a D on this exam. It's the end of the world. Nothing matters anymore. This class is stupid. I'm just going to walk out in the middle of class and slam the door really hard."*

7. *Preoccupation on regretting the past.* Focusing on past wrongs, frustrations, and mistakes, rather than what you have or can do now. *"So many things have gone wrong in my life." "The past is filled with frustration."*

   Application: *"My parents have done so many bad things to me. I just don't want to talk to them anymore. Dad's having his 50th birthday next week and the whole family is coming. Except me. I'm staying home. It's a big trip anyway. That'll make them appreciate me!"*

8. *Negative fortune telling.* Consistently predicting the future negatively, typically thinking that things will only get worse. *"I'll fail that exam or won't get the job." "I will never be really contented."*

   Application: *"Why should I even ask for a raise. I never get anywhere. Sure, I have a very good case, better than other workers who did get a raise. I think it's time to raise a stink. I'm going to march into the office and make it clear what I really think of her."*

9. *Negative spin.* Arbitrarily and pessimistically putting a negative interpretation on events, even though they may be neutral or positive. *"This is not what I really want." "I always look at the dark side of things."*

   Application: "So, my roommate didn't pick me up and drive me home from school like she promised. I guess I'm not that important in her life. Next time I see her, I won't even bring it up, especially when she has that attitude toward me."

Horrible Helplessness

10. *Hyper-neediness.* Believing you can't cope by yourself and need much help from others. *"I just deal with things by myself." "I always need help on important problems."*

    Application: *"I'm going to this hot party and hope to meet some new guys. I gotta have my roommate with me for moral support. He can tell me who to meet and what to say. I'm going to tell him that he's gotta come with me if he considers me a friend."*

11. *Fatalism.* Believing that the uncontrollable powers of fate, your "genes," or even the Divine Supreme Being, determine the present, and that there is little we can do about it. *"No use in trying to make things better; it's all been fated to happen this way." "It's my lot in life (my social background, genes, family) to have these problems, and there's not much I can do to change that."*

    Application: *"I really wanted to get on the debate team, but I wasn't selected. That's the way it was meant to be. There's a reason for everything. My friends say I should talk with the coach and see if they got all of my application materials. Why bother? What is, is."*

12. *Imperfections = unlovability.* Feeling that you are basically defective and flawed—unlovable to others if they find out. *"If people knew what I am really like, they would never like me." "I have flaws that will always keep people from accepting me."*

    Application: *"I'm such a geek, and when people find that out, that turns them off. So what happens is that when I'm at lunch with a bunch of students, I find myself getting nasty and putting others down sarcastically."*

13. *Unrealistic isolation.* Feeling that you are isolated from the rest of the world, different from other people, and are not, or cannot be part of any group or community. This terrible fact prevents you from doing anything about your frustrations. *"I just don't belong." "I'm different from others."*

    Application: *"I'm just different. I'm depressed, and everyone else is so happy. I have no friends, and don't want to be with people. They will just find me a boring downer."*

14. *Needless self-blaming.* Needlessly blaming yourself for negative events, and failing to see that some events have other, complex causes. *"The only reason my marriage ended is because I failed." "I broke my leg because God is punishing me."*

    Application: " *Whenever I get a low grade, I know I'm a screw-up. I just can't get anything right. And going to the professor for advice is so embarrassing. She'll just point out what I already know—I'm a screw-up."*

15. Needless other-blaming. Looking for someone else to blame when things don't go right. *"My husband is to blame for the way I feel." "Mother caused my problems."*

    Application: *"These people in the admissions office are so stupid. They say they sent me the application materials, but I never got them. They make an appointment, and then are 15 minutes late. I'm just going to give them a piece of my mind. Maybe if they hear me blow up, they'll think twice about being so careless."*

16. *Task exaggeration.* Treating simple barriers or challenges as overwhelming or insurmountable. *"I don't break a problem down into manageable parts. I see the whole thing as overwhelming. If I can't immediately solve it all, why try?"*

    Application: *"Things at school have gotten crazy and are really making me feel down. Courses, finances, roommate issues, everything's going wrong. I'm just going to drop out."*

Assertiveness Is a Coping Option

There is a time to be assertive and a time to be nonassertive. However, it is useful to have an assertive option available in case you want to use it. In order to have this option, you need to know what to say and do, and understand the costs and benefits.

In many cases, assertive people are more likely to get what they want, enlist the cooperation and help of others, enjoy satisfying relationships, and have a higher opinion of themselves.

Passive (and passive-aggressive) people, because they keep their wants, thoughts, and feelings to themselves, are more likely to be frustrated and not get what they want. They are more likely to be manipulated and injured by others. The passive person is more likely to experience stress and distorted thinking, and less likely to resolve stressful problems. As a result, he or she may have difficulties with deep relaxation exercises and not experience the benefits of relaxation states of mind in everyday life.

However, sometimes passivity has its benefits. If you are discussing your parking ticket and believe your police officer used an unpleasant tone of voice, perhaps it would be better to passively keep that complaint to yourself. If you are the repeated victim of a racial slur by the neighborhood bully, perhaps giving him or her a piece of your mind (and getting the anger off your chest) wouldn't be such a bad idea.

Aggressive (and passive-aggressive) people may temporarily get what they want and feel satisfied and powerful. Others are more likely to feel resentful and not cooperative, relationships are injured, and some wants may not be fulfilled. Long-term problem-solving is not enhanced and self-serving distorted thinking may persist. Generally, the aggressive person carries an additional burden of physical and psychological tension that can interfere with both practicing a relaxation exercise and enjoying relaxation throughout work and leisure.

But, like passivity, there might be a time to be aggressive. Can you think of examples?

One important key to assertiveness is knowing to consider and weigh the costs and benefits of each before making a decision.

Assertiveness and Nonverbal Behaviors

The way you stand, the postures you assume, and your tone of voice can do much to clearly communicate assertiveness, passivity, aggressiveness, and passive-aggressiveness. For example, the assertive person stands up straight, looks you straight in the eye, speaks clearly and confidently, and uses appropriate gestures.

A passive person is more likely to slouch, look aside, speak quietly, and not use gestures. An aggressive person shows hostility in posture, voice, and gesture. Make sure your nonverbal behaviors go with the assertive option you select.

Mindful Assertiveness

How can assertiveness be mindful? How can passivity, aggressiveness, and passive-aggressiveness be unmindful? First, ask which approach to coping involves the greatest focus on what matters, on the true issue of the moment? Second, which involves the least amount of needless mind wandering, worry, and rumination?

EXERCISES

The Mindfulness Exercise Challenge. Try practicing a five-minute version of your home mindfulness exercise before completing any chapter exercise.

26.1 Thoughts and Beliefs

What we think and believe can lead to or get in the way of being assertive. Alberti and Emmons (1982) and Jakubowski and Lange (1978) have listed beliefs and thoughts that may be conducive to behavior that is assertive or nonassertive. Below are some of what they have suggested. Indicate which are most conducive to behavior that is:

Assertive Passive Aggressive Passive-Aggressive

Then explain why.

1. You have the right to dignity and self-respect.
2. If you express your anger indirectly, others will get your point.
3. It is cool not to say what you want, but cause trouble for others who cause problems.
4. You must have the approval of others.
5. The world is a dangerous, hostile place where one always has to be on guard.
6. It is better to pretend that things are OK, and hurt the other person indirectly.
7. You have the right not to feel guilty.
8. You have the right to say no.
9. The world is a dangerous place, it is best to keep quiet.
10. Just in case your anger and frustration is not justified, it is better to express it in such a way that others won't know who is responsible.
11. If you compromise, you won't get what you want.
12. If people are punished, they will figure out on their own what they did wrong.
13. It's really not that important.
14. You must win in order for others to accept you.
15. You have the right to have and express feelings, even those that others might not approve of.
16. Others can usually figure out what you want, think, or feel.
17. You have the right to change your mind.
18. If you can't get what you want, get even.
19. If you are honest with others, they will retaliate.
20. You have the right to ask for help and for what you want.

21. Things will get better on their own.

22. Asking for something is selfish and needlessly inconveniences others. It is better just to keep your wants to yourself.

23. You have the right to be less than what others expect of you.

24. People who hold in their own wants, thoughts, and feelings are more likable.

26.2 What's Your Assertive Reply?

Here are some situations. For each indicate if the described response is assertive, passive, aggressive, or passive-aggressive. Then give your own assertive reply.

Situation 1: The Cancelled Trip

You and your roommate have planned to go on a trip to the woods. Unexpectedly, your friend calls and cancels.

You say: *"Gee. This is really unexpected. I need some time to think about where this puts me. Let me call you back."*

☐ Assertive
☐ Passive
☐ Aggressive
☐ Passive-Aggressive

2: Pigpen Roommate

Your roommate leaves the kitchen in a mess whenever she uses it. Dirty dishes are piled up in the sink. Open food is rotting in the fridge. Food is left on the stove.

You say: *"This kitchen is a mess! Just like you! How can you live with yourself? You must be more considerate of others."*

☐ Assertive
☐ Passive
☐ Aggressive
☐ Passive-Aggressive

Situation 3: Tacos or Hotrods

Your girl/boyfriend wants to watch a rerun of a cooking show on making bean tacos. You really want to watch a special on hotrods.

You say: *"Oh, honey. You can watch your taco show. I don't really want to watch my special show anyway. It really doesn't mean that much to me. The way you cook, you need as much help as you can get."*

☐ Assertive
☐ Passive
☐ Aggressive
☐ Passive-Aggressive

Situation 4: Oily Kid

Your 12-year-old son just finished fixing his bike and hasn't picked up all the dirt and oil he left behind. You step in the mess and get your white shoes dirty.

You say, *"You are the most inconsiderate kid I know. You just don't think about how your actions affect others."*

☐ Assertive
☐ Passive
☐ Aggressive
☐ Passive-Aggressive

Situation 5: Bully Girls

Your son gets punched out by a bunch of big girls several times each week just after school. You are concerned that his grade school teacher hasn't done anything about it. You have a meeting with the teacher.

You say, *"My son got hit three times this week, and twice last week after school. This is not acceptable, especially since I have written the school principle about the problem. I must insist that something be done. When can we meet so we can come up with an answer?"*

☐ Assertive
☐ Passive
☐ Aggressive
☐ Passive-Aggressive

Situation 6: The Secretary Issue

You are the only guy in a church group of 12 women. The group has to discuss church finances. Before the meeting, they have to select a secretary. The women turn to you and say, "We gals have done this type of work all our lives. It's time a man is secretary. You're it!"

You say, *"Hey, I understand your concerns about discrimination against women. But let's be fair. You're guilty of reverse discrimination. Wouldn't it be more reasonable to rotate the job, so everyone gets to do it once?"*

☐ Assertive
☐ Passive
☐ Aggressive
☐ Passive-Aggressive

Situation 7: Overtime Bummer

You have worked overtime every day this week, often missing dinner. Your boss asks you to work on Saturday, even though that is your official day off.

You say, *"Ooo, that hurts. Sure, I'll come in. Sure."*

☐ Assertive
☐ Passive
☐ Aggressive
☐ Passive-Aggressive

Situation 8: Help! Here Comes Mom!

Your mother wants to visit you on Saturday, the same day you have planned a special trip to the park with your friends. She springs this on you at the last moment. She lives only a mile away from you.

You say, *"Mom, I need to have my own time. I'm 23 and not your little kid anymore. You need to respect this."*

☐ Assertive
☐ Passive
☐ Aggressive
☐ Passive-Aggressive

Situation 9: The Drug Bust

Your buddy wants you to do cocaine with him. You tried it, but have made a firm decision not to do any more. Your buddy insists and accuses you of being not cool and not liking him anymore.

You say, *"Listen, buddy, I hope we're still friends. But I've made a decision that's right for me. I want you to respect that."*

☐ Assertive
☐ Passive
☐ Aggressive
☐ Passive-Aggressive

Situation 10: Late Date

You have planned a date at a nice local pizza restaurant. Your date is 20 minutes late, and arrives with no excuse. You don't have access to a phone and feel pissed off.

You say, *"Why are you always late? Do you have any idea how I feel?"*

☐ Assertive
☐ Passive
☐ Aggressive
☐ Passive-Aggressive

Situation 11: Pushy Shopper

You are waiting in a long line at the drugstore to pay for your one bottle of orange soda. A middle-aged lady in a nice suit shoves in front of you and pays for her things out of turn.

You say, *"Excuse me, lady, I'm sorry I was taking up your space. Maybe I could carry your things out to your car for you."*

☐ Assertive
☐ Passive
☐ Aggressive
☐ Passive-Aggressive

Situation 12: The Wonderful Book

A friend who often borrows money without returning it asks for $40 to buy a hot new book on Stress Management he saw in the bookstore. You have the money in your pocket, but really don't want to give him any more until he pays back what he owes you.

You say, *"Gosh, I wish I could help you. Please ask me later."*

☐ Assertive
☐ Passive
☐ Aggressive
☐ Passive-Aggressive

Situation 13: Too Close for Comfort

Someone you like and have known for a year wants to thank you for your gift. This person touches you in a way that is a bit too intimate and makes you uncomfortable.

You say, *"I'll have to charge you $50 for that."*

☐ Assertive
☐ Passive
☐ Aggressive
☐ Passive-Aggressive

Situation 14: Embarrassed at Work

Your work supervisor has criticized your performance in front of other workers. You feel really embarrassed and wish she wouldn't have done that.

You say, *"I have a request. Sometimes it is helpful to get your feedback about my work, but could you possibly give it to me alone, and not in front of others. It makes me feel a little funny."*

☐ Assertive
☐ Passive
☐ Aggressive
☐ Passive-Aggressive

Situation 15: Beer Boy

You live in a dormitory and enjoy the party your floor has every month. However, you are always the one who has to go out and buy the beer. Sometimes you get reimbursed, sometimes only partly reimbursed. However, you are the best choice to get the beer given that your family's home is right next to the store.

You say, *"You know, you guys still owe me some money. This is getting a little tiresome."*

☐ Assertive
☐ Passive
☐ Aggressive
☐ Passive-Aggressive

26.3 Your Situation

Think of a situation in which you were not as assertive as you might have been. Describe all the details. Then present an assertive alternative, including what you would say.

List the costs and benefits of what actually happened and the assertive alternative.

Stress & Coping
Eye of Mindfulness Journal

Chapter 27

Super-Assertiveness: Making Difficult Requests

© Everett Collection/Shutterstock.com

Sometimes it is not enough to assertively state what is on your mind. Some situations call for a more powerful approach, super-assertiveness. Super-assertiveness can be used when you are making a difficult request, that is, asking for something another person may not want to give. This can include asking another person to change or stop what they are doing, do something new, or give something they may hesitate giving: Life is filled with situations calling for difficult requests, for example:

- You are waiting in a grocery store checkout line. Someone has clumsily stepped in front of you. You want to bring this to their attention.
- Time is ready for a raise or promotion. You have decided to ask for one.
- It is Sunday and your neighbors are making far too much noise You want to ask them to quiet down.
- Your daughter comes home late every Saturday. You want that to stop.
- Your 8-year-old son is using foul language, and you want him to change.
- You and your friend are spending the weekend together. However, you have different plans.
- You want to return an item purchased.
- You want more time to pay back money to a friend.
- Your neighbor has not returned the frying pan he borrowed.

Consider super-assertiveness when:

- There is a good chance your request may not be heard or taken seriously.
- You are dealing with someone who may misunderstand what you are saying or take your requests the wrong way (as an insult or joke, for example).

- Your request is very important and you want to maximize the likelihood that it will be honored.
- There is a possibility of a hostile reply.
- You want to establish an atmosphere of openness and honesty (for example, with a spouse or friend).

The Key to Super-Assertiveness The DESC Script

The key to super-assertiveness is to go beyond assertively stating what is on your mind; instead, you carefully spell out all the facts relevant to the situation. For example, if you want a friend to return your bicycle, a simple assertion might go like this:

> *"I want my bike back, please."*

But imagine your friend has a habit of not returning what he borrows, doesn't seem to take your requests seriously, and sometimes blames you of picking on him when you do ask for your things back. Then you might try a super-assertion:

> *"Last Monday you borrowed my bike and promised to return it the next day. One week has passed, and I feel really frustrated and a bit irritated. I want my bike today. Hey, I need my bike today to visit my mother. And frankly, I'm getting a little tired of lending you things and not knowing when I'll get them back. You're my friend, and I want to help you when you ask, but you make it hard by not returning things."*

A super-assertion lays all the facts on the table—what the problem is, how you feel about it, what you want, and what's going to happen. Bower and Bower (1991) offer a classic tool for doing this, called the **DESC script.** There are four steps:

Describe. Clearly and objectively state the other person's behavior or words that are an issue to you or a problem.

Express. State your thoughts and feelings in reaction to the described behavior.

Specify. Make a specific, concrete request.

Consequences. Outline the positive consequences for oneself and the other person if the request is followed.

Examples

Helping a Friend Type Assignments

Describe: *"For five days in a week you have asked me to type your homework for you. Each assignment takes about an hour. I notice that you have not attended your typing class for a month."*

Express: *"I am beginning to feel frustrated at doing all this work. I feel like I am being used and that you aren't doing your share."*

Specify: *"I want you to start going back to typing class and start typing your assignments tomorrow."*

Consequences: *"If you can do at least some of your typing yourself, I'll be happy to help you do more work."*

Eating My Food

Describe: *"Wednesday I did my grocery shopping and put my week's food in the bottom shelf of our shared refrigerator. I saw you eating my food yesterday and today, so it's almost gone."*

Express: *"This gets me angry. We share the same refrigerator so we have to respect each other's food space."*

Specify: *"Please eat your food, and if you want to eat some of mine, ask."*

Consequences: *"That way I'll know if I have enough to eat this week. I won't have to worry about where my food is going. And I won't get angry."*

DESC Script Dos and Don'ts

Describe

Describe the other person's behavior, not your own feelings. Don't get overemotional; just stick to the facts. Use concrete terms, stating who, when, what, and where. Don't guess at the other person's feelings or reasons.

✔ Correct: *"Yesterday at noon you promised to meet me for breakfast. You did not arrive."*
⃠ Incorrect: *"I am upset because you did not show up for breakfast today as you promised."*

✔ Correct: *"Last week you complained to the supervisor that I have been answering your phone calls."*
⃠ Incorrect: *"Please address your complaints to me in the future rather than to my supervisor."*

✔ Correct: *"This lamp I purchased yesterday doesn't light up when I turn it on."*
⃠ Incorrect: *"I want a new lamp. This one is junk!"*

Express

Calmly state your own feelings, relating them to the specific behavior, not the whole person.

✔ Correct: *"I am frustrated and a little confused by your not showing up for breakfast."*
⃠ Incorrect: *"You know, I would appreciate it if you could be a little more considerate of your friends."*

✔ Correct: *"Frankly, I an irritated and angry."*
⃠ Incorrect: *"Frankly, please keep your feelings to yourself."*

✔ Correct: *"I was disappointed when I found this out."*
⃠ Incorrect: *"I feel you should check more carefully the merchandise you sell."*

Specify

Ask for realistic concrete, behavioral change, indicating again who, what, when, and where. Acknowledge the other person's wants.

✔ Correct: *"Next time you can't make a breakfast date, at least call me on your cell phone. "*
⃠ Incorrect: *"I want you to be more considerate of the concerns and time of your friends."*

✔ Correct: *"I understand we may have disagreements. I think it is fair to ask that if you have concerns about things I am doing, you bring them up to me."*
⃠ Incorrect: *"You are not contributing to a good work environment. I feel uncomfortable working with you."*

✔ Correct: *"I want a new lamp for the defective one. "*
⃠ Incorrect: *"Correct this immediately."*

Consequences

Be honest, realistic, concrete, and explicit. Don't bribe, threaten, or promise too much.

✔ Correct: *"We'll call each other if we can't show up. At least I'll know what's going on and won't worry."*
⊘ Incorrect: *"Don't worry. I still like you!"*

✔ Correct: *"I enjoy working with you, and will certainly feel I can trust you to be honest with me."*
⊘ Incorrect: *"You know, there's lots of stuff I could complain to the boss about you."*

✔ Correct: *"If we can work this out, I will certainly enjoy continue shopping here."*
⊘ Incorrect: *"You have to replace the defective lamp I bought here."*

Don't Make These Mistakes!

Students often make these two mistakes with DESC scripts. First, remember that you are writing a *script.* That is, actually put down the words you would say in an assertive encounter. Do not explain what or why you might say something.

⊘ Incorrect Describe Line: *"My boyfriend was saying one thing and doing another. He said he was going to call my mother to arrange for dinner for us all. But he didn't and failed to tell me."*

✔ Correct Describe Line: *"Last week you said you would call my mother to arrange for dinner. My mother tells me this didn't happen."*

Second, sometimes students have trouble with their DESCRIBE lines. Often they try to put too much into it. Simply state the problem behaviors (or words) of the other person.

⊘ Incorrect Describe Line: *"My boyfriend was saying one thing and doing another. He frustrated and confused me and I wanted to tell him to be more clear. He said he was going to call my mother to arrange for dinner for us all. But he didn't and failed to tell me."*

✔ Correct Describe Line: *"Last week you said you would call my mother to arrange for dinner. My mother tells me this didn't happen."*

The Positive DESC Script

One way of making a good DESC script more effective is to precede it with a compliment. However make sure your compliment is honest, specific, and related to the request you wish to make. For example, imagine you are returning an item to a store for a refund. You are not completely sure you will get a refund. A positive DESC script might go like this:

> *"I enjoy shopping at your store. Last week I was really pleased with how courteous and prompt your service was."*
>
> *"However, I do have a request. The lamp I purchased is broken. It simply doesn't work. I was a bit frustrated because of the long trip I made just to come to this store. I would like a refund, and would feel much relieved if I could receive it today so I could continue shopping."*

Note how the beginning compliment is specific (it identifies why the person was pleased). And it is relevant, related to the store and its service. The following positive DESC script has a problem. It isn't specific or particularly relevant. Can you see why?

> *"John, we've been friends for over a year. You are a really nice person."*
>
> *"Last week you borrowed my CD player and promised to return it the next day. I still don't have it and am getting worried. I need my CD player for my party tonight. I would like to have it today. I really want my party to be hot!"*

EXERCISES

> ***The Mindfulness Exercise Challenge.*** *Try practicing a five-minute version of your home mindfulness exercise before completing any chapter exercise.*

27.1 What's Wrong with These Scripts?

The most frequent mistake in creating DESC scripts is getting lines mixed up. People frequently put Describe line information in a Specify line, express emotions in a Describe line, and so on. See if you can identify how these lines are mixed up. Then for each create a correct DESC script.

Poor Service

"Waitress, I'm sorry, but I am getting really frustrated about your service. I am seriously considering never coming here again for a meal. I have been waiting over 20 minutes for service."

Describe:
Express:
Specify:
Consequences:

Party Drinker

"I am going to have to ask you to leave if you don't stop drinking. You have had 12 beers in the last hour and our party has just started. I think you've had your limit, so please, no more beer. I've reached my limit."

Describe:
Express:
Specify:
Consequences:

Unfaithful Lover

Sara has been dating Brian for about six months. Both have been taking their relationship very seriously, and it seems to be growing. Recently one of Sara's friends informed her that she saw Brian go out with another woman. A few days later, another friend had the same story, noting that Brian was bragging about how he took his date home. Yesterday Brian calls and invites Sara out for a date that weekend. The next day he calls and cancels, saying "some business has come up." Sara is crushed, fearing that Brian has been unfaithful and is not honest. She calls him to cancel the date:

"Brian, I know what you're doing and I think we're through. We have to get together tonight and talk. You better have a good excuse."

Describe:
Express:
Specify:
Consequences:

No Promotion

> *Brian works as a clerk in a local gourmet grocery. He is gradually building a record and hopes to be promoted to assistant manager. This year he receives a notice that not only has he been passed over for a promotion, but also a raise. He expected something, given that he has had a stellar work record, never missing a day. So he walks into his boss's office and demands, "You know I deserve a raise. I do everyone else's work. In fact I should get more. Otherwise I will have to quit."*

Describe:
Express:
Specify:
Consequences:

The Gossip

> *Jan's best friend Henrietta has been talking about her behind her back. Information is getting out about the men she dates, what men she dislikes and why, and even some rather personal information, like shoe size, pet peeves, and something about barbecue-scented deodorants. So Jan confronts her friend: "Henrietta, I am absolutely crushed and angry. You are not treating me with respect. Please treat me like I treat you. That's how friendships grow."*

Describe:
Express:
Specify:
Consequences:

27.2 Fill in the Gaps

Roommate Loan

You and your roommate are about to get into an argument. You want to remain friends, or at least on good terms. But he has been asking for money every two weeks, forgetting to pay you back. You have reminded him that he owes you $50, and he apologizes, saying he will pay you back next week. Then nothing happens.

Describe: *"Three weeks ago I loaned you $10 and you promised to pay me back in a week. That didn't happen. Then you asked for $10 more last week, and promised to pay back both loans. That hasn't happened."*

Express: ____

Specify: ____

Consequences: *"If I get my loan repaid, I'll feel better about you as a roommate, and will be happy to loan you more money in the future."*

Noisy Neighbor

The guy living in the apartment next to you plays his music very loud, even late into the night. You've tried banging on the wall, and he just cranks the music up. You've left him a polite note asking him to "please turn your music down after 9 PM so I can study." This has no effect. Not only are you very upset, but you are totally at a loss as what the next step should be. You don't know him well. Maybe he's drunk. Maybe he's just a rude person and thinks he owns the world. But you want action, and you're angry. You bump into him in the hallway.

Describe: ____

Express: ____

Specify: *"Is there any way we can talk about how to solve this problem, some way that works for both of us? What would you suggest?"*

Consequences: ____

27.3 Missing Information

Another mistake people make with DESC scripts is leaving out important information, or not presenting information in a way that is concrete and specific (what, where, when, who). Here are some scripts with missing information. Indicate what is missing and give an example of the type of information that is needed.

The Book Salesman Who Will Not Stop

> *"Listen, I don't want your stupid book. Leave me alone. What part of "no" do you not understand?"*

The Cheating Boyfriend

> *"I think you are no longer interested in me. Maybe we should call it quits. I just get the feeling your interests are elsewhere."*

Your Lab Partner Needs Help

> *"Last week I helped you clean your room. Now it's your turn. Just let me see your math homework answers so I can get a better idea of how to do the assignment. I'll remember this favor on our next date and do something special."*

27.4 Your DESC Script

Think of a difficult request you have had to make of another person. Present this request in terms of a DESC script.

Your Situation:

Describe:

Express:

Specify:

Consequences:

27.5 Your Positive DESC Script

Now try writing a positive DESC script. Make sure your beginning compliment is honest, specific, and relevant.

Your Situation:

COMPLIMENT:

Describe:

Express:

Specify:

Consequences:

27.6 Costs and Benefits

What are the costs and benefits of using a DESC script?

Costs:

Benefits:

What are the costs and benefits of using a positive DESC script?

Costs:

Benefits:

27.7 Fix This DESC Script

What's wrong with this script? Fix it, please.

OSCAR WORKS AT A TACO STAND WITH HIS BROTHER, EDEL. FOR THE LAST FIVE WEEKS HIS BROTHER HAS PROMISED TO PAY HIM. HOWEVER, OSCAR HAS YET TO BE PAID. HE DECIDES TO CONFRONT HIS BROTHER WITH A DESC SCRIPT. HERE IT IS. EVALUATE AND REWRITE EACH STEP.

I'VE GIVEN YOU EXTRA SPACE ON THE RIGHT FOR YOUR RESPONSE.

D: *"Edel, I'm pissed off. You've been taking me for granted for too long. I feel like I'm your servant. We agreed that this would be a business arrange-*

ment, an actual job. Instead, I feel like I'm doing you a favor, helping you out with cooking. It's always this way. I have to do all your chores."

E: "What I want is really simple. I just want you to treat me with a little to ask? Just don't treat me like an unpaid servant. Everyone needs some recognition."

S: "I can't continue under these conditions. You're going to make me quit. Then what will you do? I'd like to see how you get along in life without your little Oscar!"

C: "I don't know why I'm even telling you this. You never listen. But get this: If you keep treating me like your pet puppy, some day this doggie is going to bite back!"

Stress & Coping
Eye of Mindfulness Journal

Chapter 28

Shyness, Starting Relationships

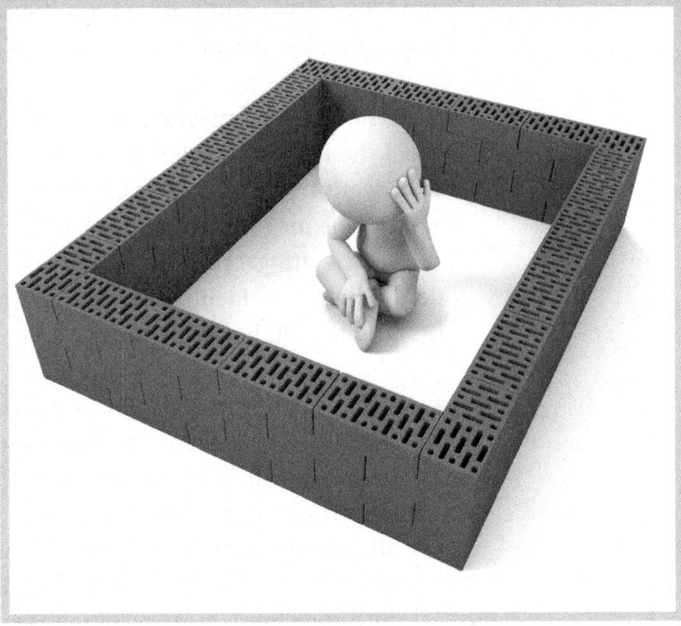

© Jane0606 / Shutterstock.com

This chapter considers a special type of stress, that which arises from not making and pursuing relationships—namely, shyness. There are many excellent books on shyness (Antony & Swinson, 2000; Bower & Bower, 1991; Curran, Wallander, & Farrell, 1985; Hope, Heimberg, Juster, & Turk, 2000; Jakubowski & Lange, 1978; West, Goethe, & Kallman, 1980). The most popular strategy is to cultivate brainstorming new ways of meeting people, following up an introduction, ending a conversations, and dealing with rejection. The ideas generated can then be combined with relaxation/mindfulness, rethinking resistance to taking action, and desensitization, all topics covered elsewhere in this book.

Brainstorming Ways of Meeting People

We begin with a setting where there are opportunities for meeting others, for example, at work, at school, in a lunchroom, a pub, a party, or church or temple. If you need help in thinking of meeting places, try brainstorming.

Distorted thinking. Often it is hard to take the first step and introduce yourself. Typically, a distorted belief or excess tension gets in the way. You may harbor such unrealistic thoughts as assuming others will reject you, thinking you will appear foolish, assuming it is a very terrible thing if you indeed appear foolish, fearing that the person will not be your ideal match and you will have difficulty getting out of the conversation, and so on. Identify and do a reality check on whatever thoughts may interfere.

Relaxation/Mindfulness. Spot relaxation is an ideal way of preparing for taking the first step and meeting someone. First you need to learn your preferred forms of relaxation, and then select a mini- relaxation to use before your meeting. You might, for example, take a few slow deep breaths, stretch a few times, or entertain a brief positive fantasy.

Desensitization. If meeting others causes enough tension and anxiety that you either avoid the task or bungle your attempts, then a little preliminary practice through desensitization might be useful. I recommend a variation called in vivo ("live") desensitization. The idea is to practice meeting others in very safe and nonthreatening settings (real, live settings, rather than those that are imagined), and practice relaxation while doing this. First, identify some practice meeting rehearsal tasks, and rank them from easy to difficult. For example, one brief hierarchy might include:

1. Go to a party with a friend and meet someone he/she introduces you to.
2. Introduce yourself to three people who pose no threat to you. Pick people you probably will never meet again. These should be people whose opinion of you doesn't matter at all. Whether they think you are silly, pushy, uninteresting, or stupid, should mean little to you, because (a) you aren't going to reveal anything seriously personal and (b) you will never see them again. Then plan your opening lines and some lines of conversation very carefully.
3. Play a game with a friend at school in which both of you see how many people you can meet in an hour. The winner buys dinner.
4. Practice with a friend. Explain that you want to role-play meeting and using opening lines, with him/her playing the part of the person being met.

Opening Lines: What to Say First

Brainstorm and practice possible opening lines. An opening line doesn't have to be particularly profound, insightful, or clever. Indeed, openers that appear exceptionally polished can be threatening to others. Simple lines are best. One might want to first think of a set of opening lines. Here are some researchers (Kleinke, Meeker, & Staneski, 1986) have found useful:

> *"Hi."*
> *"Can you give me directions to ________?"*
> *"Can you help me with __________?"*
> *"Did you see (name a movie or TV show)?"*
> *"Have you read (name an article or book)?"*
> *"I feel a bit embarrassed about this—I'd like to meet you."*
> *"That's a very pretty (sweater, shirt, etc.) you have on."*
> *"You have really nice (hair, eyes, etc.)"*
> *"Since we're both sitting alone, care to join me?"*
> *"Is it OK if I sit with you?"*

Less effective opening lines include:

> *"I'm easy. Are you?"*
> *"I've got an offer you can't refuse."*

"What's your sign?"
"Didn't we meet in a previous life?"
"Your place or mine?"
"Is that really your hair?"
"You remind me of a woman (man) I used to date."
"Isn't it cold? Let's make some body heat."
"What's that hanging from your nose?"

Your opening line should feel safe for yourself and the other person. Think of something that the other person can answer or decline easily. Often experts recommend avoiding opening lines that:

- Include cute statements
- Involve asking inappropriately intimate or probing questions
- Fill the air with empty talk
- Put oneself down
- Involve perfunctory ice-breakers and waiting for the other person to jump in and save the conversation.

Asking an open-ended question can be a good opening line. An open-ended question is one that cannot be answered with a simple "yes" or "no." They make it very easy for the other person to continue the conversation. In contrast, closed-ended questions can be answered with a single "yes" or "no," often resulting in awkward silence. Here are some examples of open-ended questions:

"That looks like an interesting magazine. What is that cover about?"
"What do you think about this place? I have mixed feelings."

Don't forget to think up what to say after your opening line.

Going Beyond Small Talk

Tom Boomer offers a useful idea about small talk. He begins by sharing the frustrations of re-entering the dating world after breaking up: "I decided to experiment with a no-small-talk policy: Not that I would insist that we talk only about heartfelt subjects . . . I simply wanted to eliminate the dull droning on about facts and figures – whether it's snowing or raiing how cold it is, what we do for work, how long it takes to get, where we went to school – all those things we think we have to talk about with someone new but that tell us little about who the person really is. Why can't we replace small talk with big talk and ask each other profound questions right from the start. Replace mindless chatter about commuting time with a conversation about our weightiest beliefs and most potent fears? Questions that reveal who we are and where we want to go."

How might one do this? Rather than ask "Where have you travelled?" ask "What place most inspired you and why?" Rather than say "Tell me about your job" ask "What work are you passionate about?" Instead of asking about one's past relationship, ask "What's the most in love you've ever felt?"

In sum, going beyond small talk opens the door for further connection and exploration. We need a "willingness to dive into conversations that may make us uncomfortable or that many believe to be inappropriate for first encounters. After a while, though it becomes natural to skip the facts and instead seek out our deepest thoughts and feelings." (downloaded 1.17.2016 from: https://www.nytimes.com/2016/01/17/fashion/dating-the-end-of-small-talk.html)

Following Up and Maintaining a Conversation

Once you've started a conversation, it can be hard to continue. Some people worry about being too pushy or saying the wrong thing. Here are some hints others have suggested:

- Can you tell if the other person really wants to continue the conversation? Is she giving you "free information" about herself, such as what she thinks or feels. Is he smiling and facing you, or turning away, looking at his watch, yawning?
- Listen to what the person is saying. Paraphrase the gist of what is being said. This shows you are interested.

Antony and Swinson (2000) and McKay, Davis, and Fanning (1995) suggest some "don'ts" to avoid:

- Don't compare yourself to others. ("I make more money than my brother.")
- Don't ignore key points of what the other person is saying.
- Don't abruptly change topics. This might be perceived as a rude, self-centered interruption.
- Don't over rehearse.
- Don't "butter up" the other person. You might think that you can make other people like you more if you constantly agree with them or praise them. This might work with some people. It turns many people off.
- Avoid body language that suggests you don't like the other person or aren't interested. This may include leaning back in your chair, standing far away, avoiding eye contact, frowning, or crossing your arms.

Dealing with Rejection

Sometimes shy people avoid meeting others because of fear of rejection. If this is a concern, consider if you are engaging in any distorted thinking.

EXERCISES

The Mindfulness Exercise Challenge. *Try practicing a five-minute version of your home mindfulness exercise before completing any chapter exercise.*

28.1 Observe Others

Spend the week listening to others, in real life and in movies or television shows. Pay particular attention to people who seem to be meeting someone for the first time. Take note of what they are saying and doing.

What are their opening lines? How would you evaluate their opening lines using the concepts of this chapter? What good ideas did you note? Why were they good? What strategies did you notice that weren't so good? Why?

Good Ideas

Why?

Not so Good Ideas

Look at their body language and nonverbal cues. Describe the appropriateness and impact of what you note.

28.2 When Have You Been Shy?

Think of several situations in which you could have tried to meet others, but did not. What were you thinking? Did any of your thoughts get in the way?

28.3 Shyness Practice

Think of some safe situations where you can practice meeting others and using opening lines. Rank these from easy to more challenging:

Difficult and challenging practice situations

Moderate-level difficulty situations

Easy practice situations

28.4 Opening Lines

Brainstorm some possible opening lines as well as follow-up lines. Ask your friends and people you know what works best for them. For each, indicate whether it is an "open ended" or "yes-no" opening line. Rank them according to which you think are best for you.

Stress & Coping
Eye of Mindfulness Journal

Chapter 29

Autogenic Body Suggestion

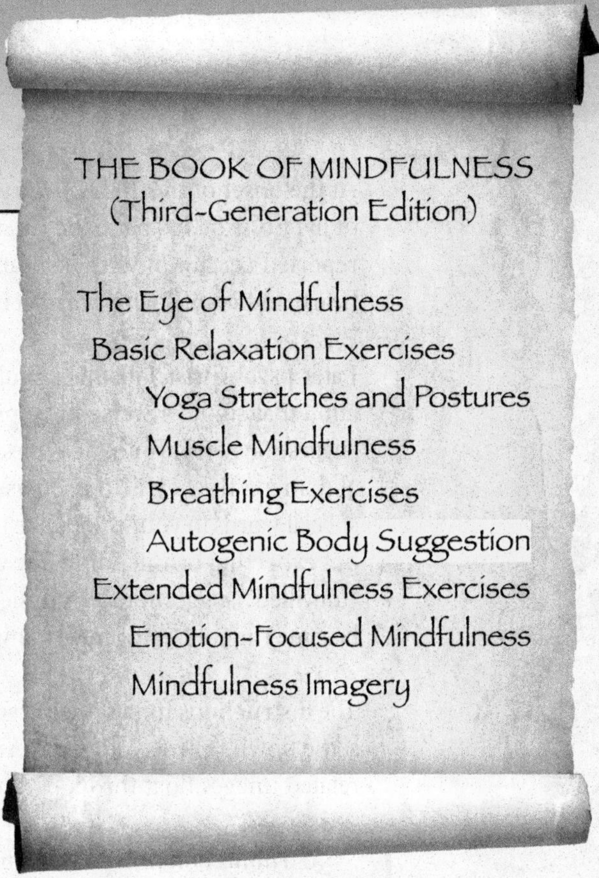

© Vadim Sadovski / Shutterstock.com

Can you simply think your body into relaxation? At first, this may seem like a type of wishful thinking. However, since 1900, relaxation therapists have the powers of the mind to evoke physical relaxation.

We experience the powers of the mind and the body every day. Imagine you are resting on the beach. Think of the warm sun soothing your skin. Your body rests comfortably in the sand. Tension dissolves and floats away. If you spend the next 60 seconds fantasizing about sunbathing, chances are that you will start feeling a bit warm and relaxed—a physiological response! Simple thoughts have the capacity to evoke a physiological reaction.

Now think about a stressful encounter. Imagine a recent confrontation that made you a bit angry. Think about everything that happened, what they did and said, what you said and did, what was unfair, and so on. Quite likely you might feel some physical changes as your blood begins to "boil," and perhaps your stomach tightens up. Or picture the most frightening thing that ever happened to you.

Replay this fantasy in your mind, including every detail. Does your stomach begin to feel queasy? Does your heart begin to beat more quickly? These fantasies illustrate the power of the mind, thoughts, and words to stir body reactions. This is the key idea underlying autogenic suggestion.

The Beginnings of Autogenic Training

At the onset of the 20th century, neurophysiologist Oskar Vogt was studying the effect of hypnosis on his patients. He noticed that when his patients began to relax, they often reported certain physical sensations, such as feeling warm and heavy, a slowly beating heart, and comforting warmth in the abdominal area.

Later psychiatrist Johannes Shultz took this idea and developed an approach to relaxation that simply reversed this process. Patients were instructed to passively repeat body suggestions of warmth, heaviness, a slowly beating heart, and comforting warmth in the abdomen. The key is to use **passive volition**, or willing without willing. Simply repeat special words in your mind, like meaningless nursery rhymes or echoes in a canyon, without expecting or intending any effect. Repeat them like a mantra. He found that such "unwilled" suggestions of physical relaxation could evoke physical relaxation. This idea became the core autogenic training, as presented in this book, autogenic suggestion.

The instructions for autogenic suggestion are very simple. Find a quiet relaxing place to settle down. Close your eyes. And then let any of the following sets of body words and related images float through your mind:

> *"Hands and arms warm and heavy."*
> *"Hand and arms in the warm sun (or sand or water).*
> *"Heart beating calm and easy.*
> *"Heart beating like a lazy clock."*
> *"Abdomen warm and soothed."*
> *"Abdomen warm and soothed, like after drinking soup or hot chocolate, or sitting in the sun."*

However, there is a trick in doing this to make it work. It is important not to exert any effort when repeating your words or pictures. Do not actively try to obtain the result you suggest. In fact, be completely indifferent as to whether or not the suggestions actually work. Let the words or pictures simply float lazily through your mind, like meaningless echoes.

It is easy to see why it is important to take this stance of easy indifference. Let's try this experiment. First, rest your hands on a table or your lap. Now, for the next minute or so, try to deliberately and effortfully create feelings of warmth and heaviness in your hands and arms. Here is an exercise script:

> *Try to make your hands and arms warm and heavy. Work really hard at it. Concentrate! Order your hands and arms to feel warm and heavy. In your mind, speak with considerable force and effort. Now continue with this for a minute.*

Now, let go and try something completely different. It doesn't matter a bit if your arms and hands actually get warm and heavy. Not a bit. Simply imagine some meaningless words and pictures slowly floating through your mind, "hands and arms warm and heavy . . . hands and arms warm and heavy . . . hands and arms warm and heavy." Let these phrases slowly go over and over and over.

I find that about 80 percent of those who try this exercise actually feel their hands and arms grow warm and heavy when they let go and passively let phrases and images float through their mind. And that is the secret to autogenic suggestion. Don't try. Don't exert effort. Let words and images float through your mind easily and lazily.

What happens with autogenic suggestion? Each suggestion seems to target a slightly different aspect of physical stress. For example, when aroused with stress, less blood flows to our extremities, our hands, arms, legs, and feet, so they feel cold and clammy. So thinking warmth counters this part of the stress response.

What about feelings of heaviness? Have you ever been so relaxed that your body felt heavy, and you just couldn't get yourself to move out of bed? If you think about it, each part of the body weighs something. A hand weighs as much as, perhaps, a baseball. When we're tense, we rarely notice this weight. When we are relaxed, and less distracted by other sensations, we are more likely to notice sensations that remain, including the sensation of the heaviness of our hands, arms, legs, and feet. When deeply relaxed, we feel heavy. Thinking suggestions of heaviness reverses the process and helps relax the muscles.

The heart obviously beats harder and faster when under stress. Autogenic suggestions of a calmly and easily beating heart counter this. And, when feeling a stressful emotion, nerves deep in our abdomen, our "gut brain," evoke certain stress sensations, such as queasiness, butterflies, and even upset. Autogenic suggestions of feeling comforting warmth in the abdomen counter this. Targeting these autogenic suggestions not only helps us relax specific parts of the body, but eventually it leads to overall relaxation.

The following autogenic suggestions are not to be used as a precise formula or chant. Instead, they are gentle suggestions of what types of thoughts or images to let float through your mind. Simply read over one category of suggestion, then close your eyes, lean back, and for about five minutes let suggestions like these float through your mind.

Whenever your mind wanders, that's fine. Gently return to letting your autogenic suggestions float through your mind. Spend up to five minutes with each category of suggestion.

Once you have mastered the idea of autogenic suggestion, try suggestions targeted to specific parts of the body other than the limbs, heart, or abdomen. If you feel the beginnings of a headache, you may want to think "head and neck, cool and relaxed." For stomach distress, "stomach soothed and calm." If you are getting a tooth filled at a dentist, you might think of pain sensations as "cool, like an ice cube." There are two general principles when inventing new autogenic suggestions:

1. Be sure you have identified a specific body part that feels uncomfortable. Therefore, do not pick "My body feels unwell" or "I feel sick."

2. Invent a suggestion that identifies a sensation or image that is either the opposite of the target discomfort ("my burning stomach feels cool") or transforms the uncomfortable sensation into a sensation that may well be similar, but not as uncomfortable. That is, instead of focusing on all the negative associations of a stomachache, think how the ache can be made into a positive fantasy ("My stomach burns as healing blood rushes to it, burning off toxins"). This is a popular strategy for managing pain ("The sensation of a dentist drilling . . . cool water flowing on my tooth")

DOING IT MINDFULLY

Treat each autogenic target sensation as a meditation. Focus on the feelings of "warmth" for example. Whenever your mind wanders, return.

Autogenic exercises provide excellent training in letting go. Indeed, the entire point of autogenics is "passive thinking," that is, letting suggestions pass through one's mind, like a mantra, without effort. Any effort or expectation would be considered mind wandering, something to gently put aside as you refocus your attention.

AUTOGENIC SUGGESTIONS

MAKING YOUR OWN RECORDING: Read very slowly and calmly. Your voice should be monotonous with little inflection. Voice should be "warm" and comforting.

Time: 15 minutes.

(Do every day. After one session fill out an R/M Tracker)

Warmth and Heaviness

Let these words go over and over in your mind:

Hands and arms, warm and heavy. Like resting in the sun. Like feeling warm water. Like magnets are pulling them down. Tension dissolves and flows away. You feel distant and far away. Indifferent.

(Repeat for legs and feet.)

[CONTINUE 3 MINUTES]

Calmly Beating Heart

Let these words go over and over in your mind:

Heart is beating calmly and evenly. Soft and easy, calm and easy. Tension dissolves and flows away.

[CONTINUE 2 MINUTES]

Abdomen

Attend to an area above your abdomen.

Let these words go over and over in your mind:

Warm and soothed. Comfortable and warm. Like feeling warm and good after drinking warm hot chocolate, or good soup.

~ END OF SCRIPT ~

EYE OF MINDFULNESS
BRIEF SCRIPT
(Practice this until you select your home exercise)
Do every day. After one session fill out an R/M Tracker

BODY/BREATH SCANNING

Imagine tension flowing from your body with every out-going breath. Flowing from the top of your head to your toes. Flowing from your head, neck, shoulders, arms, hands, back, abdomen, legs, and feet.

[PAUSE 60 SECONDS]

Attend to the easy flow of breath, in and out through your nose, throat, chest, and belly.

[PAUSE 60 SECONDS]

FOCUSED ATTENTION MEDITATION

Select your preferred meditation focus, perhaps the word "One. . . one . . . one" slowing going over and over in your mind like an echo.
Attend to it for the next few minutes.

Whenever your mind wanders, that's OK. You can change if you want.
You are always the quiet observer. Accept what comes and goes. Return to your focus again and again.

[PAUSE 6 MINUTES]

MINDFULNESS

And now we move on to mindfulness meditation. Simply attend to sounds that come and go. Or open your eyes halfway and attend to all stimuli that come and go. Or do both.

If you slip into body/breath work, that's ok.

If you slip into centered focus meditation, that's ok.

Return to mindfulness.

You are the quiet observer.

[PAUSE 6 MINUTES]

Gently let go of what you are attending to.

~ END OF SCRIPT ~

THE R/M TRACKER

WHAT DID YOU FEEL OR EXPERIENCE DURING **AUTOGENIC EXERCISES?**

CLICK BOXES USING THIS KEY

(SKIP ITEMS YOU DON'T UNDERSTAND OR DIDN'T FEEL OR EXPERIENCE)

☒ ❑ ❑ ❑	☒ ☒ ❑ ❑	☒ ☒ ☒ ❑	☒ ☒ ☒ ☒
Felt this SLIGHTLY	Felt this MODERATELY	Felt this VERY MUCH	Felt this EXTREMELY (the most ever)

1. FAR AWAY *and distant from the troubles around me.*	❑❑❑❑
2. PHYSICALLY RELAXED. *Muscles relaxed, loose, limp, warm and heavy. Breathing slow, even, and easy.*	❑❑❑❑
3 AT EASE, AT PEACE.	❑❑❑❑
4. REFRESHED.	❑❑❑❑
5. PLEASANT MIND WANDERING. *Undirected, random positive thoughts.*	❑❑❑❑
6. *Lost in* ***FANTASY*** *and* ***DAYDREAMING.***	❑❑❑❑
7. *Periods of sustained, continuous* ***FOCUS. ABSORPTION.***	❑❑❑❑
8. CENTERED, GROUNDED.	❑❑❑❑
9. QUIET. *Still, few thoughts. Little mind wandering.*	❑❑❑❑
10. UNBOTHERED. *Accepting. When I had a negative thought or feeling, I didn't get caught up in it. No judging, clinging, pushing away, figuring things out.*	❑❑❑❑
11. EASY, EFFORTLESS. *Effortless to let go, put thoughts aside, sustain focus.*	❑❑❑❑
12. *I felt like an* ***OBSERVER*** *standing aside and watching what happens.*	❑❑❑❑
13. CLEAR, AWAKE, AWARE. *I saw things as they really are.*	❑❑❑❑
14. INTERESTED, CURIOUS, FASCINATED.	❑❑❑❑
15. *Things seemed* ***BEAUTIFUL.***	❑❑❑❑
16. GOING DEEPER. *Things seemed unexpected, new, changing, opening up,being revealed. Felt like I was in a different place or space.*	❑❑❑❑
17. *Sense of* ***SPACIOUSNESS, EXPANSIVENESS.***	❑❑❑❑
18. *I felt the* ***SENSE OF SOMETHING GREATER*** *than myself (God, a higher power, spirit, energy, love, or consciousness.); God is with me.*	❑❑❑❑
19. *A sense of* ***MEANING, PURPOSE, DIRECTION.***	❑❑❑❑
20. *I felt* ***REVERENT, PRAYERFUL.***	❑❑❑❑
21. AWE / WONDER, DEEP MYSTERY *of things beyond my understanding.*	❑❑❑❑
22. *I felt a profound personal meaningful "****SPIRITUAL****" or "****MYSTICAL****" experience -- sudden awakening or insight.* • *Felt an underlying hidden* ***TRUTH.*** • *Feeling* ***AT ONE.*** • *Feelings so profound they* ***COULD NOT BE PUT INTO WORDS.***	❑❑❑❑
23. HAPPY, OPTIMISTIC, TRUSTING.	❑❑❑❑
24. LOVING, CARING.	❑❑❑❑
25. THANKFUL. *Grateful.*	❑❑❑❑

Stress & Coping

Eye of Mindfulness Journal

LESSON 7

ANGER AND AGGRESSION

Chapter 30

Turning Anger Into Powerful Coping

© Antonio Guillem/Shutterstock.com

Think of an encounter that has gone wrong, one that has turned into an "anger incident" or "aggression incident." Perhaps you have experienced one of the following:

A friend repeatedly accuses you of something you did not do. You lose it and explode.

You are in the checkout line at a store. Someone slips in front of you. You say something rude.

You are having a political discussion about two candidates for office. The person you are having a discussion with completely disagrees with you. The discussion degrades into name-calling.

Someone has been rude to you and refuses to acknowledge it. You start accusing the individual of being insensitive.

In preparing for this lesson, you might begin by considering these questions:

What kinds of situations or people are most likely to make you irritated, angry, or frustrated? What have you done in the past that shows your irritation, anger, or frustration? What inappropriate things are you tempted to say or do?

Right now, name one person who has been irritated, angry, or frustrated with you. What have they done in the past that showed their irritation, anger, or frustration? What inappropriate things did they say or do?

Do you ever get angry and later regret it? Do some of your conversations quickly turn into heated arguments? Do you sometimes "fly off the handle," only to later regret it? Do you sometimes think of yourself as a "touchy" or "irritable" person? These are just some of the signs of an anger-prone person. In this chapter we examine some powerful skills for transforming the wasted energy of anger and aggression into productive coping.

Use Your Anger as an Early Warning Alarm

To convert wasted anger energy into productive coping, you need to catch anger in the bud, before it builds. It is easier to redirect the flow of a river close to its source than at the end point where it flows into a waterfall. It is easier to put out a fire in the wastebasket than to wait until the whole house is up in flames.

To catch anger in the bud, you need to discover your anger early warning alarms, the early warning signs that anger might build. It makes no sense having a fire alarm when you don't know what it sounds like. You may think that a whining siren is from some car across the street when in fact the wastebasket is burning. Here are some common anger alarm signs:

1. Someone else has or is about to violate your expectations of what is right and expected.
2. Someone else has or is about to insult, hurt, or provoke another person significant to you.
3. Someone else has or is about to insult, hurt, or provoke you.
4. You have met a serious frustration to your goals.
5. You have encountered an appropriate target for expressing irrational/habitual or religion-based feelings of prejudice, bigotry, homophobia, or dislike.

Any of these thoughts may be a good early anger alarm.

When you are closer to erupting with anger, your emotions and body may provide you with urgent warning signs. Emotional cues include, of course, feelings of anger, hostility, irritation, frustration, rage, and so on. Physiological cues of anger arousal include those related to muscle tension (making a fist, raising one's shoulders, puffing up one's chest, tightening one's muscles, standing tall, frowning, furrowing one's brow, clenching and grinding one's teeth, squinting, etc.). Other cues are related to breathing (holding one's breath) and arousal (rapid heart beat, stomach difficulties, feeling warm).

Early Coping Strategies (Catching Anger in the Bud)

Once your anger alarm has suggested a problem about to arise, early coping strategies can quickly turn the potential of wasted anger into productive energy.

Relaxation/Mindfulness. Relaxation and mindfulness can be effective early anger reducers. Simply counting to 10 is the easiest for many people. I suggest passive breathing exercises or progressive muscle relaxation. Here's a mindful breathing exercise:

> *Let yourself breathe easily and naturally. When you are ready, take in a full deep breath, filling your lungs and abdomen with good, refreshing air. Pause. And when you are ready, relax. And slowly let the air flow out, very smoothly and gently. And now, just continue breathing normally for a while.*

Reality Checking. Much anger is the result of unrealistic expectations, distorted perceptions, or failure to consider all the possible causes of a problem. Simply pausing and taking time to consider all aspects of a provocative situation can be enough to reduce the potential for anger.

Novoco's Anger Management Program

The above strategies are useful at those times you unexpectedly encounter a provoking situation. Novaco (1975) has proposed an anger management program that can be useful when you can anticipate ahead a possible provocative situation that is likely to arouse excessive anger. He suggests breaking a potential anger situation into four stages:

1. *Preparing for provocation (pre-stress).* Prepare ahead for possible provocation. Preparations should include active coping plans, specific courses of action you can take ("I can plan what to do ahead," "I can call my supervisor," "I can repeat my main point"), possible reality checks that identify and defuse distorted thoughts ("I need to remember that a criticism of my behavior isn't necessarily a personal attack," "I might blow this out of perspective, so I should maintain perspective of what is important and what is not"), and relaxation and defensive strategies to reduce or avoid tension ("I can do my breathing exercises," "I can just excuse myself and leave the situation").
2. *Impact and confrontation (onset-stress).* Plan what you will do when your provocative incident is just beginning and the confrontation has occurred. Once again, you may consider active coping strategies, realistic and practical appraisal, and relaxation and defensive strategies.
3. *Coping with arousal (mid-stress).* When the confrontation is well underway, you unexpected anger. Again, plan ahead with active coping, reality- checking, and relaxation/defensive strategies.
4. *Reflecting on the provocation (post-stress).* Anticipate what happens after the confrontation. Think about what you will think and do if the conflict is resolved, or unresolved?

EXERCISES

The Mindfulness Exercise Challenge. *Try practicing a five-minute version of your home mindfulness exercise before completing any chapter exercise.*

30.1 Anger Early Warning Signs.

What are your anger early warning alarms? If you can't think of any, describe a recent provocation in which you responded with too much anger. Describe the details:

When:
Where:
What:
Who:

What did you want?

Then, think about the time just before this provocation. Can you detect any ways you could have figured out that the situation was about to happen, or turn angry?

30.2 Apply Novoco's System

Select an aggressive encounter you have had. Write a movie script presenting all of the details, including what was said, thought, and felt. Give enough details that an actor could actually act out your incident.

Then, rewrite your script using Novoco's system. First break your incident into four stages. Then, write an ideal script for each script. Skip stages that don't fit.

Stress & Coping

Eye of Mindfulness Journal

Chapter 31

Dealing With Aggression

© Luis Louro/Shutterstock.com

Making difficult requests can be especially challenging when the possibility of aggression is involved. In these situations you are either responding to a threat of attack, or are making a request that may trigger verbal or physical violence.

The first goal of dealing with aggressive and manipulative behavior is to conduct a reality check and determine if the aggression or manipulation is real or imagined. What more information do you need in order to decide? If the threat is real, a number of experts (Goldstein & Keller, 1987; Jakubowski & Lange, 1987) suggest strategies for limiting the other person's aggressive behavior and dealing with the threat in general. These strategies involve:

- Introduce calm/Mindfulness
- Get to the source of the problem

Introduce Calm/Mindfulness (Smith, 2001)

Goldstein and Keller (1987) offer some very useful advice for relaxing a potentially hostile or aggressive person. I have somewhat revised their suggestions on the following pages:

Change to a neutral and more relaxed/mindful setting. Imagine a coworker has accused you of being rude and argumentative. Both of you are standing next to his office desk. People are waiting outside for their appointments with both of you. The pressure is building. Clearly this is not the time or place to sort things out. Suggest a neutral and quiet setting, perhaps over coffee at the local coffee house after work.

Model calm and mindfulness. Make a simple effort to be relaxed and mindful, this can help introduce an atmosphere that can defuse anger and enhance problem-solving. Be careful not to do a visible relaxation/mindfulness exercise during a threatening encounter (by deliberately taking slow deep breaths, tensing up and releasing tension, or closing your eyes to meditate). These efforts work best before a potential encounter when one is alone. When done during an encounter, they can be misinterpreted as behavior that is hostile or defensive. During an encounter, take a relaxed posture. Do not cross your arms, make a fist, hold something tightly, or clench your teeth. Assume a relaxed posture with your shoulders loose and slightly sloped. Your arms, ands, and legs should be slightly open and not clenched. Don't Let yourself breathe in a relaxed way. If you notice your shoulders or arms getting tense, just let go.

Encourage rational and problem-solving talk. Set the stage for calm discussion by asking the other person what both of you might do to constructively deal with the problem. Note that if you ask the person to explain his or her anger, that may actually increase the anger ("*Isn't it obvious, stupid . . .* "). You might ask, *"If you speak more slowly and quietly, I can understand you better."*

Listen empathically. Honestly attempt to paraphrase what the other person is saying. Make it clear you are interested and listening. At least restate or rephrase their comments. If possible, focus on underlying feelings. But do not dwell on feelings, because this might aggravate anger. Move quickly to attempting to address the problem. *("Now that I understand where you are coming from, let's get to business. What are our options?")*

Reward calm and mindful behavior. Gently praise or reinforce the other person when they show less anger or aggression, and an increased willingness to engage in mature problem-solving. Try not to be patronizing. You might say, *"Thanks for being open; that helps me know where you are coming from so we can work this thing out." "I appreciate your patience. I know this is difficult, but I want to solve this as quickly as you do."*

Getting to the Source of the Problem

Ask for a clarification. Note if the angry person seems to be so overwhelmed with emotion that he or she ignores the specific problem. Simply acknowledge the emotion ("*I can tell you are really irritated*") and quickly focus on what you understand the concrete problem to be.

Focus on the concrete issue. Try to consistently approach your problem using the skills of problem-solving. That is, focus on what you realistically want. What can you realistically seek for now? When do you want it? Where? The other person may engage in emotional outburst, blaming, self-pity, and so on. Such efforts obscure the issue or divert attention from the real problem. Basically, acknowledge and respect what the other person is saying, and then suggest that it would be better for both of you to get right to the real problem. Then suggest your perception of the concrete issues that need to be addressed.

Tell the other person the message you hear. Honestly let the other person know the message that you are getting:

> *Person A: "So far, what I have heard is that I am 'ruthless, insensitive, and arrogant.' I'm confused. That doesn't tell me exactly what I need to do to help fix the problem."*
>
> *Person B: "It's your insensitivity to the rules we have at work."*
>
> *Person A: "The rules? That helps somewhat, but which rules are you talking about?"*
>
> *Person B: "We all have to be here at 8:30 AM. Yesterday you were here at 9 AM. In fact every day last week you came in after 9 AM. That upsets me."*

When Problem-Solving Doesn't Work

Sometimes, problem-solving is going nowhere and is clearly escalating to dangerous proportions. At some point one may have to take emergency action to defuse the situation. The ideas of this chapter can be applied to such emergencies. Specifically:

- *Aggression focus.* Ask questions to prompt awareness of the other person's aggressive behavior. Provide direct and specific negative feedback, identifying the specific problems and issues you see.
- *Fact focus and ignore.* Treat putdowns as neutral comments (ignore emotional words; focus on what might be true). Sort out fact from judgment and interpretation.
- *Escalate.* Announce your intent to escalate your assertive comments.
- *Bail out.* State your intent to end the encounter.
- *Apply a terminal DESC script.* Some differences simply cannot be reconciled and both parties may have to settle with accepting no resolution. Here, a reasonable goal can be to assertively express oneself, rethink one's goals, and go on living. One might choose to terminate an unsuccessful negotiation with a clear and concise summary of what has transpired, focusing on both one's own wants, thoughts, feelings, and behavior as well as those of the other person. Again, a DESC script can be a useful tool, with the Describe line focusing on the failed negotiation process:

  Describe (summarizes both positions): *"We have negotiated this problem for three days. Both of us have made a reasonable attempt to offer solutions and compromises. But we still haven't reached a solution."*

  Express (what you feel): *"I feel very frustrated when I can't negotiate a solution. But I also feel resigned that perhaps that is how it will have to be."*

Specify (make a specific request): *"Let me suggest that we stop our negotiations and accept that we both have legitimate, but irreconcilable, differences."*

Consequences: *"I would like to leave feeling that we made our best effort to resolve our differences, and that we respect each other."*

EXERCISES

> *The Mindfulness Exercise Challenge.* *Try practicing a five-minute version of your home mindfulness exercise before completing any chapter exercise.*

31.1 What's Going On in This Angry Encounter?

Here is a tense exchange between Gil and Lois, a couple that has been married for about a year. Identify where techniques used in Chapters 30 and 31 are illustrated. Use the AAA Checklist (end of chapter).

THE FAMILY VISIT

Gil has just announced to Lois that his mother and family are coming to stay with them for a week. Lois is extremely upset and is close to moving out, or worse.

Lois: *"How could you do such a thing? Don't you care for me at all? Everyday something like this happens. You constantly do things without asking or telling me. You just don't love me anymore! How can I put up with this behavior?"*

Gil (takes a deep breath, and sits down; invites Lois to sit): *"You're really getting upset, and I understand that. I'm not sure what the issue is for you really."*

Lois: *"You don't? It's simple. You're always too inconsiderate and I can't take it anymore. Stupid!"*

Gil: *"Please help me out. Inconsiderate? I need some specifics."*

Lois: *"You know. You just don't talk to me anymore, like you don't care."*

Gil: *"This isn't helping. I can see you're upset. That's making me upset, and I don't think we can sort this out when we're both so stirred up."*

Lois: *"You asked your parents to stay with us for a week. You didn't ask me. What am I going to do? How am I supposed to feel? Do you want me to just obey all of your commands?"*

Gil: *"One thing at a time, otherwise I get confused. It's hard for me to deal with name-calling, although I understand how you feel. I hear you saying you're angry I asked my parents to stay without talking to you first. Am I getting the point?"*

Lois: *"Duhh. Yes, that's exactly it. And you're a selfish pig to boot."*

Gil: *"I apologize for not asking you, and I know you're frustrated. I promise I will ask you in the future. But I'm not sure that is all that's going on here."*

Lois: *"Isn't it obvious? Where are they going to stay? Who is going to feed them? Where are we going to put our four children? And we're going on vacation two weeks from now. How can we plan with your parents always around."*

Gil:*" I guess I hadn't thought that through. By the way, it helps when you explain to me exactly what's going on. I can think things through more clearly. But I'm not sure where to begin. You and I have a problem, and I'm really sorry I caused it. But what's done is done? Where do you suggest we begin?"*

Lois: *"Well, for starters, is it a done deal that they're coming? Have they bought their plane tickets? Could their trip be delayed until after our vacation? Is there any chance they could stay in the motel on the corner?"*

Gil: *" Hmm, those concrete ideas get me thinking. There's got to be an answer to this. Maybe I could call them up today and tell them the situation, and see what kind of compromise we all can live with."*

Lois: *"Yes, I think we should call them up as soon as possible. But I also think we should think through ahead of time what we want, what we can live with, and what just won't work with them. If we call them and treat this as just one of those unexpected problems that happen, we can figure it out as mature adults."*

Gil: *"Good idea. Let's start after breakfast. You know, you're so sexy when you're angry!"*

Lois: *"You pig!"*

31.2 Examples of Tense Encounters in Entertainment

Find a story, television show, or movie that illustrates an angry encounter between at least two people. Show how it illustrates the concepts in Chapters 30 and 31, using the AAA Checklist.

31.3 Observations of Angry Encounters

This week keep your eye out for an angry or aggressive encounter. Carefully note which of the ideas from Chapters 30 and 31 were used, using the AAA Checklist.

31.4 Your Angry Encounter

Think of a recent angry encounter that either went well or didn't go so well. Write a "movie script" for this encounter, including everything that was done, said, thought, and felt. Does this script illustrate any of the ideas in Chapters 30 and 31 (AAA Checklist)?

Now rewrite your script. In your do-over, include ideas from the AAA Checklist.

THE AAA (ANGER /AGGRESSION ANALYSIS) CHECKLIST

<u>WARNING SIGNS</u> What Anger Early Warning Signs Did You Encounter?

- ☐ **Warning 1. Situational Cues**
  - Incident violates your expectations of what is right or expected.
  - Someone is or is about to insult, hurt, or provoke.
  - You have met a serious frustration.
  - You are a target of prejudice, bigotry, homophobia, or dislike.
- ☐ **Warning 2. Emotional Signs**
  - Anger, hostility, irritation, frustration
- ☐ **Warning 3. Physical Signs**
  - Making fist, raising shoulders; Frowning, furrowing brow, clenching teeth; Holding breath; Rapid heartbeat; Stomach difficulties

<u>PRE-COPING</u> How Did You, or Could You Catch Anger Before It Starts?

- ☐ **Pre-Coping 1. Relax/Be Mindful**
- ☐ **Pre-Coping 2. Reality Check: What is realistic, undistorted, wasted effort?**
- ☐ **Pre-Coping 3. Focus on Anger Stage**
  - Pre-stress: Preparing for provocation
  - Onset-stress: Preparing for incident
  - Mid-stress: Preparing for the incident when it's happening
  - Post-stress: Reflecting on the incident

<u>AGGRESSION COPING</u> How Did You or Could You Deal with Aggression?

- ☐ **AGG 1. Introduce Calm/Mindfulness**
  - Change to neutral, relaxed, mindful setting
  - Model calm and mindfulness
  - Encourage rational problem-solving talk
  - Listen empathically
  - Reward calm and mindful behavior
- ☐ **AGG 2. Get to source of problem**
  - Ask for clarification
  - Focus on the concrete issue
  - Tell the other person the message you hear

<u>WHEN PROBLEM-SOLVING DOESN'T WORK</u>

- ☐ AGGRESSION FOCUS
  - Ask questions to prompt awareness of other person's aggressive behavior.
  - Provide direct and specific negative feedback.
- ☐ FACT FOCUS AND IGNORE
  - Treat putdown as neutral comment (ignore emotional words; focus on what might be true).
  - Sort out fact from judgment and interpretation.
- ☐ ESCALATE
  - Announce intent to escalate your assertions, and ask for a contract to end the aggression.
- ☐ BAIL OUT
  - State your intent to end the encounter.
- ☐ APPLY A TERMINAL DESC SCRIPT

© iunewind / Shutterstock.com

Chapter 32

Emotion-Focused Mindfulness

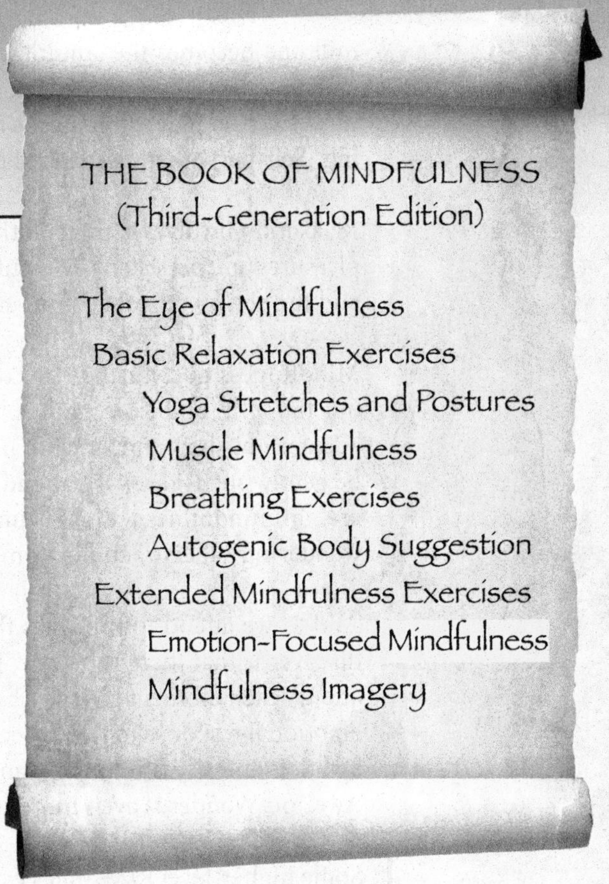

© Vadim Sadovski / Shutterstock.com

In this chapter we step back from our exploration of relaxation and mindfulness exercises. In our journey we have been exploring ways of mastering the relaxation and mindfulness response in order to develop basic skills. But growth in mindfulness goes beyond developing quiet sustained simple focus. One additional skill is that of deliberately contemplating themes that embody mindful emotion. This is emotion-focused mindfulness. It, along with quiet focus, is a core mindfulness skill.

The Hedonic and Stress Treadmills

Positive emotions can wear off. Our brains like newness, novelty, and change. Repeated experience of a good thing leads to adaptation. The first bite of an ice cream cone is the best. Then the goodness and newness wears off. Similarly, the fun of a new job, or a new college class, gets old. One may even grow tired of love and, yes, sex. This overall process is called **hedonic adaptation** (Brickman & Campbell, 1971), something of a **hedonic treadmill**. It is the opposite of mindfulness, of seeing things fresh and new.

© Michael D Brown / Shutterstock.com

At times stress can become a treadmill. Problems we think we have solved come back again and again. Negative emotions return. This can be something of a cycle, one fueled by self-centered and preoccupied mind wandering. On the treadmill one becomes the "multitasking observer," distracted from mindful singletasking (Chapter 13). Mind wandering churns up rumination about more stress, more that is unsatisfactory, more that needs to be done. This in turn churns up more mind wandering. Self-perpetuating stressful mind wandering is the opposite of mindful single focus.

Relaxation involves getting off the hedonic or stress treadmill, taking a break from both pleasures and persistent stressful mind wandering. Once off the treadmill, one recovers, and can return refreshed and renewed.

Mindfulness goes further by cultivating a simple awareness of the world apart from our thoughts and expectations. In mindfulness, the thoughts and feelings of hedonic adaptation—boredom, lack of interest—constitute mind wandering and distraction to be gently put aside as we attend to things with fresh eyes and see things as they really are. In mindfulness, stress is unnecessary effort and judgment, rumination and mind wandering, all distractions from simple focus and single tasking.

And as we attend to things as they are, simply on their own terms, the first thing we discover is that there is more. The world changes. Things come and go. If we simply attend, each moment is new. The R/M State Interested, Curious, Fascinated reflects our emotional response to this aspect of "things as they are" when the cloud of hedonic adaptation and stressful mind wandering distraction are gently put aside. The R/M State Awe and Wonder is even more so.

Some higher-level R/M States can be understood as mindful emotions, or having emotion-like qualities, that counter adaptation and stressful mind wandering. They do so in several ways. First, they are nonverbal experiences. Hedonic adaptation and stressful mind wandering are perpetual motion word machines, sources of continuing preoccupation and worry. Second, mindful emotions are focus-prompting. They command our mindful, singular attention. Lastly, mindful emotions center us on what might lie beyond self-referential thinking, our bubble of self-centered preoccupied mind wandering. They prompt "other-referential thinking" and point to a larger and greater world. Students frequently see mindful emotion in higher-level R/M States:

I felt like an ***OBSERVER*** *standing aside and watching what happens.*
CLEAR, AWAKE, AWARE. *I saw things as they really are.*
INTERESTED, CURIOUS, FASCINATED.
Things seemed ***BEAUTIFUL.***

GOING DEEPER. *Things seemed unexpected, new, changing, opening up, being revealed. Felt like I was in a different place or space.*
Sense of ***SPACIOUSNESS, EXPANSIVENESS.***
I felt the ***SENSE OF SOMETHING GREATER*** *than myself (God, a higher power, spirit, energy, love, or consciousness.)*
A sense of ***MEANING, PURPOSE, DIRECTION.***

I felt ***REVERENT, PRAYERFUL.***
AWE / WONDER, DEEP MYSTERY *of things beyond my understanding.*
I felt a profound personal meaningful ***"SPIRITUAL"*** *or* ***"MYSTICAL"*** *experience -- sudden awakening or insight.* • *Felt an underlying hidden* ***TRUTH.*** • *Felt* ***AT ONE.*** • *Feelings so profound they* ***COULD NOT BE PUT INTO WORDS.***

HAPPY, OPTIMISTIC, TRUSTING.
LOVING, CARING.
THANKFUL. *Grateful.*

Emotion-Focused Mindfulness

Emotion-focused mindfulness exercises start with the core instructions of *sustaining simple focus while minimizing judgment and effort.* However, one sustains focus on a mindful emotion. Perhaps the most popular examples of this are loving kindness (*metta)* meditation and gratitude meditation.

Loving Kindness Meditation

Loving kindness meditation is an ancient Buddhist imagery meditation that involves quietly cultivating feelings of compassion toward oneself and others (including our adversaries). Actually, most world religions have incorporated love, kindness, and compassion in their mindful contemplations. And of course there is a vast secular literature of writings on love.

In loving kindness meditation one may in sequence have fantasies about selflessly loving, being kind toward, and having compassion for a sequence of increasingly challenging "targets":

- Oneself
- A good friend
- A neutral person
- An adversary
- Everyone else
- Deities, or lack thereof
- The entire universe

At first you might think this is a silly thing to do. But loving kindness meditation isn't easy. When we enjoy a moment of love or care for someone, it is usually fleeting, lasting less than a minute. In loving kindness meditation, you sustain your imagery progression for an entire practice session, perhaps 15 to 20 minutes. Every time your mind wanders and you think about a selfish need or something you like less about the object of your attention, you let go of your mind wandering, and return focus to your target.

How do you focus? You might visualize the person receiving your loving kindness. Think of all the details and specifics you appreciate. You may repeat the person's name, over and over, like a mantra. You might imagine "radiating" a kind of "love energy," perhaps flowing from your heart. Doing this might be something like practicing an autogenic "warmth" or "heart" focus exercise, adding "love" to the experience of energy.

What does this have to do with the hedonic treadmill? When you love someone genuinely, your attention is taken away from yourself. Think about what this means. You let go of mind wandering about self-centered concerns and preoccupations, both good and bad. You let go of what might make the object of your experience seem ordinary or boring. You see people for who they are, ever new, unclouded by the fog of your habitual expectations. You truly focus in a mindful way. Loving kindness is mindfulness. We can cultivate loving kindness through loving kindness meditation.

As an example, the University of New Hampshire Health Services has an excellent loving kindness meditation: https://www.youtube.com/watch?v=sz7cpV7ERsM.

Gratitude Meditation

What does it mean to experience gratitude for something? Someone gives you a gift, a wonderful diamond, a cute kitten, a brand new car. It is unexpected. It is beautiful. For a moment you forget yourself completely and are filled with appreciation of the gift. It may even fill you with feelings of awe and wonder. And you feel gratitude for the gift, and thankfulness to the person who gave it to you.

In this moment of gratitude you are off the hedonic treadmill. You are off the stress treadmill. You are very much mindful. You are fully aware of your gift. So aware that you don't even have words to express yourself. You feel mindful awe and wonder. You have spontaneously put all self-centered mind wandering aside. You are fully focused on how thankful you are that someone has given you such a gift.

Gratitude is a way of rediscovering a world that has grown tired and ordinary. Gratitude is a way of discovering what is truly new in the moment. Gratitude is mindfulness. And we can cultivate gratitude with a simple gratitude meditation.

Breaking the Cycle

Mindfulness and relaxation are ways of taking a break from the treadmill cycle and hopefully returning to life refreshed and renewed. Loving kindness and gratitude mindfulness break the cycle in a different way. One makes a deliberate choice to put oneself aside, one's self-centered thoughts and preoccupations, and genuinely direct one's care and gratitude toward another. Each act of loving kindness, each act of sincere gratitude, can be something of a giving, a small sacrifice, in the name of something or someone larger or greater than your mind wandering, larger than yourself.

Other Emotion-Focused Approaches

Loving kindness and gratitude meditation are among the most popular of emotion-focused approaches. However, they reflect two general strategies. In **associative meditation,** one selects a word or phrase for meditative focus. Here mind wandering is put to use. One waits for associations to come and go related to the word or phrase. After each association emerges, one mindfully lets go and returns focus. Alternatively one might let go "what is the gist or most important thing about what I am feeling?" and simply wait without deliberately trying to answer.

Target words might be any word from the R/M Tracker. You might focus on the word "wonder," "quiet," and so on. Or you might focus on a poem or passage that seems to convey R/M States. One very popular passage is the Serenity Prayer (Reinhold Neibuhr):

God grant me the serenity
to accept the things I cannot change;
courage to change the things I can;
and wisdom to know the difference.

You read the passage very slowly and select one word to be the target of your mindful focus, perhaps "accept" or "wisdom."

In **expressive meditation** you perform a simple expressive act to honestly say what mindfulness might mean to you at the time. Your act could be taking notes in a journal, silently speaking to oneself, or perhaps prayer.

LOVING MINDNESS MEDITATION
(Do every day. After one session fill out an R/M Tracker)

Oneself

May I be safe and free.

May I be free from pain and suffering.

May I be healthy.

I care and love myself, as a mother loves a child.

I picture myself holding and caring for myself, as a child.

Safe and free.

Cradling and loving.

With care and compassion.

Without conditions. Loving myself as I am.

I am good. I am worthy.

[REFLECT ON THIS 2 MINUTES]

A Good Friend

I think of my good friend.

I care for and love this person.

I care for and love this person as is, without condition.

With care and compassion.

I imagine all the things I love about this person.

[PAUSE 2 MINUTES]

I repeat this person's name in my mind, like a mantra, over and over.

[PAUSE 2 MINUTES]

I feel energy of compassion radiating toward this person.

[PAUSE 2 MINUTES]

A Neutral Person

I think of a person I do not know. Perhaps someone nearby or someone I have read about.

I care for and love this person.

I care for and love this person as is, without condition.

With care and compassion.

I imagine all the things I love about this person.

[PAUSE 2 MINUTES]

I repeat one word that best depicts this person in my mind, like a mantra, over and over.

[PAUSE 2 MINUTES]

I feel energy of compassion radiating toward this person.

[PAUSE 2 MINUTES]

An Adversary

I think of an adversary in my life.

I care for and love this person.

I care for and love this person as is, without condition.

With care and compassion.

I imagine all the things I love about this person.

[PAUSE 2 MINUTES]

I repeat one word that best depicts this person in my mind, like a mantra, over and over.

[PAUSE 2 MINUTES]

I feel energy of compassion radiating toward this person.

[PAUSE 2 MINUTES]

God or the universe as it is, "What is truly deep and real for me?"

I care for and love "What is truly deep and real for me."

I care for and love "What is truly deep and real for me" as is, without condition.

With care and compassion.

I imagine all the things I love about this.

[PAUSE 2 MINUTES]

I repeat one word that best depicts this, like a mantra, over and over.

[PAUSE 2 MINUTES]

I feel energy of compassion radiating toward this.

[PAUSE 2 MINUTES]

GRATITUDE MEDITATION

(Do every day. After one session fill out an R/M Tracker)

I list and think of three blessings I have received.

[PAUSE 2 MINUTES]

I imagine myself expressing thanks and gratitude for these three things.

[PAUSE 2 MINUTES]

I imagine something wonderful and positive that may be ending in the near future.

[PAUSE 2 MINUTES]

I imagine myself expressing thanks and gratitude for this.

[PAUSE 2 MINUTES]

I imagine a positive experience that quite possibly may not have happened.

[PAUSE 2 MINUTES]

I imagine myself expressing thanks and gratitude for this.

[PAUSE 2 MINUTES]

I imagine the most important thing in my life I can feel gratitude for. The one thing more important than anything else. I imagine myself expressing thanks for this in whatever way feels most honest and real.

[PAUSE 4 MINUTES]

THE R/M TRACKER

WHAT DID YOU FEEL OR EXPERIENCE DURING **LOVING KINDNESS MEDITATION?**

CLICK BOXES USING THIS KEY

(SKIP ITEMS YOU DON'T UNDERSTAND OR DIDN'T FEEL OR EXPERIENCE)

☒☐☐☐	☒☒☐☐	☒☒☒☐	☒☒☒☒
Felt this SLIGHTLY	Felt this MODERATELY	Felt this VERY MUCH	Felt this EXTREMELY (the most ever)

1. ***FAR AWAY*** *and distant from the troubles around me.*	☐☐☐☐
2. ***PHYSICALLY RELAXED.*** *Muscles relaxed, loose, limp, warm and heavy. Breathing slow, even, and easy.*	☐☐☐☐
3 ***AT EASE, AT PEACE.***	☐☐☐☐
4. ***REFRESHED.***	☐☐☐☐
5. ***PLEASANT MIND WANDERING.*** *Undirected, random positive thoughts.*	☐☐☐☐
6. *Lost in* ***FANTASY*** *and* ***DAYDREAMING.***	☐☐☐☐
7. *Periods of sustained, continuous* ***FOCUS. ABSORPTION.***	☐☐☐☐
8. ***CENTERED, GROUNDED.***	☐☐☐☐
9. ***QUIET.*** *Still, few thoughts. Little mind wandering.*	☐☐☐☐
10. ***UNBOTHERED.*** *Accepting. When I had a negative thought or feeling, I didn't get caught up in it. No judging, clinging, pushing away, figuring things out.*	☐☐☐☐
11. ***EASY, EFFORTLESS.*** *Effortless to let go, put thoughts aside, sustain focus.*	☐☐☐☐
12. *I felt like an* ***OBSERVER*** *standing aside and watching what happens.*	☐☐☐☐
13. ***CLEAR, AWAKE, AWARE.*** *I saw things as they really are.*	☐☐☐☐
14. ***INTERESTED, CURIOUS, FASCINATED.***	☐☐☐☐
15. *Things seemed* ***BEAUTIFUL.***	☐☐☐☐
16. ***GOING DEEPER.*** *Things seemed unexpected, new, changing, opening up,being revealed. Felt like I was in a different place or space.*	☐☐☐☐
17. *Sense of* ***SPACIOUSNESS, EXPANSIVENESS.***	☐☐☐☐
18. *I felt the* ***SENSE OF SOMETHING GREATER*** *than myself (God, a higher power, spirit, energy, love, or consciousness.); God is with me.*	☐☐☐☐
19. *A sense of* ***MEANING, PURPOSE, DIRECTION.***	☐☐☐☐
20. *I felt* ***REVERENT, PRAYERFUL.***	☐☐☐☐
21. ***AWE / WONDER, DEEP MYSTERY*** *of things beyond my understanding.*	☐☐☐☐
22. *I felt a profound personal meaningful* ***"SPIRITUAL"*** *or* ***"MYSTICAL"*** *experience -- sudden awakening or insight.* • *Felt an underlying hidden* ***TRUTH.*** • *Feeling* ***AT ONE.*** • *Feelings so profound they* ***COULD NOT BE PUT INTO WORDS.***	☐☐☐☐
23. ***HAPPY, OPTIMISTIC, TRUSTING.***	☐☐☐☐
24. ***LOVING, CARING.***	☐☐☐☐
25. ***THANKFUL.*** *Grateful.*	☐☐☐☐

© iunewind / Shutterstock.com

LESSON 8

SPECIAL TOPICS

Chapter 33

Stress at Work

© ivector/Shutterstock.com

Job stress comes in many forms. However, often different stressful types of work share the same stressful characteristics. Consider the following story.

Steve is waiting nervously in his doctor's office. For weeks he has been suffering from a variety of stress-related physical symptoms, including fatigue, stomach distress, and headaches. To make things work, his home life has suffered. Steve has become something of an angry tyrant at home, complaining and arguing with his wife and two children. And the grandparents have moved on and another child is on the way.

Steve's most frequent complaint is work. For the past five years he has been a customer complaint officer at a department store. He used to enjoy his job and looked forward to a managerial position. Every day had its challenges, calling for creative solutions. However, things have changed. Steve's store is downsizing, and the management is cutting corners. The first "efficiency steps" seemed minor. The cleaning staff was cut back and assigned to clean once a week rather than once a day. The water cooler was removed. Extra workers were moved into Steve's office space and some had to double-up on desks. The workplace became noisy, dirty, and uncomfortable.

Soon it became clear that economizing and downsizing meant that no one's job was safe. As people left, others had to take over. Steve found himself doing the work of two or three people. His hours became unpredictable. Sometimes he worked evenings, sometimes early mornings. Steve hoped for some flexibility in scheduling hours. Even here he had to follow the rules rigidly given by his supervisors. Steve used to enjoy socializing with his friends at work. Now many have left or there's no time. However, nearly everyone complains how the new management just doesn't listen. They feel stuck in something of a rat race, working hard just to keep up. Many feel there is no way out, and no future in a downsizing organization that is poorly run. (http://www.cdc.gov/niosh/topics/stress/)

Steve's story is becoming increasingly common. Job stress can become a serious and costly problem. Problems at work are more strongly associated with health complaints than are any other life stressor, more so than even financial problems or family difficulties.

Often we complain about our jobs. Sometimes our complaining becomes a source of continuous mind wandering. In this chapter we will learn how to stand back as a mindful observer, and look at job stress calmly and objectively. We will learn how to become a job stress analyst. Specifically, we will learn the system suggested by the National Institute for Occupational Safety and Health (NIOSH).

NIOSH is the federal agency responsible for conducting research and making recommendations for the prevention of work-related illness and injury. As part of its mandate, NIOSH is directed by Congress to study the psychological aspects of occupational safety and health, including stress and work. NIOSH works with industry, labor, and universities to better understand the nature of stress at worry, its effects on worker safety and health, and ways of reducing workplace stress. This chapter presents material and examples from NIOSH (http://www.cdc.gov/niosh/topics/stress/). Given its importance, it is presented in a form that you may freely copy, reprint, and distribute in any way you wish. You may wish to acquire and distribute copies of "Stress at Work," a free booklet from NIOSH (1999), that presents the information in this chapter.

What Is Job Stress?

Job stress can be defined as the harmful physical and emotional responses that occur when the *requirements of the job do not meet the capabilities, resources, or needs of the workers.* In other words, the problem is job/worker fit, which can lead to poor health and injury.

Job stress is not the same as challenge. Challenge energizes and motivates us to learn new job skills. When a challenge is met, we're relaxed and satisfied. Thus challenge is an important part of healthy and productive work. Indeed, a little bit of job stress is good for you.

In our example of Steve, we see how a possibly challenging job can become a source of stress, possibly leading to illness, frustration, and poor performance.

Causes of Job Stress

There are two causes of job stress: work conditions and worker characteristics. **Stressful working conditions** (job stressors such as too much work, little control, noisy environments) can directly influence safety and health. **Individual and situational factors** may intensify or weaken the effects. Steve's physical complaints, as well as his busy family life, are individual and situational factors that can aggravate the impact of stressful working conditions.

The NIOSH model of job stress is summarized in this widely cited illustration presented here (https://www.cdc.gov/niosh/docs/99-101).

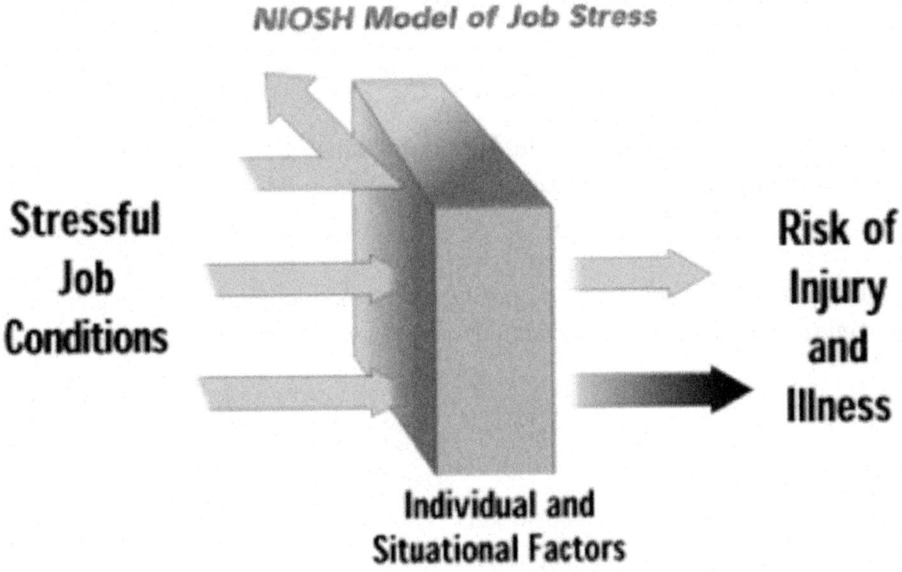

Stressful Job Conditions

When conducting your job stress analysis, ask if you work under stressful conditions? NIOSH has summarized six things to look for:

1. The Design of Work Tasks
2. Management Style
3. Interpersonal Relationships
4. Work Roles
5. Career Concerns
6. Environmental Conditions

To these I have added a seventh, "Feedback and Communication."

1. The Design of Tasks

- Heavy workload
- Infrequent rest breaks
- Long work hours and shift work
- Hectic/routine tasks with little meaning
- Work that underutilizes your skills
- Work that provides little sense of control

Example: *Steve has to do the work of several people, with few rest breaks. Often he works long hours, and feels little control over his hours.*

2. Management Style

- Lack of participation by workers in decision-making
- Poor communication in the organization
- Lack of family-friendly policies

Example: *Steve and his coworkers do not take part in creating work schedules. Assignments come down from supervisors without discussion.*

3. Interpersonal Relationships

- Poor social environment
- Lack of support or help from coworkers
- Lack of support or help from supervisors

Example: *Steve's workload is so hectic that he has little chance to socialize, or seek help.*

4. Work Roles

Conflicting or uncertain job expectations
Too much responsibility
Too many "hats to wear"

Example: *As Steve's workplace downsizes, he takes on uncertain jobs from others. Often he does two jobs at once.*

5. Career Concerns

- Job insecurity
- Lack of opportunity for growth, advancement, or promotion
- Rapid changes for which workers are unprepared

Example: *Steve and his coworkers worry about their future in the organization. Things change without warning.*

6. Environmental Conditions

- Unpleasant work conditions
- Dangerous physical conditions such as crowding, noise, air pollution, or ergonomic problems.

Example: *Steve's work space has deteriorated and is uncomfortable and possibly even unsafe.*

7. Feedback and Communication

Many of these problems are made worse by poor feedback and communication. Often, simply letting workers know the facts can reduce uncertainty and a sense of helpless. Knowing what's really going on also gives workers the best opportunity to consider realistic coping options. Signs of poor feedback and communication include:

- Not receiving clear, specific, and immediate constructive feedback when you make a mistake or can do something better.
- Not receiving clear, specific, and immediate praise and positive feedback when you have done something right or completed a job particularly well.
- Not being informed of the full extent of challenges or problems that may be present at work.

Individual and Situational Factors

NIOSH provides three examples of individual and situational factors that can help to reduce the effects of stressful working conditions:

1. Balance between work and family or personal life
2. A support network of friends and coworkers
3. A relaxed and mindful outlook

To these I believe it is important to add maintaining a healthy lifestyle, including:

- Getting enough sleep
- Eating properly
- Getting enough exercise
- Conscientiously taking care of medical problems (taking medications, following doctor's orders)

However, the perspective of this book personal coping skills, specifically the basic skills of:

- Learning relaxation and mindfulness
- Applying effective problem-solving skills
- Thinking rationally and realistically

To this we can add the following major application skills:

- Desensitization and relapse prevention
- Assertiveness
- Dealing with shyness
- Managing anger and aggression

The Costs and Warning Signs of Job Stress

Illness and Productivity Loss

NIOSH identifies the following early warning signs of job stress:

- Headache
- Sleep disturbances
- Difficulty in concentrating
- Short temper
- Upset stomach
- Low morale

In addition, we add high scores on the Stress Symptoms Scale presented earlier. Low morale, health and job complaints, and employee turnover often provide the first signs of job stress. But sometimes there are no clues, especially if employees are fearful of losing their jobs. Lack of obvious or widespread signs is not a good reason to dismiss concerns about job stress or minimize the importance of a prevention program. Left unchecked, job stress can contribute to:

Cardiovascular disease. Many studies suggest that psychologically demanding jobs that allow employees little control over the work process increase the risk of cardiovascular disease.

Musculoskeletal disorders. On the basis of research by NIOSH and many other organizations, it is widely believed that job stress increases the risk for development of back and upper-extremity musculoskeletal disorders.

Psychological disorders. Several studies suggest that differences in rates of mental health problems (such a depression and burnout) for various occupations are due partly to differences in job stress levels. (Economic and lifestyle differences between occupations may also contribute to some of these problems.)

Suicide, cancers, ulcers, and impaired immune function. Some studies suggest a relationship between stressful working conditions and these health problems. However, more research is needed.

Workplace injury. Although more study is needed, there is a growing concern that stressful working conditions interfere with safe work practices and set the stage for injuries at work.

Productivity loss. Some employers assume that stressful working conditions are a necessary evil, that companies must turn up the pressure on workers and set aside health concerns to remain productive and profitable in today's economy. But research findings challenge this belief. Studies show that stressful working conditions are actually associated with increased absenteeism, tardiness, and intentions by workers to quit their jobs, all of which have a negative effect on the bottom line.

© iunewind / Shutterstock.com

Chapter 34

Preventing Stress at Work

© Siberian Art/Shutterstock.com

Job stress management focuses on individual/ situational problems and stressful job conditions. NIOSH (1999) concludes that partial approaches aren't enough. For example, often businesses use "stress workshop" seminars that offer information about stress. Various approaches to relaxation, especially yoga and time management, are also popular. But such strategies have limited effectiveness. One needs to include other approaches to individual/situational stress management as well as modifying stressful job conditions through organizational change. NIOSH recommends that a combination of organization change and [individual/situational] stress management is often the most useful approach to preventing stress at work.

This book covers the basic approaches to individual/situational stress management. A wide range of organizational changes may also be considered. This chapter presents material offered by NIOSH (http://www.cdc.gov/niosh/topics/stress/).

Stress Management Target Goals

First, consider the following specific target goals (adapted from Sauter, Murphy, & Hurrell, 1990):

- Recognize employees for good work performance
- Increase opportunities for career development
- Cultivate an organizational culture that values the individual worker

- Ensure consistency between management actions and stated organizational values
- Ensure that the workload is in line with workers' capabilities and resources
- Design jobs to provide meaning, stimulation, and opportunities for workers to use their skills
- Clearly define workers' roles and responsibilities
- Give workers opportunities to participate in decisions and actions affecting their jobs
- Improve communications—reduce uncertainty about career development and future employment prospects
- Provide opportunities for social interaction among workers
- Establish work schedules that are compatible with demands and responsibilities outside the job

The NIOSH Program for Minimizing Stressful Job Conditions

This chapter presents a three-step program recommended by NIOSH. In order for this program to work, organizations must first be prepared.

Before Attempting Job Stress Management

- Provide a basic introduction on stress, its causes and costs, and how it can be controlled. Copies of the NIOSH (1999) publication "Stress at Work" may be distributed and discussed at a workshop.
- Meet with top management, explain the program, and seek their support.
- Management must understand and sincerely support whatever stress management program is initiated.
- Involve employees at all phases of the program.
- Know what you are doing. Study this book. For others working with you, introduce in-house training for workers who plan to participate as assistants.

It can be particularly useful to have workers and managers work together in task-oriented problem-solving and brainstorming sessions. Such participation is effective and works by making use of the direct experience and differences in perspective of workers and managers.

When creating such work groups, make sure that they comply with current labor laws. The National Labor Relations Act may limit the form and structure of employee involvement in worker management teams or groups. Employers should seek legal assistance if they are unsure of their responsibilities or obligations under the National Labor Relations Act.

The Three-Step NIOSH Stress Prevention Program

Step 1: Identify the problem. The best method to explore the scope and source of a suspected stress problem in an organization depends partly on the size of the organization and the available resources. Group discussions among managers, labor representatives, and employees can provide rich sources of information.

Discussions may be all that is needed to find and fix problems in a small company. In a larger organization, such discussions can be used to help design formal surveys for gathering input about stressful job conditions from large numbers of employees. Regardless of the method used to collect data, information should be obtained about employee perceptions of their job conditions and perceived levels of stress, health, and satisfaction. The list of job conditions that may lead to stress and the warning signs and effects of stress (Chapters 2 and 3) provided starting points for deciding what information to collect. You may consider using the Stress Test at the end of Chapter 3. I offer a possible additional inventory at the end of this chapter.

Objective measures such as absenteeism, illness and turnover rates, or performance problems can also be examined to gauge the presence and scope of job stress. However, these measures are only rough indicators of job stress.

Data from discussions, surveys, and other sources should be summarized and analyzed to answer questions about the location of a stress problem and job conditions that may be responsible—for example, are problems present throughout the organization or confined to single department or specific jobs? In summary:

- Hold group discussions with employees
- Design an employee survey
- Measure employee perceptions of job conditions, stress, health, and satisfaction
- Collect objective data
- Analyze data to identify problem locations and stressful job conditions

Step 2: Design and implement interventions. Once the sources of stress at work have been identified and the scope of the problem is understood, the stage is set for design and implementation of an intervention strategy.

In small organizations, the informal discussions that helped identify stress problems may also produce fruitful ideas for prevention. In large organizations a more formal process may be needed. Frequently, a team is asked to develop recommendations based on analysis of data from step 1 and consultation with outside experts.

Certain problems, such as a hostile work environment, may be pervasive in the organization and require company-wide interventions. Other problems such as excessive workload may exist only in some departments and thus require more narrow solutions such as redesign of the way a job is performed. Still other problems may be specific to certain employees and resistant to any kind of organizational change, calling instead for stress management or employee assistance interventions. Some interventions might be implemented rapidly (e.g., improved communication, individual stress management training), but others may require additional time to put into place (e.g., redesign of a manufacturing process).

Before any intervention occurs, employees should be informed about actions that will be taken and when they will occur. A kickoff event, such as an all-hands meeting, is often useful for this purpose. To summarize:

- Target the source of stress for change
- Propose and prioritize intervention strategies
- Communicate planned interventions to employees
- Implement interventions

Step 3: Evaluate the interventions. Evaluation is an essential step in the intervention process. Evaluation is necessary to determine whether the intervention is producing desired effects and whether changes in direction are needed.

Time frames for evaluating interventions should be established. Interventions involving organizational change should receive both short and long-term scrutiny. Short-term evaluations might be done quarterly to provide an early indication of program effectiveness or possible need for redirection. Many interventions produce initial effects that do not persist. Long-term evaluations are often conducted annually and are necessary to determine whether interventions produce lasting effects.

Evaluations should focus on the same types of information collected during the problem identification phase of the intervention, including information from employees about working conditions, levels of perceived stress, health problems, and satisfaction. Employee perceptions are usually the most sensitive measure of stressful working conditions and often provide the first indication of intervention effectiveness. Adding objective measures such as absenteeism and health care costs may also be useful. However, the effects of job stress interventions on such measures tend to be less clear-cut and can take a long time to appear. The process does not end with evaluation. Rather, job stress prevention should be seen as a continuous process that uses evaluation data to refine or redirect the intervention strategy. To summarize:

- Conduct both short- and long-term evaluations.
- Measure employee perceptions of job conditions, stress, health, and satisfaction.
- Include objective measures.
- Refine the intervention strategy.

Smith Job Stress Inventory on the next page adapted from: National Institute for Occupational Safety and Health (NIOSH; 1999). Stress at work. (DHHS Publication No. 99-101). Washington, DC: US Government Printing Office.
Note: Examples in this chapter are based on adaptations of actual situations. For other examples of job stress interventions, see the Conditions of Work Digest, Vol 11/2, pp. 139-275.
This publication may be obtained by contacting the ILO Publications Center at P.O. Box 753, Waldorf, MD 20604 (Telephone: 301-638-3152). Or call NIOSH at 1-800-35-NIOSH.

SMITH JOB STRESS INVENTORY
(Describe your current job)

PART 1: PERSONAL SYMPTOMS

❑ 1. I am dissatisfied with my job.
❑ 2. I have low morale at work.
❑ 3. I have symptoms which seem to be related to job stress.
❑ 4. I have an illness which job stress seems to be making worse.
❑ 5. I find myself taking a lot of "mental health holidays" or not showing up for work.
❑ 6. I find it hard to get myself "psyched up" or motivated for work, and often arrive at work late.
❑ 7. I frequently think about quitting my job.

PART II: SOURCES OF JOB STRESS

Design of Work Tasks

❑ 1. My workload is too heavy.
❑ 2. I need more rest breaks at work.
❑ 3. My work day is too long.
❑ 4. I'm having trouble coping with shift work (sometimes working nights, sometimes days).
❑ 5. Things are too hectic at work.
❑ 6. I find my job too routine with little meaning.
❑ 7. My job underutilizes my skills.
❑ 8. My job gives me little sense of control; I have little "say" about things.

Management style

❑ 1. Workers do not participate enough in decision-making.
❑ 2. There is poor communication at work. I don't know what's going on or what's expected.
❑ 3. This job lacks family-friendly policies.

Interpersonal relationships

❑ 1. Where I work does not provide a friendly or comfortable social environment.
❑ 2. I do not get enough support or help from coworkers.
❑ 3. I do not get enough support or help from supervisors.

Work roles

❑ 1. I have to deal with conflicting or uncertain job expectations.
❑ 2. I am burdened with too much responsibility.
❑ 3. I have many "hats to wear" at work.

Career concerns

❑ 1. I feel I have to worry too much about job insecurity.
❑ 2. My job has a lack of opportunity for growth, advancement, or promotion.
❑ 3. I am confronted with rapid changes for which workers are unprepared.

Environmental conditions

❑ 1. There are unpleasant or dangerous physical conditions such as crowding, noise, or air pollution.
❑ 2. The equipment I work with, including chairs, desks, computers, etc., are uncomfortable and poorly designed.

Feedback

❑ 1. I do not get clear, specific, and immediate constructive feedback when I make a mistake or could do better.
❑ 2. I do not get clear, specific, and immediate praise and positive feedback when I do something right or well.
❑ 3. I am not informed of the full extent of challenges or problems that may be present at work.

PART III: I THINK THIS JOB NEEDS . . .

❑ 1. More recognition of employees for good work performance.
❑ 2. More opportunities for career development.
❑ 3. More of a culture that values the individual worker.
❑ 4. More consistency between management actions and stated organizational values.
❑ 5. Workload that is in line with workers' capabilities and resources.
❑ 6. Work that is meaningful, stimulating, and gives me a chance to use my skills.
❑ 7. A clear definition of my roles and responsibilities.
❑ 8. More opportunities to participate in decisions and actions affecting my job.
❑ 9. Improved communications.
❑ 10. Reduced uncertainty about career development and future employment prospects.
❑ 11. More opportunities for social interaction among workers.
❑ 12. Work schedules that are compatible with demands and responsibilities outside work.

EXERCISES

The Mindfulness Exercise Challenge. *Try practicing a five-minute version of your home mindfulness exercise before completing any chapter exercise.*

33-34.1 My Job from Hell (My "Official" NIOSH Job Stress Analysis)

Think about a stressful job you currently have, or had in the past. Describe it. Imagine you have been hired to perform a "NIOSH Job Stress Analysis." List and describe all the concepts in the assigned textbook chapters that help explain why the job is stressful.

As preparation, complete the "Smith Job Stress Inventory" in Chapter 34.

The more concepts you mention, the higher your total score will be. WARNING: YOU MUST NOT NAME THE ACTUAL JOB SITE. INSTEAD, USE THE WORD "ACME" TO NAME THE JOB." FOR EXAMPLE, IF YOU WANT TO DESCRIBE "CITY OF CHICAGO POLICE DEPARTMENT," NEVER IDENTIFY THE CITY OF CHICAGO POLICE DEPARTMENT BY NAME; INSTEAD, CALL IT THE "ACME POLICE DEPARTMENT." ALSO, NEVER GIVE ANY SPECIFIC IDENTIFYING INFORMATION THAT CAN BE USED TO UNCOVER THE REAL IDENTITY OF THE WORKPLACE YOU ARE DESCRIBING. FOR EXAMPLE, DON'T SAY "I WORK AT ACME DEPARTMENT STORE, THE FANCY BUILDING AT 900 N. MICHIGAN AVENUE IN CHICAGO." Also, it is not enough just to list concepts. For example, don't say:

Environmental conditions: "*When I was working as a cook at a local university cafeteria, the conditions were just too hectic and pressing.*"

A better answer:

Environmental conditions: "*When I was working as a cook at a local university cafeteria, the environmental work conditions made the job more stressful. For example, there was no ventilation. So with all the ovens heating and smelling up the place, we all felt like we were being baked along with the food. Also, the kitchen was small. Lots had to be done in a small space. So we were constantly bumping into each other. And the noise! Dishes banging in the sink, grinding noises from the ovens, yelling supervisors, and so on. My ears were ringing. It was so stressful that every hour or so I had to take a break.*"

33-34.2 The Most Important NIOSH Dimension

Consider the Smith Job Stress Checklist. Which dimension is most important? If you could change one, what would it be? Why?

Stress & Coping
Eye of Mindfulness Journal

Chapter 35

Crises and Catastrophes

© Romolo Tavani/Shutterstock.com

In times of war, crisis, and terrorist attacks and threats, we are often confronted with stressors that are unusually severe and traumatic. Even in more ordinary times, people encounter crises and catastrophes. In this chapter we consider traumatic stressors, defined as events outside the realm of ordinary experience associated with feelings of intense fear, helplessness, or horror. Unfortunately, many events fall into this category (Smith, 2001).

Examples of Crises and Catastrophes

Deliberate Human Activities

- Wartime violence, destruction, injury, and death
- Terrorist attacks
- Breakdown of social infrastructure (mail delivery system; health system; air transportation; communication network; energy, food, and water resources)
- Bombing
- Riot
- Military combat
- Sexual assault
- Sexual abuse
- Physical attack
- Serious physical abuse

- Robbery
- Mugging
- Kidnaping
- Being taken hostage
- Torture
- Involuntary incarceration
- Suicide/death

Unintentional Human Activities (Accidents, Technological Disasters)

- Serious automobile accident
- Serious industrial accident
- Serious sports/recreational accident
- Breakdown of social infrastructure (mail delivery system, health system, air transportation, communication network), if not due to terrorist attack
- Nuclear power plant disaster
- Surgical damage to body
- Fires and explosions
- Plane crash
- Train wreck
- Boating accident/shipwreck
- Building/major structure collapse

Acts of Nature/Natural Disasters

- Earthquake
- Flood
- Global warming
- Epidemic/plague (not human origin)
- Meteor/comet catastrophe
- Hurricane/tornado
- Heat wave
- Severe snow/rain
- Avalanche/mudslide
- Brush fire
- Famine
- Sinkholes
- Animal (wild dog/cat, bear) attack
- Severe illness or medical incident
- Death of loved one

One need not be a direct victim to experience the impact of crises and catastrophes; traumatic events can be witnessed or learned about through word of mouth, television, radio, the Internet, or the print media.

Symptoms

Health professionals have a name for the reactions we often have when confronting a trauma—namely, **acute stress disorder** (American Psychiatric Association, 2014). Five symptoms are involved: intrusion, negative mood, dissociation, avoidance, and arousal. These symptoms are often a normal response to an abnormal situation, and can pass within a month or so. If they are exceptionally severe (interfering with work or school) and persist, then professional help is required.

1. Intrusion: Reexperiencing the Trauma

There are many ways a crisis or catastrophe can stick in your mind, including fantasies about the trauma, worrisome thoughts, and nightmares.

You may experience flashbacks or recurrent, involuntary, and intrusive memories in which the trauma is reexperienced or "replayed" mentally. Flashbacks are predominantly visual, and can be so vivid that you think you are reliving an event. They can be triggered by lack of sleep, fatigue, stress arousal, drugs, or deep relaxation.

Also, you may find that stimuli that remind you of the trauma creates distress. These can include people who look like or wear the same clothes as those involved in the trauma, places, objects, weather conditions, and so on. Sometimes you may be confronted with such a reminder quite unexpectedly, or even distort what you are seeing or hearing so they become trauma reminders. Someone who in fact may look very little like a lost loved one may suddenly resemble the loved one.

2. Negative Mood

One persistently experiences negative moods such as anxiety or depression, and is unable to experience happiness, satisfaction, or loving feelings.

3. Dissociation

Sometimes victims avoid things without knowing it. Such unconscious avoidance is called dissociation. One can dissociate in several ways.

Psychic (or "psychological") numbing. This has nothing to do with "psychics" or the occult. "Psychic numbing" is a state in which you feel numb, detached, uninvolved in life.

You may have difficulty loving, crying, laughing, caring, or even feeling anger. You may no longer find fun and pleasure in activities you used to like. Numbing is a psychological defense mechanism in which one tunes out all feelings in order to "tune out" painful feelings related to a trauma.

Reduced awareness of surroundings. You simply might not notice or respond to other people or events. People might say you seem to be "in a daze," "spaced out," or "in one's own private world." As with numbing, this is a way to tune out traumatic pain. If you are less aware of everything, you are less aware of memories and reminders of your trauma.

Derealization. This strange psychiatric term is hard to describe. Have you ever seen a long, engaging, and strange movie, walked into the daylight sun, and found that things and people seemed different—perhaps more vivid, perhaps unfamiliar, strange, unreal, dreamlike, or mechanical. Your perception of what's real has been slightly altered, and you experience derealization.

Maybe you overslept, and when waking up felt a little confused. You may have wondered, "What day is this? What time is it?" Again, you have tasted a bit of derealization, in that parts of the normal ordinary world seem different.

And perhaps you have witnessed a friend having a mildly distressing reaction to marijuana or some other drug. He or she may report feeling detached from the familiar world. Things might seem like they are not real, or not really happening. The person may feel like a stranger or an outsider, even in familiar places. Maybe events seem speeded up or slowed down. Again, one's reality has been altered, and one is experiencing a type of derealization.

Most people have had mild experiences of derealization from time to time. Derealization may be both an attempt to distance oneself from a trauma and a secondary effect of numbing and reduced awareness.

Depersonalization. Another psychiatric term, depersonalization is a little like derealization, except that the experience of your body or self is distorted. Examples include "out of body experiences" in which one has the experience of being separated from one's body, perhaps looking down from above or across the room, or watching a movie of oneself. The body might seem like it's split into parts, or one part of the body might feel numb, warm, or cold. Depersonalization, like derealization, serves to distance oneself from trauma.

Amnesia. Amnesia is both a psychiatric term and a word in everyday language. When you experience amnesia, you simply can't remember something. This is common in times of stress. You often read or hear of people who can't remember details of a traumatic crime, attack, or accident. Often, memory returns.

4. Avoidance

After a severe trauma, it is understand that a victim might want to avoid all memories and reminders of the event. This can involve avoiding places related to or similar to where the event occurred, or avoiding conversations or people related to the trauma. You might not want to think about the event at all, and put it out of mind.

5. Arousal

A fundamental part of all stress is arousal/distress. Arousal/distress can be exaggerated in victims of crisis or catastrophe. There are many symptoms:

- Sleep disturbance (difficulty falling or staying asleep or restlessness during sleep)
- Irritable behavior and angry outbursts (with little or no provocation), typically expressed as verbal or physical aggression toward people or objects
- Hypervigilance
- Problems with concentration
- Exaggerated startle response

What's Going On?

An acute stress reaction is a serious response to trauma. It can take time to recover. Avoidance, dissociation, and reexperiencing the trauma can be seen as part of a process of working through the trauma (Horowitz, 1982).

One's first reaction may be an intense emotional outcry, such as fainting, weeping, or panic. Physical and mental arousal may increase, potentially disrupting the working through process. When this happens, it can be very helpful to share your feelings with someone you trust.

The real "work" of working through often involves a two-part process in which one cycles between avoidance/dissociation and reexperiencing the trauma. One withdraws, approaches, withdraws, and then again approaches the trauma, reminders of the trauma, feelings associated with the trauma, and ramifications of the trauma.

What is important to recognize is alternating phases of approach and withdrawal helps one deal with manageable pieces of a crisis. Put differently, a terrorist attack, disaster, loss of a loved one, or illness may be too big to deal with at once. For example, after losing one's house to a fire one might have to deal with the emotions of fear, rage, and depression as well as the tasks of finding new housing, dealing with the feelings of family and loved ones, and so on. The phases of working through enable you to deal with pieces of the trauma in manageable doses, one at a time, and then withdraw to recover and regroup. When this happens, symptoms of reexperiencing a trauma help us take on a piece of a trauma; whereas withdrawal and dissociation are ways of taking a break.

Coping with and Resolving a Crisis or Catastrophe

If you seem to be stuck at any part of this working through process, or things are not getting better after a month, seek professional help. Generally, coping with crisis and catastrophe has short- and long-term goals. The short-term goals are to remove any threat or danger to life, health, or well-being. Longer-term goals involve mindfully:

1. Accepting the crisis or catastrophe—it happened and can't be undone
2. Learning to put the event aside so it is no longer a pressing concern
3. Going on coping and live a full, satisfying life

Coping with a crisis or catastrophe can be an act of mindfulness. Indeed, many of the techniques and strategies in this book can be very useful in dealing with a crisis or catastrophe.

EXERCISES

The Mindfulness Exercise Challenge. Try practicing a five-minute version of your home mindfulness exercise before completing any chapter exercise.

35.1 In the News

Find an example of a crisis or catastrophe in the news. Can you find any of this chapter's concepts illustrated?

35.2 A Familiar Crisis or Catastrophe

Every student can think of a crisis or catastrophe in their life, or the lives of loved ones. Select a crisis or catastrophe you feel comfortable sharing with others, one that happened some time ago. Be sure to select an incident you have recovered from.

1. What textbook concepts did this incident illustrate?
2. How do you know you recovered?
3. Did you use any of the textbook concepts and tools to cope?

Stress & Coping
Eye of Mindfulness Journal

LESSON 9

YOUR MINDFULNESS PROGRAM

Chapter 36

Mindfulness Imagery

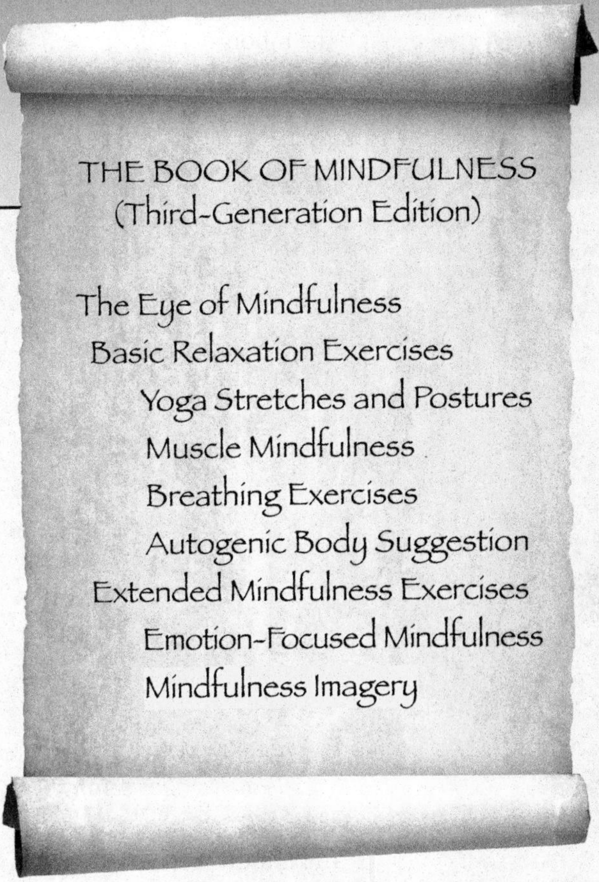

What is mindfulness to you? What is your vision of mindfulness? What is its value? Its promise? Where might it go? In Lesson 9 we consider our journey from a variety of perspectives. We begin with imagery.

In simple terms, imagery is a popular approach to relaxation. In addition, imagery is central to many contemplative poems, parables, stories, chants, song lyrics, prayers, and literary wisdom passages people read before or after meditation or mindfulness. Most important, imagery can help us go beyond words in understanding the nature and promise of mindfulness.

Descriptive Imagery: The Mindfulness Snapshot

Most people know how to daydream or fantasize. However, mindfulness imagery is a little different. In a daydream or fantasy you may engage in an intense emotional activity, think about winning a game, or rehearse or review some stressful event.

With mindfulness *descriptive imagery* you select a mindful situation or setting that does not involve strong emotion or achievement. You simply enjoy all that you see, hear, feel, and smell. Descriptive imagery is simple sense imagery. It is what we might experience as a mindful observer. Examples might include:

A tree on a hill
A sunset
A flower

The moon
The night sky
The seashore

© Shutterstock, Inc.

Here's a descriptive imagery script of a tree on a hill. Note how it focuses simply on sense impressions, not on doing or getting anything. You are simply a mindful observer in a relaxing situation or setting.

Imagine a solitary tree on a gentle hill. Its soft branches reach and touch the roaming clouds in the clear blue sky. A quiet breeze caresses your skin. In the distance you hear the leaves rustle. You feel the warm sun. The refreshing scent of new grass fills the air. The tree sits quietly, centered on the earth. With all your senses you mindfully savor the beauty of this setting.

The mindfulness literature abounds with wonderful examples of mindfulness descriptive imagery. In all you are a mindful observer. Here are instructions for creating imagery which you can contemplate or read in a group session.

1. Pick a Theme

What type of image theme appeals to you most? It should be very quiet, with little activity. Instead of doing something, you simply imagine all of the sense details of a relaxing setting or situation.

Generally I have found the students pick from five types of imagery themes. Which works for you?

Travel
Airplane, bird, blimp, bus, car, cruise ship, horse-drawn carriage, floating in air, floating dandelion seed, flying saucer, flying like a bird, hot-air balloon, jet, kite, magic cow, motorcycle, ocean liner, raft, parachute, rocket into space, ship, roller blades, skateboard, submarine, train, wagon, walking.

Outdoor/Nature
Church retreat, campgrounds, clouds, desert, forest, garden, island, meadow, monastery, mountain, nature preserve, nudist camp, outer space, park, planet (Mars, etc.), spa, valley, storybook land, zoo

Water
Bath house, beach, brook, creek, glacier, hot tub, lake, ocean, pond, rain, rain forest, mist, river, sauna, ski slopes, shower, snow, steam bath, stream, swimming pool, wading pond, waterfall

Indoor
Cabin, castle, cave, cavern, childhood house, church, dream house, meditation room, mosque, palace, prayer room, skyscraper, school room, secret hiding place, synagogue, tavern, temple, tree house, vacation home

Person/Animal
A good friend, relative, famous individual, holy person, mythical individual, character in a story or movie, a pet

Now, select a specific theme. For example, if you picked "Outdoor /Nature," name the setting. You might prefer outdoor/nature imagery and select as a specific image "resting in a beautiful park with tree, grass, and flowers."

2. Fill in the Sense Details

You are ready to fill in the sense details. Let your mind wander. Have some fun. Think freely. There is no reason to come up with a "correct" or "complete" list. Just think of a handful of details for each of the following sense modalities:

- What do you see? (List about five things)
- What do you hear? (List about five things)
- What do you feel touching your skin? (List about three things)
- What fragrances do you smell? (List two or three things)

3. Check for Problems or Booby Traps

You are just about ready to begin your imagery exercise; however, just to be careful, review what you have selected. Sometimes people select an imagery topic that stirs up an unexpected negative association. For example, perhaps you selected "resting on the ocean beach" as your peaceful image, only to realize during the image that you once were seriously sunburned on the beach. It would be better to adjust this imagery by inserting a shade tree. Do you foresee any such booby traps in your image? Here are some examples of complete planned imagery exercises:

EXAMPLE: TRAVEL

My Preferred Type of Imagery
TRAVEL

My Specific Imagery Topic

RIDING HORSEBACK THROUGH THE WOODS

What do you see? (List about five things)

I am riding my very trusted old friend, Duke.
I see the soft brown hair on his head and his ears flopping.
The fields of peaceful green grass pass by.
From time to time we pass under a huge, arching tree.
The sky is pure blue, without a cloud.
I see birds overhead.

What do you hear? (List about five things)

I hear the gentle stepping of my horse.
I hear my horse breathing easily.
I hear the wind passing by my ears.
I hear birds in the air.
The breeze brushes through the trees.

What do you feel touching your skin? (List about three things)

I feel the pressure of my horse supporting my body.
I feel the wind on my skin.
I feel the soothing sun.

What fragrances do you smell? (List about two or three things)

I smell the fresh grass.
I smell the pleasant aroma of leather.

EXAMPLE: WATER

My Preferred Type of Imagery

WATER

My Specific Imagery Topic

RESTING NEXT TO A GENTLE WATERFALL

What do you see? (List about five things)

I see the water flowing down rocks above.
I see the waterfall splashing into a pond.
I see the rippling pond next to me.
I see patches of flowers next to the pond.
I see a few tiny goldfish in the pond.

What do you hear? (List about five things)

I hear the gentle gurgle of water flowing.

I hear the water flowing under my feet.
I hear the soft spray of water as it touches the surrounding ground.
I hear an occasional fish splash.
I hear my feet as they dangle in the pond.
I hear the breeze brushing the trees.

What do you feel touching your skin? (List about three things)
I feel spray of water on my face.
I feel the cool air evaporating the water.
I feel the warm sun.

What fragrances do you smell? (List about two or three things)
I smell the clean scent of water.
I smell the flowers.

To summarize, mindfulness descriptive imagery is a snapshot in which we saver and enjoy a quiet situation or setting. We do so with all our senses. We are a mindful observer.

© andreiuc88 / Shutterstock.com

Narrative Imagery: The Evolving Story

Mindfulness descriptive imagery is static and unchanging. You are a quiet observer and little else. This is indeed where much of the creative literature of mindfulness stops. But we are only beginning.

The goal of mindfulness *narrative imagery* is to transform an unchanging image into one that evolves in such a way that suggests changes that occur or might occur during mindfulness. Your image becomes a story that tells where mindfulness might go. It is your personal vision of mindfulness. However, your story is not a typical story with characters, plot, conflicts, and conclusion. Instead, it is an evolving image. It is dynamic.

In narrative imagery, your focus is moving deeper, expanding, discovering. But you are not deliberately planning what is happening. You put effort and control aside, and mindfully observe the journey and what it has to reveal. Your stance shifts from that of a mindful observer to that of a mindful observer-participant.

Consider this mindfulness narrative of a tree:

> *The solitary tree is alive in the evening air. The rustling breeze. The fleeing clouds. The chorus of birds. And the sun begins to set. The tree grows quiet in silent anticipation. Ground and sky become dark. Clouds evaporate into the night. A hushed glow of final sunlight says farewell to the hustle of the day. Behind the tree the heavens open to a brilliant field of stars. The tree stands, silent and aware.*

Notice how our narrative image evolves. How is this achieved? A mindfulness narrative can be achieved through four deepening strategies (Smith, 2005). These can be particularly powerful when creating a mindfulness narrative imagery to read in group.

Deepening Strategies

Deepening imagery begins relatively
1. Deliberate/planned
2. Effortful
3. Moving/changing
4. Complex

It becomes progressively
1. Spontaneous/unplanned
2. Effortless
3. Still/unchanging
4. Simple

Here are the four elements in detail.

Deliberate / Planned - - - Spontaneous / Unplanned

A fantasy displaying deliberate planning is active and willful. You make choices and decide to do things. In contrast, in a spontaneous and unplanned fantasy things happen on their own, outside of your decisions. Perhaps someone or something else is calling the shots. Maybe things are happening spontaneously and you are just the observer.

DELIBERATE / PLANNED	SPONTANEOUS / UNPLANNED
I decide to walk into a peaceful forest. There are two paths ahead. I chose to take the path lined by trees and carefully step through the leaves.	*I find myself deep in the forest. Suddenly the branches ahead open in front of me and reveal a stream leading to a lake. A bird sings almost as if it were calling me to continue.*

Effortful - - - Effortless

In an effortful fantasy work, strain and effort are displayed. This could be your effort, or that of someone or something else. You are working hard. Perhaps the subject of your fantasy is struggling or trying to do something. In contrast, in an effortless fantasy you are aware of not having to exert any work. The characters in your fantasy are equally free of strain.

EFFORTFUL	EFFORTLESS
It is not an easy walk. The leaves are thick and I have to push my legs through. The path leads up a hill and I climb.	*The path becomes easier. I am sitting on a log floating freely on the shore of the river. With a very slight push, the log begins to float. I do nothing as I gently float away.*

Moving / Changing - - - Still / Unchanging

In a fantasy that is moving or changing, elements are quickly traveling from one place to another, transforming one thing to another, or simply changing in appearance. There is much energy. In a fantasy that is still and unchanging little is going on. Focus is sustained in one direction. Things and people aren't going places. They stay the same. Things are calm.

MOVING / CHANGING	STILL / UNCHANGING
As I move through the forest I notice many things. The leaves, birds, squirrels. Above clouds peak through the leaves. A brisk breeze brushes against my skin. Birds all about sing their songs.	*Things become still. The sun is beginning to set. The breeze has grown quiet. The clouds no longer move. The birds are now quiet. The forest is in hushed silence.*

Complex - - - Simple

Finally, a complex fantasy has many different parts. There are numerous details, many pieces. A simple fantasy is focused and singular. There is just one target image that has few parts.

COMPLEX	SIMPLE
The forest is alive with details. Birds, squirrels, many types of trees, bushes, and flowers. Below a rich mat of leaves of many colors form my path.	*As dusk comes, things drop out of sight into the shadows. I am floating on the lake and simply aware of the reflection of the moon.*

The following example of mindfulness deepening imagery weaves all four elements together. The theme is resting by the ocean on a beach. Notice how the imagery changes.

You are relaxing on a beach.

As you sit up [DELIBERATE / PLANNED] and look around [EFFORTFUL], you notice the blue water and sky [COMPLEX].

The sun is directly overhead, its warm rays pierce your skin and dissolve tension in your body [EFFORTFUL].

You can feel the wind and hear the soothing waves splash against the shore. Birds are everywhere. The sky is full of clouds [MOVING, CHANGING; COMPLEX] which move quickly.

As you become more relaxed, you recline on the beach [EFFORTLESS].

The wind dies down to a gentle breeze. Your attention narrows to the sky above and the peaceful clouds slowly floating by [EFFORTLESS; STILL / UNCHANGING; SIMPLE].

There is nothing you have to think about or do [EFFORTLESS].

The air is now completely still [STILL / UNCHANGING; SIMPLE].

The sky is pure blue and empty. There are no clouds. The sea is silent. [SIMPLE]. Simply attend to the sea and nothing else [EFFORTLESS, STILL / UNCHANGING; SIMPLE].

Few distractions come to mind. You are focused. You listen to the quiet song of the ocean waves [SPONTANEOUS].

© VOJTa Herout / Shutterstock.com

Deepening Markers

A deepening marker is an image you repeat a few times throughout an exercise sequence. Each time it is repeated, it symbolizes the concrete meaning of the surrounding exercise elements and becomes more mindful. The marker acquires a new connotation each time it appears. In other words, deepening markers are colored by and illuminate their surroundings. As such they are something like lanterns along a path. Although each marking light is the same, the area it reveals is different at different places. And changing surroundings color and shade the light differently.

The following examples use the image of a dove as a marker.

> *Imagine a dove beginning to lift off.*
>
> *Tense and let go of your shoulders, like a dove lifting its wings.*
>
> *The dove begins to float in the sky.*
>
> *Breathe slowly and deeply, as the dove floats easily.*
>
> *The dove moves far away.*
>
> *Thoughts come to mind, and you let them go, let them float away.*
>
> *Your attention centers meditatively on the small dove in the distance.*

Notice what is happening in this brief evolving image. First the dove symbolizes letting go, like in progressive muscle relaxation. Then it symbolizes the flow of breath as in breathing relaxation. The dove next becomes a symbol of letting go of distracting thoughts. Finally, it symbolizes a singular meditation focus. In this way, our deepening image reminds us, or shines a light on, how our exercise has changed and evolved. First it is just physical letting go. Then relaxed breathing. Then beginning mindfulness. Then mindful focus. A mindful image is a subtle reminder that change is happening, that one is moving in a direction.

Imagery Priming and Intercentering

R/M States often shift and change within a practice session through a process I have called **intercentering** (Smith, 2005) Here one R/M State sets the stage or leads to another. Once an inner conflict has been put aside, one might feel at ease, which might lead to inner silence. In terms of R/M States, AT EASE, AT PEACE → QUIET. One might experience a brief moment of muscle relaxation, followed by a sense of awareness, or PHYSICALLY RELAXED → CLEAR, AWAKE, AWARE.

Here are some intercentering sequences my students have discovered. (Can you figure out how one might lead to another?)

FAR AWAY → REFRESHED

PLEASANT MIND WANDERING → GOING DEEPER

QUIET → SENSE OF SOMETHING DEEPER → REVERENT, PRAYERFUL

FOCUS, ABSORPTION → GOING DEEPER

One can cultivate such sequences in mindfulness by suggesting them in preceding imagery. I call this strategy **imagery priming**.

One can find numerous examples of imagery priming in the meditation and mindfulness literature, especially through wisdom stories, parables, lyrics, poetry, and song. Some images are even more explicit, such as directions to compassionately imagine loved ones (metta meditation). When teaching mindfulness, I often select preparatory passages or images that evoke the sequence of R/M States I am emphasizing. In this text I encourage practitioners to discover or invent their own.

This brief imagery script targets R/M State Far Away followed by Going Deeper and Centered, Grounded.

> *You are floating far above the world in your own private balloon. All your cares are a distant concern.* ***[FAR AWAY]*** *You slowly float away from the busy landmarks of your world into quiet and peaceful spaces. You move higher and*

higher into the clouds. The people, trees, and houses below become smaller and smaller. Each cloud that floats by reminds you that you are drifting farther and farther away. ***[GOING DEEPER]*** *Your balloon settles into a quiet space above the world. You firmly and safely land on your silent observation cabin, observing below. The world is centered, and you are the observer.* ***[CENTERED, GROUNDED]***

This script moves from R/M State Beautiful as well as Happy, Optimistic, Trusting to Thankful, Grateful, and Unbothered.

> *Enjoy the beautiful temple you have entered. Beautiful music surrounds you* ***[BEAUTIFUL]*** *filling you with happiness* ***[HAPPY . . .]*** *and trust that you are in a safe place. You are in God's place and feel loved and accepted.* ***[LOVING, CARING]*** *You are thankful for this moment.* ***[THANKFUL, GRATEFUL]*** *As all grows still, you find it easy to let go of your petty worries and distractions.* ***[UNBOTHERED]***

One way of adding interest and variety to mindfulness practice is to identify R/M State sequences present in poems, parables, stories, chants, song lyrics, prayers, and literary wisdom passages one has found conducive to mindfulness.

DOING IT MINDFULLY

To practice imagery mindfully, become a neutral observer. Let images come and go on their own, without your interference. Once your images start becoming goal-directed or effortful, let go of this as mind wandering. And if your images start becoming negative, this too is mind wandering.

MAKING YOUR OWN RECORDING: Slowly and calmly. Voice should be relaxed and "interesting," as if you were reading a colorful nature story to a child. Use inflection and voice tone to highlight specific images. In sum, use your fanciful "storytelling voice."

MINDFULNESS NARRATIVE IMAGERY SCRIPT

First make sure you are seated upright with your feet flat on the floor. Through the magical powers of imagery we will take a journey, one that is enjoyable and refreshing. In this journey you explore special questions: What is the deepest purpose of doing mindfulness? What is the most important reason for mastering mindfulness? We will meet these questions later, at a special part of our journey. Now is the time to put them aside and enjoy our time together.

The Setting

Imagine a beautiful outdoor setting, quiet and distant from the concerns of everyday life. This outdoor setting can be any place you choose: a vast garden, extending without end; a park with trees and bushes; perhaps you see a forest.

Your setting is a world full of life and energy. The wind, the glowing sun, trees waving in the wind, rippling grass, flowing water. There is much to experience.

What do you see? The clear blue sky above? Soft, fluffy clouds floating by? Waving leaves and grass that are healthy and green? Trees in the deep green forest?

[PAUSE 5 SECONDS]

What do you feel touching your skin? A cool breeze? The warm sun? Brushing leaves of grass?

[PAUSE 5 SECONDS]

What do you hear? A gentle breeze flowing through grass or leaves? Waves gently touching the shore? The gentle flight of birds in the distance.

[PAUSE 5 SECONDS]

What fragrances are there? Freshly cut grass? Green trees? Clean, fresh air?

[PAUSE 5 SECONDS]

For the next few minutes, there is nothing you need to do. Simply enjoy the life and energy in your beautiful nature setting. Enjoy all of your senses.

[PAUSE 2 MINUTES]

Release of Tension

The world around you becomes more quiet. Wind settles into a gentle breeze. Clouds in the sky move more slowly. The grass and trees are more still. Branches move more slowly.

Now it is the time to let go of excess burdens that weigh you down and keep you from moving deeper, keep you from seeing things clearly.

Attend to your body. Let any tensions you may feel dissolve and flow away. A breeze touches your skin, and tension flows. Away. Tension melts in the warm and soothing sun. For the next minute or so, let tensions flow away.

[PAUSE 1 MINUTE]

Release your tension and concerns.

The Path.

We are ready to move on.

You are relaxed and standing.

In front of you is a long path through the grass and trees.

The path starts at your feet, and extends into the distance out of sight, perhaps hidden by trees, rocks, or water.

The path may be paved with smooth stones. Or it may be a path of sand or grass. The path can be anything. For the next minute or so, simply attend to your path, and when you feel comfortable, begin moving along the path.

[PAUSE 1 MINUTE]

Slowly begin to move down your path.

You are moving away from your everyday concerns into

the world of silence.
You are guided by an inner wisdom, the song of a distant bird, or perhaps a glowing light in the distance.
I will begin to count backwards from five to one.
With each count, you find yourself moving deeper and deeper along the path.
Five.
Breathe in deeply, pause and let go. Release the tensions and concerns of the day.
Four.
You are moving deeper along your path.
Three.
Deeper and deeper, far away from the everyday world.
Two.
The world grows more quiet and still, the farther you move.
One.
And your path ends.
You have arrived at a special place of wisdom. The air is completely still. Complete silence. Complete calm.
In this place is a magic pond, illuminated only by the faint light of the moon.
It is here you can find answers, or deeper questions.

The Question
And now is the time for your questions. What is the deepest reason for practicing mindfulness? What is the most important reason?
Do not try to figure out your answers.

Simply attend to the magic pond.
Let the answer appear in any way it wants. As a light. A reflection. A message written in gentle ripples.

[PAUSE 90 SECONDS]

The reason for mindfulness.
At this time, select for you what seems like the best answer.

[PAUSE 60]

Let go of what you are thinking. We are ready to move on.

A Moment of Gratitude.
In whatever way feels right for you, express your thanks for wherever your journey has taken you. You may simply nod your head in appreciation, or actually say a few words in your mind. You may do this now.

[PAUSE 30 SECONDS]

Gently let go of what you are attending to. Slowly open your eyes, take a deep breath, and stretch. We have completed our journey and are ready to move on to life's tasks.

~ END OF SCRIPT ~

ALTERNTIVE IMAGERY EXRCISE
A MINDFUL OR MEDITATIVE
LITERARY PASSAGE

(Do every day. After one session fill out an R/M Tracker)

Select a poem, prayer, or meditative or mindful literary passage. Let yourself settle into relaxation. Read a few words. Pause for a few minutes to let the words sink in. Do not figure them out. You are simply the observer, like watching a river float by. Let thoughts and feelings come and go. Then after a few minutes, read the next few words.

Select your own poem, prayer, passage. Many people start out with the "Serenity Prayer." There are many versions, including the following secular one:

Grant me the serenity
to accept the things
I cannot change

Courage to change the
things I can, and the
wisdom to know the
difference.
Living one day at a time.

Enjoying one moment at a time.

Accepting hardship as the
pathway to peace

Taking the world as it is
not as I would have it.

EYE OF MINDFULNESS
BRIEF SCRIPT
(Practice this until you select your home exercise)
Do every day. After one session fill out an R/M Tracker

BODY/BREATH SCANNING

Imagine tension flowing from your body with every outgoing breath. Flowing from the top of your head to your toes. Flowing from your head, neck, shoulders, arms, hands, back, abdomen, legs, and feet.

[PAUSE 60 SECONDS]

Attend to the easy flow of breath, in and out through your nose, throat, chest, and belly.

[PAUSE 60 SECONDS]

FOCUSED ATTENTION MEDITATION

Select your preferred meditation focus, perhaps the word "One. . . one . . . one" slowing going over and over in your mind like an echo.
Attend to it for the next few minutes.

Whenever your mind wanders, that's OK. You can change if you want.
You are always the quiet observer. Accept what comes and goes. Return to your focus again and again.

[PAUSE 6 MINUTES]

MINDFULNESS

And now we move on to mindfulness meditation. Simply attend to sounds that come and go. Or open your eyes halfway and attend to all stimuli that come and go. Or do both.

If you slip into body/breath work, that's ok.

If you slip into centered focus meditation, that's ok.

Return to mindfulness.
You are the quiet observer.

[PAUSE 6 MINUTES]

Gently let go of what you are attending to.

~ END OF SCRIPT ~

THE R/M TRACKER

WHAT DID YOU FEEL OR EXPERIENCE DURING **IMAGERY**?

CLICK BOXES USING THIS KEY

(SKIP ITEMS YOU DON'T UNDERSTAND OR DIDN'T FEEL OR EXPERIENCE)

☒☐☐☐	☒☒☐☐	☒☒☒☐	☒☒☒☒
Felt this SLIGHTLY	Felt this MODERATELY	Felt this VERY MUCH	Felt this EXTREMELY (the most ever)

***1. FAR AWAY** and distant from the troubles around me.*	☐☐☐☐
***2. PHYSICALLY RELAXED**. Muscles relaxed, loose, limp, warm and heavy. Breathing slow, even, and easy.*	☐☐☐☐
3 AT EASE, AT PEACE.	☐☐☐☐
4. REFRESHED.	☐☐☐☐
***5. PLEASANT MIND WANDERING**. Undirected, random positive thoughts.*	☐☐☐☐
6.** Lost in **FANTASY** and **DAYDREAMING.	☐☐☐☐
7.** Periods of sustained, continuous **FOCUS. ABSORPTION.	☐☐☐☐
8. CENTERED, GROUNDED.	☐☐☐☐
***9. QUIET.** Still, few thoughts. Little mind wandering.*	☐☐☐☐
***10. UNBOTHERED.** Accepting. When I had a negative thought or feeling, I didn't get caught up in it. No judging, clinging, pushing away, figuring things out.*	☐☐☐☐
***11. EASY, EFFORTLESS.** Effortless to let go, put thoughts aside, sustain focus.*	☐☐☐☐
***12.** I felt like an **OBSERVER** standing aside and watching what happens.*	☐☐☐☐
***13. CLEAR, AWAKE, AWARE.** I saw things as they really are.*	☐☐☐☐
14. INTERESTED, CURIOUS, FASCINATED.	☐☐☐☐
15.** Things seemed **BEAUTIFUL.	☐☐☐☐
***16. GOING DEEPER**. Things seemed unexpected, new, changing, opening up,being revealed. Felt like I was in a different place or space.*	☐☐☐☐
17.** Sense of **SPACIOUSNESS, EXPANSIVENESS.	☐☐☐☐
***18.** I felt the **SENSE OF SOMETHING GREATER** than myself (God, a higher power, spirit, energy, love, or consciousness.); God is with me.*	☐☐☐☐
19.** A sense of **MEANING, PURPOSE, DIRECTION.	☐☐☐☐
20.** I felt **REVERENT, PRAYERFUL.	☐☐☐☐
***21. AWE / WONDER, DEEP MYSTERY** of things beyond my understanding.*	☐☐☐☐
22.** I felt a profound personal meaningful "**SPIRITUAL**" or "**MYSTICAL**" experience -- sudden awakening or insight.* • *Felt an underlying hidden **TRUTH. • *Feeling **AT ONE.*** • *Feelings so profound they **COULD NOT BE PUT INTO WORDS.***	☐☐☐☐
23. HAPPY, OPTIMISTIC, TRUSTING.	☐☐☐☐
24. LOVING, CARING.	☐☐☐☐
***25. THANKFUL.** Grateful.*	☐☐☐☐

EXERCISES

> *The Mindfulness Exercise Challenge. Try practicing a five-minute version of your home mindfulness exercise before completing any chapter exercise.*

EXERCISE 36.1 Create Your Own Narrative Imagery

Create a narrative imagery script using the instructions and model provided in your text. This is a script you can read to yourself before or after an exercise session, or read to a group. As in the example, indicate where your script instructions are deliberate/planned, effortful, moving/changing, and complex. Indicate where they become progressively spontaneous/unplanned, effortless, still/unchanging, and simple.

EXERCISE 36.2 Create an Imagery Script Using Deepening Markers

Create a narrative script using deepening markers. First, select a marker. Then introduce it at least four times. After your script explain how it works. Specifically, how the words surrounding each marker alter its meaning?

EXERCISE 36.3 Find an Example of Mindfulness Descriptive or Narrative Imagery

Imagery is central to many contemplative poems, parables, stories, chants, song lyrics, prayers, and literary wisdom passages people read before or after meditation or mindfulness. Most important, imagery can help us go beyond words in understanding the nature and promise of mindfulness.

In this exercise, find an example of descriptive or narrative imagery. Describe how it illustrates the tools discussed in this chapter. How do these tools contribute to mindfulness?

© iunewind / Shutterstock.com

Chapter 37

Combination Exercises and Spot Relaxation

© Dzulius/Shutterstock.com

When you wake up from sleep, perhaps you stretch. After moving heavy furniture, perhaps you rub your arms. These are examples of **spot relaxation**, one of the most useful applications of the approaches taught in this book. Spot relaxation is a one- to five-minute exercise targeted to a specific problem or goal. The exercises in this book provide a rich source of possible types of spot relaxation. Simply take one or two exercises and try them in a situation that might call for relaxation.

Combining Exercises

It can be particularly effective to combine exercises. For example, if your neck is stiff after a hour of typing, you might first practice the neck squeeze from progressive muscle relaxation followed by a neck stretch.

Here are some suggestions:

- Progressive muscle relaxation (PMR) and autogenic warmth and heaviness exercises evoke somatic sensations and can be combined and sequenced: "Tense up . . . let go . . . feel warm and heavy as the tension flows away."
- Autogenic exercises work best after PMR or breathing, and may be combined with imagery.
- PMR and imagery can both be designed to target muscles.
- PMR and breathing exercises both directly instruct one to "let go" or "release." Combination option: "Breathe in . . . tense up . . . and as you let go, exhale, letting the air easily flow through your lips."

- PMR and stretching both involve movement of muscles. Combination option: "Tense up your fingers and make a fist. Release the tension. Then slowly stretch open your fingers all the way, and slowly release the stretch."
- Slowly pace breathing with active yoga stretches. Inhale as your stretch expands (like reaching up). Exhale as you release your stretch (bowing down).
- Passive breathing exercises can be combined with any other family of techniques.
- PMR and imagery can both target muscles.
- Combination option: "Tense up your muscles, as if you were squeezing a wad of paper. Let go, and let the wad of paper slowly relax and open."
- Yoga stretching and rocking meditation can involve movement of the torso. Combination option: "Bow over and stretch your back . . . reach up to the sky . . . and now sit and gently rock back and forth, attending to your rocking."
- Imagery and autogenic visual suggestions (visualize a warm fireplace instead of repeating the words "warm") are both visual. Combination option: "Imagine relaxing on a beach. You can see the soft clouds, hear waves, and smell the clean water. The sun on your skin; warm and heavy."

Spot Relaxation Situations

The possibilities for spot relaxation are nearly endless. Here are some examples. Read them, then see what you can think of.

Situation: *"I work in a day care center and spend lots of time holding the kids. This wears me out, especially when a child starts crying in my arms."*

Spot Relaxation: *"I gently rock a child while I breathe slowly and evenly. I try to pace my rocking with my breathing. This has a way of calming both the baby and me."*

Situation: *"I am at my dentist's for a filling. Usually, the drilling and poking in my mouth makes me very tense."*

Spot Relaxation: *"I imagine a cool ice cube touching my gums and cheeks. That seems to take away the discomfort."*

Situation: *"I drive several hours a day, two and from work. After a long drive, my shoulders and arms are very knotted up."*

Spot Relaxation: *"I do the PMR Shoulder squeeze followed by a yoga shoulder stretch."*

Situation: *"I go to my doctor's office twice a month for a blood test. The idea of sticking me with a needle really upsets me. Here's what I do."*

Spot Relaxation: *"I imagine myself at a peaceful, faraway island. I think of a friendly little monkey grabbing on my arm where I am actually getting stuck. This way I turn the sensations of getting stuck into sensations of being grabbed."*

Situation: *"When driving home, I often get stuck in a traffic jam. For about 30 minutes everyone moves very slowly. Usually, my temper rises and my arms get very tense."*

Spot Relaxation: *"I see how slowly and evenly I can breathe. When I breathe out, I let go of tension in my arms."*

Situation: *"In the middle of the morning, after reading many reports, I need a refresher break."*

Spot Relaxation: *"I close my eyes and meditate for about 5 minutes."*

EXERCISES

The Mindfulness Exercise Challenge. *Try practicing a five-minute version of your home mindfulness exercise before completing any chapter exercise.*

37.1 Your Spot Relaxation Exercises

Experiment with different types and combinations of spot relaxation. Over the week see if you can think of something different for six situations.

Situation

Spot Relaxation

Situation

Spot Relaxation

Situation

Spot Relaxation

Situation

Spot Relaxation

Situation

Spot Relaxation

Situation

Spot Relaxation

37.2 Your Combo Exercises

Describe what exercises you might combine.

Stress & Coping
Eye of Mindfulness Journal

Chapter 38

Mindfulness and You

© The Clay Machine Gun/Shutterstock.com

This is a chapter you write yourself. What approaches to stress and coping worked best? What approaches to relaxation and mindfulness worked best? Why? How is mindfulness related to what we have been doing?

Mindful Coping

Let's begin with a simple tally. Here's a list of the coping strategies we have considered. Check those that seemed to fit you best:

- ☐ Finding Social Support
- ☐ Brainstorming and Problem-Solving
- ☐ Time Management and Setting Priorities
- ☐ Dealing with Procrastination
- ☐ Finding Your "Blockbuster Distortions" or Stressful Negative Thinking
- ☐ Desensitization
- ☐ Relapse Prevention
- ☐ Assertiveness
- ☐ Shyness and Starting Relationships
- ☐ Turning Your Anger into Powerful Coping
- ☐ Dealing with Others Who Are Aggressive
- ☐ Job Stress
- ☐ Crises and Catastrophes

Describe the specific coping strategies that work best for you.

My Best Specific Coping Strategy

We have learned that the secret of mindfulness is to focus on the simple task at hand (rather than many), and gently put aside mind wandering and distraction. It is clear how we do this in relaxation and meditation. For example, attend to your breathing, and refocus your attention every time your mind wanders to something else, like thoughts about eating a hamburger or doing your homework. How can your checked coping strategy be done mindfully?

How My Coping Strategy Can Be Done Mindfully

Relaxation and Mindfulness

Here's a list (feel free to add items). Check those that worked for you.

- ☐ Yoga Stretching
- ☐ Progressive Muscle Relaxation
- ☒ Active Breathing Exercises
- ☒ Passive Breathing Exercises
- ☒ Autogenic "Warm/Heaviness" Suggestions
- ☐ Emotion-Focused Mindfulness Loving Kindness/Gratitude
  Your Focus: ____________________
- ☐ Mindfulness Imagery
  Theme: ____________________
- ☐ Eye of Mindfulness – Body Scan
- ☐ Eye of Mindfulness – Breathing Scan
- ☐ Focused Attention Meditation Rocking
  Mantra: ____________________
  Simple image in mind
- ☐ Pure Mindfulness (OM Meditation)

Relaxation/Mindfulness "Quickies"

Imagine you need a five-minute stress break. Perhaps this is before an exam, an interview, a first date, or seeing the doctor. Which exercises would work best as your "relaxation/mindfulness quickies"? Feel free to combine exercises:

When I would use my "Quickie":
My Relaxation/Mindfulness "Quickie" or "Quickie combo."

Relaxation/Mindfulness Regular Exercise

If you were to continue practicing one or two relaxation/mindfulness exercises to explore where they might go, which would you include? (You don't have to have a regular exercise. Just pick one or two you might consider in the future.)

Possible Relaxation/Mindfulness Regular Exercise

Favorite R/M States You Experienced

Here are the R/M States from your R/M Tracker. Of those you actually experienced, which were the most helpful, important, and meaningful?

Basic Relaxation

☐ 1. FAR AWAY
☐ 2. PHYSICALLY RELAXED
☐ 3. AT EASE, AT PEACE
☐ 4. REFRESHED
☐ 5. PLEASANT MIND WANDERING
☐ 6. FANTASY, DAYDREAMING

Basic Mindfulness
- ☐ 7. FOCUSED, ABSORBED
- ☐ 8. CENTERED, GROUNDED
- ☐ 9. QUIET
- ☐ 10. UNBOTHERED
- ☐ 11. EASY, EFFORTLESS

Mindful Awakening
- ☐ 12. OBSERVER
- ☐ 13. CLEAR, AWAKE, AWARE
- ☐ 14. INTERESTED, CURIOUS, FASCINATED
- ☐ 15. BEAUTIFUL

Mindful Deepening
- ☐ 16. GOING DEEPER
- ☐ 17. SPACIOUSNESS, EXPANSIVENESS
- ☐ 18. SENSE OF SOMETHING GREATER
- ☐ 19. MEANING, PURPOSE, DIRECTION

Mindful Transcendence
- ☐ 20. REVERENT, PRAYERFUL
- ☐ 21 AWE/WONDER, DEEP MYSTERY
- ☐ 22. SPIRITUAL MYSTICAL

Mindful Positive Emotion
- ☐ 23. HAPPY, OPTIMISTIC, TRUSTING
- ☐ 24. LOVING, CARING
- ☐ 25. THANKFUL

Which R/M States are the best signs that mindfulness is working for you?

My Signs Mindfulness Is Working

Which R/M States did you experience early on? That is, which were the first for you?

R/M States I Experienced Early

Which R/M States changed or increased most as you continued practicing? That is, which did you experience only after practicing a while?

R/M States I Experienced Later as I Practiced

Finally, what were the most useful ideas and practices you learned?

Most Useful Ideas and Practices

Stories of Mindfulness

Each session you practice is something of a story, with a beginning, middle, and end. Some sessions are rather uneventful. But some sessions can be noteworthy. In these special sessions you move from one R/M State to another. You discover how some exercises prepare for others. For example, George practiced a session of progressive muscle relaxation and then the Eye of Mindfulness. Here's his story of this session.

George: Progressive Muscle Relaxation ---> Mindfulness

I started by tensing and letting go of my muscles, using the audio instructions. After doing this for about 30 minutes my body felt really relaxed. I felt like I was sinking in my chair. It settled my mind and helped quiet the inner noise for mindfulness.

I then played a simple eye of mindfulness exercise. My mind was really peaceful. I found it a lot easier to focus on the instructions. It was very easy to let go of each distraction and return to my meditation.

Notice how George experienced different R/M States throughout his exercise, starting with simple Physical Relaxation, then Mental Relaxation, and then mental Quiet, Focusing, and Ease of returning to his focus.

If George were to rewrite his story, he could note which R/M States emerged at different times:

George: Progressive Muscle Relaxation ---> Mindfulness

I started by tensing and letting go of my muscles, using the audio instructions. After doing this for about 30 minutes my body felt really relaxed [R/M STATE: PHYSICAL RELAXATION]. I felt like I was sinking in my chair [R/M STATE: GOING DEEPER]. It settled my mind and helped quiet the inner noise for mindfulness [R/M STATE: QUIET].

I then played a simple eye of mindfulness exercise. My mind was really peaceful [R/M STATE: AT EASE, PEACE]. I found it a lot easier to focus on the instructions. It was very easy to let go of each distraction and return to my meditation [R/M STATE: EASY TO LET GO].

In our final exercise, pick a notable or special exercise or combination of exercises. Tell the story of what you did. Most important, note the R/M States that appeared, and how they seemed to be related to each other (like George did).

Your Mindfulness Relaxation Story

© Saylakham / Shutterstock.com

Appendix

How to Use the R/M Tracker and Chart

R/M States are experiences sometimes associated with relaxation and mindfulness. These include feeling relaxed, focused, and centered as well as having deeper feelings like being thankful and spiritual. As we will see later in the chapter, together they provide a map or model of mindfulness.

On the pages that follow you will find one "R/M Tracker" and one "R/M Tracker Chart." The R/M Tracker is a simple questionnaire where you can record your "Mindfulness States," or "R/M States." Fill one out after a good practice session. You don't have to fill one out after every session. The R/M Tracker Chart enables you to rate experiences for multiple exercises. You select your best sessions for each approach attempted and record it on your charts.

First, take a look at one sample version of the blank R/M Tracker Chart presented next. (Don't fill this one out. Use the R/M Trackers at the end of this book.)

THE R/M TRACKER

WHAT DID YOU FEEL OR EXPERIENCE DURING **THE EYE OF MINDFULNESS EXERCISE?**

CLICK BOXES USING THIS KEY

(SKIP ITEMS YOU DON'T UNDERSTAND OR DIDN'T FEEL OR EXPERIENCE)

☒❑❑❑	☒☒❑❑	☒☒☒❑	☒☒☒☒
Felt this SLIGHTLY	Felt this MODERATELY	Felt this VERY MUCH	Felt this EXTREMELY (the most ever)

1. **FAR AWAY** *and distant from the troubles around me.*	❑❑❑❑
2. **PHYSICALLY RELAXED**. *Muscles relaxed, loose, limp, warm and heavy. Breathing slow, even, and easy.*	❑❑❑❑
3 **AT EASE, AT PEACE**.	❑❑❑❑
4. **REFRESHED**.	❑❑❑❑
5. **PLEASANT MIND WANDERING**. *Undirected, random positive thoughts.*	❑❑❑❑
6. *Lost in* **FANTASY** *and* **DAYDREAMING.**	❑❑❑❑
7. *Periods of sustained, continuous* **FOCUS. ABSORPTION.**	❑❑❑❑
8. **CENTERED, GROUNDED.**	❑❑❑❑
9. **QUIET.** *Still, few thoughts. Little mind wandering.*	❑❑❑❑
10. **UNBOTHERED.** *Accepting. When I had a negative thought or feeling, I didn't get caught up in it. No judging, clinging, pushing away, figuring things out.*	❑❑❑❑
11. **EASY, EFFORTLESS.** *Effortless to let go, put thoughts aside, sustain focus.*	❑❑❑❑
12. *I felt like an* **OBSERVER** *standing aside and watching what happens.*	❑❑❑❑
13. **CLEAR, AWAKE, AWARE.** *I saw things as they really are.*	❑❑❑❑
14. **INTERESTED, CURIOUS, FASCINATED.**	❑❑❑❑
15. *Things seemed* **BEAUTIFUL.**	❑❑❑❑
16. **GOING DEEPER**. *Things seemed unexpected, new, changing, opening up,being revealed. Felt like I was in a different place or space.*	❑❑❑❑
17. *Sense of* **SPACIOUSNESS, EXPANSIVENESS.**	❑❑❑❑
18. *I felt the* **SENSE OF SOMETHING GREATER** *than myself (God, a higher power, spirit, energy, love, or consciousness.); God is with me.*	❑❑❑❑
19. *A sense of* **MEANING, PURPOSE, DIRECTION.**	❑❑❑❑
20. *I felt* **REVERENT, PRAYERFUL.**	❑❑❑❑
21. **AWE / WONDER, DEEP MYSTERY** *of things beyond my understanding.*	❑❑❑❑
22. *I felt a profound personal meaningful* "**SPIRITUAL**" *or* "**MYSTICAL**" *experience -- sudden awakening or insight.* • *Felt an underlying hidden* **TRUTH.** • *Feeling* **AT ONE.** • *Feelings so profound they* **COULD NOT BE PUT INTO WORDS.**	❑❑❑❑
23. **HAPPY, OPTIMISTIC, TRUSTING.**	❑❑❑❑
24. **LOVING, CARING.**	❑❑❑❑
25. **THANKFUL.** *Grateful.*	❑❑❑❑

R/M TRACKER CHART (for summarizing R/M Trackers)

WHAT DID YOU FEEL OR EXPERIENCE IN YOUR **RELAXATION SESSION**?

CLICK BOXES USING THIS KEY

(SKIP ITEMS YOU DON'T UNDERSTAND OR DIDN'T FEEL OR EXPERIENCE)

☒❑❑❑	☒☒❑❑	☒☒☒❑	☒☒☒☒
Felt this SLIGHTLY	Felt this MODERATELY	Felt this VERY MUCH	Felt this EXTREMELY (the most ever)

NAME YOUR TECHNIQUE OR ACTIVITY HERE →						
***FAR AWAY** and distant from the troubles around me.*	❑❑❑❑	❑❑❑❑	❑❑❑❑	❑❑❑❑	❑❑❑❑	❑❑❑❑
***PHYSICALLY RELAXED**. Muscles relaxed, loose, limp, warm and heavy. Breathing slow, even, and easy.*	❑❑❑❑	❑❑❑❑	❑❑❑❑	❑❑❑❑	❑❑❑❑	❑❑❑❑
AT EASE, AT PEACE.	❑❑❑❑	❑❑❑❑	❑❑❑❑	❑❑❑❑	❑❑❑❑	❑❑❑❑
***REFRESHED**.*	❑❑❑❑	❑❑❑❑	❑❑❑❑	❑❑❑❑	❑❑❑❑	❑❑❑❑
***PLEASANT MIND WANDERING**, undirected, random positive thoughts.*	❑❑❑❑	❑❑❑❑	❑❑❑❑	❑❑❑❑	❑❑❑❑	❑❑❑❑
*Lost in **FANTASY** and **DAYDREAMING.***	❑❑❑❑	❑❑❑❑	❑❑❑❑	❑❑❑❑	❑❑❑❑	❑❑❑❑
*Periods of sustained, continuous **FOCUS. ABSORPTION.***	❑❑❑❑	❑❑❑❑	❑❑❑❑	❑❑❑❑	❑❑❑❑	❑❑❑❑
CENTERED, GROUNDED.	❑❑❑❑	❑❑❑❑	❑❑❑❑	❑❑❑❑	❑❑❑❑	❑❑❑❑
***QUIET.** Still, few thoughts. Little mind wandering.*	❑❑❑❑	❑❑❑❑	❑❑❑❑	❑❑❑❑	❑❑❑❑	❑❑❑❑
***UNBOTHERED.** Accepting. When I had a negative thought or feeling, I didn't get caught up in it. No judging, clinging, pushing away, figuring things out.*	❑❑❑❑	❑❑❑❑	❑❑❑❑	❑❑❑❑	❑❑❑❑	❑❑❑❑
***EASY, EFFORTLESS.** Effortless to let go, put thoughts aside, sustain focus.*	❑❑❑❑	❑❑❑❑	❑❑❑❑	❑❑❑❑	❑❑❑❑	❑❑❑❑
*I felt like an **OBSERVER** standing aside and watching what happens.*	❑❑❑❑	❑❑❑❑	❑❑❑❑	❑❑❑❑	❑❑❑❑	❑❑❑❑
***CLEAR, AWAKE, AWARE.** I saw things as they really are.*	❑❑❑❑	❑❑❑❑	❑❑❑❑	❑❑❑❑	❑❑❑❑	❑❑❑❑
INTERESTED, CURIOUS, FASCINATED.	❑❑❑❑	❑❑❑❑	❑❑❑❑	❑❑❑❑	❑❑❑❑	❑❑❑❑
*Things seemed **BEAUTIFUL.***	❑❑❑❑	❑❑❑❑	❑❑❑❑	❑❑❑❑	❑❑❑❑	❑❑❑❑
***GOING DEEPER.** Things seemed unexpected, new, changing, opening up, being revealed. Felt like I was in a different place or space.*	❑❑❑❑	❑❑❑❑	❑❑❑❑	❑❑❑❑	❑❑❑❑	❑❑❑❑
*Sense of **SPACIOUSNESS, EXPANSIVENESS.***	❑❑❑❑	❑❑❑❑	❑❑❑❑	❑❑❑❑	❑❑❑❑	❑❑❑❑
*I felt the **SENSE OF SOMETHING GREATER** than myself (God, a higher power, spirit, energy, love, or consciousness.)*	❑❑❑❑	❑❑❑❑	❑❑❑❑	❑❑❑❑	❑❑❑❑	❑❑❑❑
*A sense of **MEANING, PURPOSE, DIRECTION.***	❑❑❑❑	❑❑❑❑	❑❑❑❑	❑❑❑❑	❑❑❑❑	❑❑❑❑
*I felt **REVERENT, PRAYERFUL**.*	❑❑❑❑	❑❑❑❑	❑❑❑❑	❑❑❑❑	❑❑❑❑	❑❑❑❑
***AWE / WONDER, DEEP MYSTERY** of things beyond my understanding.*	❑❑❑❑	❑❑❑❑	❑❑❑❑	❑❑❑❑	❑❑❑❑	❑❑❑❑
*I felt a profound personal meaningful **"SPIRITUAL"** or **"MYSTICAL"** experience -- sudden awakening or insight.* • *Felt an underlying hidden **TRUTH.*** • *Felt **AT ONE.*** • *Feelings so profound they **COULD NOT BE PUT INTO WORDS.***	❑❑❑❑	❑❑❑❑	❑❑❑❑	❑❑❑❑	❑❑❑❑	❑❑❑❑
HAPPY, OPTIMISTIC, TRUSTING.	❑❑❑❑	❑❑❑❑	❑❑❑❑	❑❑❑❑	❑❑❑❑	❑❑❑❑
LOVING, CARING.	❑❑❑❑	❑❑❑❑	❑❑❑❑	❑❑❑❑	❑❑❑❑	❑❑❑❑
***THANKFUL.** Grateful.*	❑❑❑❑	❑❑❑❑	❑❑❑❑	❑❑❑❑	❑❑❑❑	❑❑❑❑

How to Use Your R/M Trackers

Complete one R/M Tracker after an exercise. What did you experience during the exercise? Summarize R/M Trackers for several exercises on your R/M Chart.

Rows of R/M States

Notice that there are 25 rows or "boxes." Each describes a different R/M State or experience associated with relaxation and mindfulness. Specifically, they are:

Basic Relaxation
1. FAR AWAY
2. PHYSICALLY RELAXED
3. AT EASE, AT PEACE
4. REFRESHED
5. PLEASANT MIND WANDERING
6. FANTASY, DAYDREAMING

Basic Mindfulness
7. FOCUSED, ABSORBED
8. CENTERED, GROUNDED
9. QUIET
10. UNBOTHERED
11. EASY, EFFORTLESS

Mindful Awakening
12. OBSERVER
13. CLEAR, AWAKE, AWARE
14. INTERESTED, CURIOUS, FASCINATED
15. BEAUTIFUL

Mindful Deepening
16. GOING DEEPER
17. SPACIOUSNESS, EXPANSIVENESS
18. SENSE OF SOMETHING GREATER
19. MEANING, PURPOSE, DIRECTION

Mindful Transcendence
20. REVERENT, PRAYERFUL
21 AWE/WONDER, DEEP MYSTERY
22. SPIRITUAL MYSTICAL

Mindful Positive Emotion
23. HAPPY, OPTIMISTIC, TRUSTING
24. LOVING, CARING
25. THANKFUL

Checking Boxes

To the right of each R/M State description are sets of four little boxes. After practicing an exercise, indicate how much you felt each R/M State by checking the boxes to the right.

If you felt an R/M State "SLIGHTLY," click one box, like this:

☒☐☐☐

If you felt an R/M State "MODERATELY," click two boxes:

☒☒☐☐

If you felt an R/M State "VERY MUCH," click three boxes:

☒☒☒☐

If you felt an R/M State "EXTREMELY, The Most Ever," click four boxes:

☒☒☒☒

What if you didn't experience an R/M State at all? Simply skip the item and go on to the next. What if you don't understand an item? That's fine. I don't expect some of the R/M States will make sense to some practitioners. Again, skip them. Don't rate them. Leave the boxes blank, like this:

☐☐☐☐

Imagine you've just practiced YOGA and want to rate your session. The first R/M State is "FAR AWAY." Let's say you felt moderately "FAR AWAY." If so, your rating would look like this:

FAR AWAY *and distant from the troubles around me.*	☒☒☐☐

If you felt very "PHYSICALLY RELAXED," your rating would look like this:

PHYSICALLY RELAXED. *Muscles relaxed, loose, limp, warm, and heavy. Breathing slow, even, and easy the troubles around me.*	☒☒☒☐

If you didn't feel at all "AT EASE, AT PEACE," or did not understand these words, your rating would look like this (you would simply not rate the item):

AT EASE, AT PEACE	□□□□

The R/M Tracker Chart

Now take a look at the R/M Tracker Chart. Notice that there are more than four boxes after each R/M State. Each column is for a different practice session. After you have completed many exercises, and filled out several R/M Trackers, select your best session for each approach. For example, select the R/M Tracker for your best yoga session, your best breathing session, and so on. You summarize your best sessions on your R/M Tracker Chart.

In the example below there are six columns, each for a different type of exercise the practitioner has chosen to try. She has written the name of each exercise in the top boxes (you may choose to leave these blank and fill them in only when you decide which exercise to practice):

	Eye of Mindfulness	*Yoga*	*Muscle Mindfulness*	*Breathing*	*Loving Kindness*	*Mindfulness Imagery*
***FAR AWAY** and distant from the troubles around me.*	□□□□	□□□□	□□□□	□□□□	□□□□	□□□□
***PHYSICALLY RELAXED**. Muscles relaxed, loose, limp, warm and heavy. Breathing slow, even, and easy.*	□□□□	□□□□	□□□□	□□□□	□□□□	□□□□
AT EASE, AT PEACE.	□□□□	□□□□	□□□□	□□□□	□□□□	□□□□

Below is how our student rated her Eye of Mindfulness exercise. Note that she felt very much physically relaxed and at ease and at peace. She didn't check any boxes for "FAR AWAY," because she didn't feel this at all, or didn't understand how the words applied.

	Eye of Mindfulness	*Yoga*	*Muscle Mindfulness*	*Breathing*	*Loving Kindness*	*Mindfulness Imagery*
FAR AWAY *and distant from the troubles around me.*	☐☐☐☐	☐☐☐☐	☐☐☐☐	☐☐☐☐	☐☐☐☐	☐☐☐☐
PHYSICALLY RELAXED. *Muscles relaxed, loose, limp, warm and heavy. Breathing slow, even, and easy.*	☒☒☒☐	☐☐☐☐	☐☐☐☐	☐☐☐☐	☐☐☐☐	☐☐☐☐
AT EASE, AT PEACE.	☒☒☒☐	☐☐☐☐	☐☐☐☐	☐☐☐☐	☐☐☐☐	☐☐☐☐

The next week our student practiced her yoga exercises. She added to her chart:

	Eye of Mindfulness	*Yoga*	*Muscle Mindfulness*	*Breathing*	*Loving Kindness*	*Mindfulness Imagery*
FAR AWAY *and distant from the troubles around me.*	☐☐☐☐	☒☒☐☐	☐☐☐☐	☐☐☐☐	☐☐☐☐	☐☐☐☐
PHYSICALLY RELAXED. *Muscles relaxed, loose, limp, warm and heavy. Breathing slow, even, and easy.*	☒☒☒☐	☒☒☐☐	☐☐☐☐	☐☐☐☐	☐☐☐☐	☐☐☐☐
AT EASE, AT PEACE.	☒☒☒☐	☒☒☐☐	☐☐☐☐	☐☐☐☐	☐☐☐☐	☐☐☐☐

When doing her yoga exercises, she felt the three indicated R/M States "MODERATE-LY" and checked two boxes for each.

THE R/M TRACKER

What is the Activity or Exercise you are rating?

WHAT DID YOU FEEL OR EXPERIENCE IN THIS ACTIVITY OR EXERCISE?
CLICK BOXES USING THIS KEY
(SKIP ITEMS YOU DON'T UNDERSTAND OR DIDN'T FEEL OR EXPERIENCE)

☒❑❑❑	☒☒❑❑	☒☒☒❑	☒☒☒☒
Felt this SLIGHTLY	Felt this MODERATELY	Felt this VERY MUCH	Felt this EXTREMELY (the most ever)

1. ***FAR AWAY*** *and distant from the troubles around me.*	❑❑❑❑
2. **PHYSICALLY RELAXED**. *Muscles relaxed, loose, limp, warm and heavy. Breathing slow, even, and easy.*	❑❑❑❑
3 ***AT EASE, AT PEACE.***	❑❑❑❑
4. ***REFRESHED.***	❑❑❑❑
5. **PLEASANT MIND WANDERING**. *Undirected, random positive thoughts.*	❑❑❑❑
6. *Lost in* **FANTASY** *and* **DAYDREAMING.**	❑❑❑❑
7. *Periods of sustained, continuous* **FOCUS. ABSORPTION.**	❑❑❑❑
8. ***CENTERED, GROUNDED.***	❑❑❑❑
9. **QUIET.** *Still, few thoughts. Little mind wandering.*	❑❑❑❑
10. **UNBOTHERED.** *Accepting. When I had a negative thought or feeling, I didn't get caught up in it. No judging, clinging, pushing away, figuring things out.*	❑❑❑❑
11. **EASY, EFFORTLESS.** *Effortless to let go, put thoughts aside, sustain focus.*	❑❑❑❑
12. *I felt like an* **OBSERVER** *standing aside and watching what happens.*	❑❑❑❑
13. **CLEAR, AWAKE, AWARE.** *I saw things as they really are.*	❑❑❑❑
14. ***INTERESTED, CURIOUS, FASCINATED.***	❑❑❑❑
15. *Things seemed* **BEAUTIFUL.**	❑❑❑❑
16. **GOING DEEPER**. *Things seemed unexpected, new, changing, opening up,being revealed. Felt like I was in a different place or space.*	❑❑❑❑
17. *Sense of* **SPACIOUSNESS, EXPANSIVENESS.**	❑❑❑❑
18. *I felt the* **SENSE OF SOMETHING GREATER** *than myself (God, a higher power, spirit, energy, love, or consciousness.); God is with me.*	❑❑❑❑
19. *A sense of* **MEANING, PURPOSE, DIRECTION.**	❑❑❑❑
20. *I felt* **REVERENT, PRAYERFUL.**	❑❑❑❑
21. **AWE / WONDER, DEEP MYSTERY** *of things beyond my understanding.*	❑❑❑❑
22. *I felt a profound personal meaningful* "**SPIRITUAL**" *or* "**MYSTICAL**" *experience -- sudden awakening or insight.* • *Felt an underlying hidden* **TRUTH.** • *Feeling* **AT ONE.** • *Feelings so profound they* **COULD NOT BE PUT INTO WORDS.**	❑❑❑❑
23. ***HAPPY, OPTIMISTIC, TRUSTING.***	❑❑❑❑
24. ***LOVING, CARING.***	❑❑❑❑
25. **THANKFUL.** *Grateful.*	❑❑❑❑

References

Alberti, R. E., & Emmons, M. L. (1982). *Your perfect right.* San Luis Obispo, CA: Impact Publishers.

American Psychiatric Association. (2014). *Diagnostic and statistical manual of mental disorders* (5th ed.). Washington, DC: APA.

Ansell, E. B., Rando, K., Tuit, K., Guarnaccia, J., & Sinha, R. (2012). Cumulative adversity and smaller gray matter volume in medial prefrontal, anterior cingulate, and insula regions. *Biological Psychiatry, 72*, 57–64.

Antony, M. M., & Swinson, R. P. (2000). *The shyness and social anxiety workbook.* Oakland, CA: New Harbinger.

Beck, A. T. (1993). *Cognitive therapy and the emotional disorders.* New York: American Library Trade.

Benson, H. (1975). *The relaxation response.* New York: Marrow.

Blonna, R. (2005). *Coping with stress in a changing world.* New York: McGraw-Hill.

Borkovec, T. D. (1985). What's the use of worrying. *Psychology Today, 19*, 59–64.

Borkovec, T. D., Wilkinson, L., Folensbee, R., & Lerman, C. (1983). Stimulus control applications to the treatment of worry. *Behavior Research and Therapy, 21*, 247–251.

Borgogna, N. & Smith., J.C. (May, 2016). Effects of Yoga and Meditation on Mindfulness States. Poster presented at the 2016 Annual Midwestern Psychological Association Conference, Chicago, IL.

Borgogna, N. & Smith, J.C. (June, 2016). The Factor Structure of Relaxation and Mindfulness: Two States or One? Poster to be presented at the Association For Contextual Behavioral Science Annual World Conference 14, Seattle, WA.

Bower, S. A., & Bower, G. H. (1991). *Asserting yourself.* Cambridge, MA: Perseus Books.

Bressler, S. L., & Menon, V. (2010). Large-scale brain networks in cognition: Emerging methods and principles. *Trends in Cognitive Science, 14(6)*, 277–290.

Brickman, P., & Campbell, D. T. (1971). Hedonic relativism and planning the good society. In M. H. Appley (Ed.), *Adaptation-level theory: A symposium* (pp. 287–302). New York: Academic Press.

Brown, K. W., Creswell, J. D., & Ryan, R. M. (2015). *Handbook of mindfulness: Theory, research, and practice.* New York: Guilford.

Burns, D. D. (1990). *The feeling good handbook.* New York: Plume.

Cahn, B. R., & Polich, J. (2006). Meditation states and traits: EEG, ERP, and neuroimaging studies. *Psychological Bulletin, 132*(2), 180–211.

Cannon, W. B. (1929). *Bodily changes in pain, hunger, fear, and rage.* New York: Appleton.

Cannon, W. B. (1932). *The wisdom of the body.* New York: W. W. Norton

Cautela, J. R., & Wisocki, P. A. (1977). The thought-stopping procedure: Description, applications, and learning theory interpretations. *Psychological Record, 1*, 255–264.
Cohen, S. (2004). Social relationships and health. *American Psychologist, 676–684.*
Curran, J. P., Wallander, J. L., & Farrell, A. D. (1985). Heterosocial skills training in L. L'Abate & M. A. Milan (Eds.), *Handbook of social skills training and research* (pp. 136–169). New York: Wiley.
Davis, D. M., & Hayes, J. H. (2012). What are the benefits of mindfulness. *Monitor on Psychology, 43*, 64.
Ewart, C. K., & Suchday, S. (2002). Discovering how urban poverty and violence affect health: Development and validation of a neighborhood stress index. *Health Psychology, 21*(3), 1–16.
Ferrari, J. R., Johnson, J. L., & McCown, W. G. (1995). *Procrastination and task avoidance: Theory, research, and treatment.* New York: Plenum.
Foerde, K., Knolton, B. J., & Poldrack, R. A. (2006). Modulation of competing memory systems by distraction. *Proceedings of the National Academy of Sciences, 103*, 11778–11783.
Fulton, J. F. (1932). Claude Bernard and the future of medicine. *Canadian Medical Association Journal, 27*, 427–433.
Gaspar, J. M., & McDonald, J. J. (2014). Suppression of salient objects prevents distraction in visual search. *The International Journal of Neuroscience, 34(16)*, 5658–5666.
Goldstein, A. P., & Keller, H. (1987). *Aggressive behavior: Assessment and intervention.* New York: Pergamon Press.
Greenberg, M. (2017). *The stress-proof brain: Master your emotional response to stress using mindfulness and neuroplasticity*. Oakland, CA: New Harbinger.
Greenwald, H. (1973). *Direct decision therapy*. San Diego, CA: EDITS.
Hayes, S. C., Strosahl, K. D., & Wilson, K. G. (2003). *Acceptance and commitment therapy: An experiential approach to behavior change.* New York: Guilford.
Holmes, T. H., & Rahe, R. H. (1967). The social readjustment rating scale. *Journal of Psychosomatic Research, 11*, 213–218.
Hope, D. A., Heimberg, R. G., Juster, H. R., & Turk, C. L. (2000). *Managing social anxiety: A cognitive behavioral therapy approach.* San Antonio, TX: The Psychological Corporation.
Horowitz, M. J. (1982). Psychological processes induced by illness, injury, and loss. In T. Millon, C. Green, & R. Meagher (Eds.), *Handbook of clinical health psychology.* New York: Plenum.
House, J. S., & Kahn, R. L. (1985). Measures and concepts of social support. In S. Cohen & S. L. Syme (Eds.), *Social support and health* (pp. 83–108). New York: Academic Press.
Jacobson, E. (1929). *Progressive relaxation.* Chicago: University of Chicago Press.
Jacobson, E. (1932). Electrophysiology of mental activities. *American Journal of Psychology, 44*, 677-694.
Jaffe, E. (2013). Why wait? The science behind procrastination. The Association for Psychological Science, accessed March 6, 2017, https://www.psychologicalscience.org/observer/why-wait-the-science-behind-procrastination
Jakubowski, P., & Lange, A. J. (1978). *The assertive option.* Champaign, IL: Research Press.
Juran, J. M. (1988). *Juran's quality control handbook* (4th ed.). New York: McGraw-Hill.

Kabat-Zinn, J. (1990). *Full catastrophe living.* New York: Random House.

Karren, K. J., Hafen, B. Q., Smith, N. L., & Frandsen, K. J. (2001). *Mind/body health: The effects of attitudes, emotions, and relationships* (2nd ed.). San Francisco: Benjamin Cummings.

Kasamatsu, K. H., & Hirai T. (1966). An electroencephalographic study on the Zen meditation (Zazen). *Folia Psychiatrica et Neurologica Japonica, 20,* 315–336.

Kerr, C. E., Sacchet, M. D., Lazar, S. W., Moore, C. I., & Jones, S. R. (2013, February). Mindfulness starts with the body: somatosensory attention and top-down modulation of cortical alpha rhythms in mindfulness meditation. *Frontiers of Human Neuroscience, 13*, online.

Killingsworth, M., & Gilbert, D. (2010). A wandering mind is an unhappy mind. *Science* (November 12), 932.

Kleinke, C. L, Meeker, F. B., & Staneski, R. A. (1986). Preferences for opening lines: Comparing ratings by men and women. *Sex Roles, 15*, 585–600.

Lakein, A. (1973). *How to get control of your time and your life.* New York: Signet.

Lutz, A., Brefczynski-Lewis, J., Johnstone, T., & Davidson, R.J. (2008, March 26). Regulation of the neural circuitry of emotion by compassion meditation: effects of meditative expertise. *PLOS-ONE.*

Lutz, A., Jha, A. P., Dunne, J. D., & Saron, C. D. (2015). Investigating the phenomenological matrix of mindfulness-related practices from a neurocognitive perspective. *American Psychologist,* 70(7), 632–658.

Mabuire, E. A., Gadian, D. G., Johnsrude, I. S., Good, C. D., Ashburner, J., Frackowiak, R. S. J., Frith, C. D. (2000). Navigation-related structureal change I the hippocampi of taxi drivers. *Proceedings of the National Academy of Sciences, USA. 97(8).* 4398-4403

Marlatt, A., & Gordon, J. (1984). *Relapse prevention: A self-control strategy for the maintenance of behavior change.* New York: Guilford Press.

McKay, M., Davis, M., & Fanning, P. (1995). *Messages: The communication skills book* (2nd ed.). Oakland, CA: New Harbinger Publications.

Meichenbaum, D. (1985). *Stress inoculation training.* New York: Pergamon.

Miller, E. K., & Buschman, T. J. (2014). Neural mechanisms for the executive control of attention. In K. Nobre and S. Kastner (Eds.), *The Oxford handbook of attention.* New York: Oxford University Press.

The multitasking paradox. (2013, March). *Harvard Business Review, 91*(3), 30–31.

Nasar, J .L., & Troyer, D. (2013, August). Pedestrian injuries due to mobile phone use in public places. *Accident Analysis & Prevention, 57*, 91–95.

National Highway Traffic Safety Administration. (2014, May). *The economic and societal impact of motor vehicle crashes, 2010.* Washington, DC: NHTSA.

Novaco, R. (1975). *Anger control: The development and evaluation of an experimental treatment.* Lexington, MA: D. C. Heath.

Osborn, A. F. (1963). *Applied imagination: Principles and procedures of creative problem solving* (3rd rev. ed.). New York: Charles Scribner's Sons.

Paul, A. M. (2013, May 3). The new marshmallow test: Resisting the temptations of the web. The Hechinger Report, accessed March 3, 2017, http://hechingerreport.org/the-new-marshmallow-test-resisting-the-temptations-of-the-web/

Sauter, S. L., Murphy, L. R, & Hurrell Jr., J. J. (1990). Prevention of work-related psychological disorders. *American Psychologist, 45,* 1146–1158.

Schwartz, T. (2013, Feb. 9). Relax! You'll be more productive. *New York Times Sunday Review.*

Segerstrom, S. C., & Miller, G. E. (2004). Psychological stress and the human immune system: A metaanalytic study of 30 years of inquiry. *Psychological Bulletin, 130,* 601–630.

Selye, H. (1974). *Stress without distress.* New York: Signet Classics.

Seyle, H. (1956). *The stress of life.* New York: McGraw-Hill.

Shonin, E., & Van Gordon, W. (2015). Managers' experiences of meditation awareness training. *Mindfulness, 6,* 899–909.

Smith, J. C. (1975, July). Meditation as psychotherapy: A review of the literature. *Psychological Bulletin, 82*(4), 558–564.

Smith, J. C. (1976, August). Psychotherapeutic effects of transcendental meditation with controls for expectation of relief and daily sitting. *Journal of Consulting and Clinical Psychology, 44*(4), 630–637.

Smith, J. C. (1985). *Relaxation dynamics: Nine world approaches to self-relaxation.* Champaign, IL: Research Press.

Smith, J. C. (1986). *Meditation: A sensible guide to a timeless discipline.* Champaign-Urbana, IL: Research Press.

Smith, J. C. (1988). Steps toward a cognitive-behavioral model of relaxation. *Biofeedback and Self Regulation, 13*(4), 307–329.

Smith, J. C. (1999). *ABC relaxation theory.* New York: Springer.

Smith, J. C. (2001). *Advances in ABC relaxation: Applications and inventories.* New York: Springer.

Smith, J. C. (2001). *Stress management: A comprehensive handbook of techniques and strategies.* New York: Springer.

Smith, J. C. (2005). *Relaxation, meditation, and mindfulness: A mental health practitioner's guide to new and traditional approaches.* New York: Springer.

Smith, J. C. (2007). The psychology of relaxation. In P. M. Lehrer, R. L. Woolfolk, and W. E. Sime (Eds.), *Principles and practice of stress management* (3rd ed., pp. xvii, 38–52). New York: Guilford Press.

Smith, J. C. (2010). *Pseudoscience and extraordinary claims of the paranormal: A critical thinker's toolkit.* New York: Wiley-Blackwell.

Smith, J. C. (2012). Relaxation. In V. S. Ramachandran (Ed.), *Encyclopedia of human behavior* (pp. 23–45). New York: Elsevier.

Smith, J. C. (2015). Relaxation. In M. S. Schwartz and F. Andrasik (Eds.), *Biofeedback: A practitioner's guide* (4th ed.). New York: Guilford.

Smith, J. C. (in press, 2018). *Critical thinking: Pseudoscience and the paranormal.* New York: Wiley-Blackwell.

Smith, J. C., Amutio, A., Anderson, J. P., & Aria, L. A. (1996). Relaxation: Mapping and uncharted world. *Biofeedback and Self-Regulation, 21*(1), 63–90.

Tuckman, B. W., Abry, D. A., & Smith, D. R. (2008). *Learning and motivation strategies: Your guide to success* (2nd ed.). Upper Saddle River, NJ: Pearson Prentice Hall.

United States Environmental Protection Agency; the United States Consumer Product Safety Commission Office of Radiation and Indoor Air. (1995, April). *The inside story: A guide to indoor air quality*. EPA Document 402-K-93-007.

West, B. L, Goethe, K. E., & Kallman, W. M. (1980). Heterosocial skills training: A behavioral-cognitive approach. In D. Upper & S. M. Ross (Eds.), *Behavioral group therapy, 1980: An annual review*. Champaign, IL: Research Press.

Wills, T. A. (1985). Supportive functions of interpersonal relationships. In S. Cohen & L. Syme, Social support and health (pp. 61–82). Orlando, FL: Academic Press.

Yerkes, R. M., & Dodson, J. D. (1908). The relation of strength of stimulus to rapidity of habit-formation. *Journal of Comparative Neurology and Psychology, 18*, 459–482.

Zack, D. (2015). *Singletasking*. Oakland, CA: Berrett-Koehler, Publishers.

CPSIA information can be obtained
at www.ICGtesting.com
Printed in the USA
LVOW02s1603220617
538965LV00002B/2/P

9 781524 933227